The

FOR
BY OWNER

Handbook

FSBO FAQs: From Pricing Your Home Right and Increasing Its Curb Appeal to Negotiating the Contract and Hassle-Free Closing

CAREER
PRESS
Franklin Lakes, NJ

THE FOR SALE BY OWNER HANDBOOK
EDITED AND TYPESET BY CLAYTON W. LEADBETTER
Cover design by Mada Design, Inc./NYC
Printed in the U.S.A. by Book-mart Press
The terms REALTOR® and REALTORS® are
Registered Trademarks of the National Association of REALTORS®

To order this title, please call toll-free 1-800-CAREER-1 (NJ and Canada: 201-848-0310) to order using VISA or MasterCard, or for further information on books from Career Press.

The Career Press, Inc., 3 Tice Road, PO Box 687,
Franklin Lakes, NJ 07417
www.careerpress.com

Library of Congress Cataloging-in-Publication Data

Nichole, Piper, 1981-
    The For Sale by Owner handbook : FSBO FAQs : from pricing your home right and increasing its curb appeal to negotiating the contract and hassle-free closing / by Piper Nichole.
        p. cm.
    Includes index.
    ISBN 1-56414-805-X (pbk.)
    1. House selling—Handbooks, manuals, etc. 2. House selling—United States—Handbooks, manuals, etc. I. Title.

HD1379.N52 2005
643'.12--dc22

                                                                  2005042069

With much love, this book is dedicated to
Mom, Devin, Nicholas, Sydney, Joel and Dad.

Acknowledgments

A very special THANK YOU to the many amazing participants in *The For Sale By Owner Handbook*. I really appreciate all your expertise, professionalism, charisma and enthusiasm for this project. Thank you so, so much.

Bob Diforio (Thank you very much!); to everyone at Career Press, many thanks to you all—Ron Fry, Mike Lewis, Clayton Leadbetter, Laurie Kelly-Pye, Kirsten Dalley, Michael Pye, Linda Reinecker and everyone! To Justin McDonald, thank you for doing the wonderful graphics for the book.

Coming straight from my notes, e-mails and phone logs, a special and much appreciated thank-you to: *Los-Angeles Times*'s Barbara Thornburg; *Better Homes and Gardens*' Karol DeWulf Nickell; Meredith Corporation's Katharine Robbins; *Trading Spaces*' Hildi Santo-Tomas; Virginia Shackelford; *Hearst Magazine*'s Nathan Christopher and Priyanka Hanna; *House Beautiful*'s Mark Mayfield; *Country Living*'s Larry Bilotti; *Country Living Gardener*'s Marjorie Gage; Scripps Networks Corporation's LaShonda Louallen, Dan Hurst, Jessie Mack Burns and Lynda Lyday; Julie Morgenstern; Christine Lassiter; Lauren Podber; Assist-2-Sell's Mary LaMeres-Pomin and Glennis Bishop; *This Old House*'s Leah Orfanos, Roger Cook, and Kate Hathaway; Christine Unsworth of U.S. Legal Forms, Inc.; NBC12 business analyst Randy Cost; My Linh Tran; Ethan Allen's Kelly Maicon, Jenny Morgan and Lynn Bernstein; Yale University's Lisa Kereszi; Thomas Davidoff of the University of California, Berkeley, HAAS School of Business; Wendy Tilton of New York University and Key Properties Consulting; Patrick Butler of Home Financing Center Realty, Inc.; Donna Kay and Patty Briguglio of MMI Associates, Inc.; R.T. Hayes & Associates' Richard Tom Hayes; John Byrd of *Outdoor Living* and John Byrd Garden Design; Fannie Mae Foundation's Tina McDaniel and Lynsey Wood Jeffries; Jim McHugh of Jim McHugh Photography; Rhoni Epstein of Rhoni Epstein Associates; Belinda Lynn; Mike Butler of Mike Butler Architectural Photography; W.W. DuBois, Images & Ideas ; Attorneys' Title Insurance Fund's Louis Guttmann; Edelman's John Moore and Erin Houchin; Countrywide Home Loans' Kris Yamamoto and Doug Perry; MBA Mortgage Corporation's Brian Shulman; Cowles & Thompson's Richard Barrett-Cuetara; American Society of Interior Designers' Michelle Snyder; Peterson-Arce Design Group's BJ Peterson; "Quick Turn Real Estate Millionaire" Ron LeGrand; Gregory FCA Communications' Colleen O'Boyle; American Society of Home Inspectors' Rich Matzen; Michael Kaminer Public Relations' Jill Feldman;

ForSaleByOwner.com's Colby Sambrotto; National Association of Certified Home Inspectors' Nick Gromicko; Whitney Smith of Cushman/Amberg Communications, Inc.; Dave Kowal of Kowal Communications, Inc.; ERA Key Realty Services' Nelson Zide; Robin Embry of Lovell Communications Inc.; George Pappas and Hilary Kaye of Hilary Kaye Associates, Inc.; Market Ready Redesign's Elisabeth Campbell-Westlind; Mark 1 Mortgag's Mark Prather; Re/Max Village Square's Joanna Parker-Lentz; Penske Truck Rental's Louise Moyer; Joanne Fried of U-Haul International, Inc.; Weber Shandwick's Ofer Erenfeld; Todd Krieger of Quicken Loans/Rock Financial; The GAB Group's Michelle Soudry; Cutaia Mortgage Group's Susan and Anthony Cutaia; Nicholas & Co. Mortgage Planning Solutions' Gibran Nicholas and William S. McDonald; Coldwell Banker's Ginny Leamy; RE/MAX Coastal Properties' Ed Smith; Allison & Partners' Christine Fox; Jennifer Wake; Karen Andrews; Johanna Bilodeau; Mike McNulty; The New York Institute of Photography; US Inspect's Pablo Gomez; Anthony Duffy of The Duffy Law Firm; and Thornburg Mortgage Home Loans' Ron Chicaferro.

American University's Libby Cullen; Echo Media PR's Sabrina Shannon; Potomac Communications Group's Bob Conrad; Empire Realty Associates' Sandi Mitchell; Robert Walkowicz of The Group, Inc. Real Estate; In Order of Appearance's Nancy Krueger; Sierra Communications' Susan Kohl; Mary Zentz of RE/MAX; Shorewest Realtors' Pat Ohlendorf; "Real Estate and Finance Hour" cohost Norm Bour; Premier Properties' Diane F. Matthews; Citigate Sard Verbinnen's Drew Ferguson; Becker Public Relations' Bertha Diaz; Legal PR's Rhonda Reddick; The USAA Educational Foundation's Bobbie L. Dover; and Executive Inspection Services, Inc.

Gloria Wajciechowski of the IRS; Kevin Konopik of Executive Inspection Services, Inc.; Bell Inspection Service's Greg Bell; Brian Sheeran of Investor's Savings Bank Mortgage Company, LLC; Wells Marketing Group's Petrina Fisher Wells; *Rogue Real Estate Investor Collection* coauthor Bryan Rundell, Patricia Ricci of Idea Lab, Inc.; Fagan Business Communications' Aimee Bennett; Odona Technology's Bob Anastasi; Lauren Hunter Public Relations' Lauren Hunter; Help-U-Sell's Rick O'Neil; FindLaw's Leonard Lee; Thom MacFarlane; Homebridge Mortgage Bankers' Stephen Katz.

Greg Wilson of The Greg Wilson Group; Newspaper Association of America's Mort Goldstrom and Sheila Owens; Alain Pinel Realtors' Anne Riley; Phenix & Phenix Literary Publicists' Molly Cain; RealtySecurity.com's Robert L. Siciliano; Anne Hunt; Dave Martel; PR Newswire's Maria Perez; Scotts' Ashton Ritchie; Karla Neely of Michael A. Burns & Associates; Loyal Termite and Pest Control's Nick Lupini; Emily Hallford of Burson-Marsteller; Heather Greer of Experian Public Relations; Environmental PR Group's Natalie Mealey; The R&J Group's Jason Ledder; Stacey Tepper of Robin Leedy & Associates, Inc.; OutreachPR's Connie Holubar; Steve Allen of Anthony Mora Communications; Fannie Mae's Sandra Cutts; Allison & Partners' Laurie Kamras; Fishman Public Relations' Caitlin M. Gorand; Peters, Cook & Company's Nilla Lauberts; Pantin/Beber Silverstein Public Relations' Carol Brady Blades; PR First's Colleen Cimini; The Institute for Luxury Home Marketing's Anna Marotti and Anthony Armstrong; ABA's Deborah Weixl; Georgiann Groves; Donna Brennan of Donna Brennan Associates; Nancy Tamosaitis of Vorticom Inc.; Merton G. Silbar Public Relations' Brent Roberts; Publitas' Mike Iacovella; WE (Women's Entertainment) and AMC's Tanya Saunders.

Contents

Introduction: You Have the Right to Sell Your Own Home

Everyone has the right to sell their own home.

The For Sale By Owner Handbook is a must-have guide that gives you inside real estate techniques to sell your home like a pro. This is an objective, fully informative—no hold back kind of book—that shares trade secrets. A companion website accompanies this book and you can get quick answers to your questions by e-mailing info@pipernichole.com. Our goal is to be a one-on-one source to help you sell your home fast, effectively and successfully.

In this book, you have a whole team helping you sell. Experts featured in the book are from *Better Homes and Gardens*; *Los Angeles Times*; *Trading Spaces*; *This Old House*; *Country Living*; Yale; New York University; University of California, Berkeley; and Fannie Mae Foundation, among many others.

The grab 'n' go, easy-to-read content is based on research, personal experience and interviews with national experts.

Part I

The first part of this book answers questions For Sale By Owners face: how to sell your home step by step, price it right, attract buyers, make your home irresistible, sell it from the outside and how to have a sensational open house.

Part II

In Part II you'll find tactics to turn a potential customer into a buyer: how to make sure the buyer is financially qualified and how to negotiate the contracts. This section covers what to expect with home inspections, termite inspections, appraisals, attorneys and title companies, plus it includes steps to a hassle-free closing.

Part III

Part III is about providing you with tools and information to help you succeed in the sale. For example, this part shares a sample written contract, inspection, disclosure/ disclaimer statement and the lead disclosure paperwork often associated with a sale. It also features safety tips, how to reinvest your money after a sale and your rights, with a special section on how to improve your credit, score a mortgage and purchase your next home.

Half of every venture is attitude. Know that it is possible, and you will sell your home successfully. The other half is having the inside scoop; welcome to *The For Sale By Owner Handbook*.

For every person who wants to sell your home—this is for you.

Top 10 Tips From Experts Featured in This Book

1. **Karol DeWulf Nickell of *Better Homes and Gardens* magazine:** "Consider selling yourself. While most homeowners are too busy to deal with the hassle of selling a home, it can be worth exploring, since it could save you thousands on commissions to sell by owner."

2. **Hildi Santo-Tomas of TLC's *Trading Spaces*:** "Make the house look as good as you can without going into debt to improve it."

3. **Thomas Davidoff of The University of California, Berkeley:** "People tend to be in too much of a hurry and take the lower price instead of waiting a few weeks and getting a higher price. People make the mistake of selling too low."

4. **John Byrd of *Outdoor Living* magazine:** "The first impression is most important in life; you want the visitor to feel they have come home."

5. **Larry Bilotti of *Country Living* magazine:** "When you come into a home, I think there's a need to know who's living there has a sense of pride and has loved living there."

6. **Attorney Louis Guttmann of Attorneys' Title Insurance Fund:** "Prior to selling the property, it's important to show the property accurately and represent things accurately to prevent problems later."

7. **Roger Cook of *This Old House*:** "Right away, easy fixes for your yard include mulching beds, fertilizing the grass and having perennials. Make sure your shrubs are pruned, take them out if they are dead or overgrown. Mature plantings block windows or destroy the body of the home. Notice if your walkways or driveways are cracked, irregular or bumpy. Seal coat your driveway or power wash your walkways. You can do it instantly and you can do it yourself."

8. **Attorney Tom Hayes of R.T. Hayes & Associates:** "If it's not in writing, it's not binding."

9. **Lynsey Wood Jeffries of the Fannie Mae Foundation:** "A prospective seller may want to consider the potential prices of their future home

(will they buy or rent?), estimate the current value of their current home by examining the home prices of similar homes and consider how much equity is in their current home before deciding to sell."

10. **Mark Mayfield of** *House Beautiful* **magazine:** "Moving is a great time to edit yourself. It's a great opportunity to have a new decorating look or a garage sale. If people look at it more as an opportunity than drudgery, it's a great opportunity to change your life."

It's the American dream to buy a home—and cash in on the investment.

When I helped my friends buy their first home before they got married, it was one of my most rewarding experiences. They say we have 10 important changes in our lives; buying a home and getting married are two of those. Fast-forward to a year later: My friends and I were standing in their kitchen at their last bash before having twins. Kelly and Rick were thinking of one day selling their home themselves as For Sale By Owners. As a young couple, they could make money when selling their home because it was in a nice location and a good neighborhood and they were keeping the home nice.

As my friend Trisha and I were talking one day during lunch, she asked: "How easy is it to sell your own home? Can you do it?"

"It's really easy," I nodded my head.

She smiled, "I can't wait to read your book."

So, here we are. I want to give you insight into selling your home like the professionals do. The first chapter is designed to take you step by step through the process. The following chapters help carry you through pricing your home, preparing it for sale, tips for stress-control, negotiating the contract and a hassle-free closing. I share how to sail through the home inspection process—where most deals fall apart—and how to ensure that buyers can afford your home. I also have included a special section on tips for buying your next home, scoring a mortgage and improving your credit.

I will never forget one For Sale By Owner family. They really needed to sell their home because they could no longer afford the payments. They needed the extra funds, and they needed to sell fast. There was a curiosity in the man's blue eyes, his wife at his side and toddler in the playpen. He asked: "How do I price my home? How do I find buyers? How do I write the contract? I want to sell my home fast, but I also want to make money."

Everyone has different needs for selling solo. And this book is meant to help you achieve your desire to sell your home.

I asked incredible national experts to participate in sharing must-have advice to help you sell your home—editors-in-chief at major magazines, TV show personalities, faculty and employees at top universities, leaders and investors. I also spoke to one of the best investors in the world. His keys to success include 20 directional signs pointing to your home, pre-screening buyers to make sure they can afford your home (check out Chapter 8) and being a pleasant person during negotiating. He really lives up to being pleasant. I enjoyed our conversation. He's sold hundreds of homes and what he says about home selling is: "It's a simple process."

It truly is. Are you ready to sell your home? Let's do it!

PART ONE

Preparation Is Key

Chapter 1

Step-by-Step Guide to Sell It Yourself

Jennifer Wake is banking $45,000 from selling her home solo. This nurse by day, For Sale By Owner by night says, "It really paid off."

She had countless showings, numerous calls and worked it like a walking ad. Now, she says, "It's sold."

What was key to the sale? Preparation. Like a well-polished Realtor, she and her husband looked at their yard with a critical eye. Jennifer repainted the interior and exterior, landscaped the front yard, replaced a couple of windows and added new carpet. They priced it to sell, did cost-effective advertising and paid a flat fee to list their home on the Multiple Listing Service and get maximum exposure for snagging buyers.

Belinda Lynn wants to sell her home, but she faces the same questions many For Sale By Owners have: "How do I sell my house? How does the process work? Where do I start?"

The first thing you must know is *Selling is simple.*

Here are the five easy steps:

1. **Price it:** Get a free CMA from area Realtors or online. A CMA (Comparable Market Analysis) will tell you what homes are selling for in your area, how long it's taking them to sell and the going price per square foot. You will see homes that are sold, pending and currently on the market. You can also get an appraisal to see what your home is worth. Do grassroots research. Visit homes for sale in person, look online or glance at the newspaper—see what price they are selling for, how it compares to your home and how long it took to sell (then you get a feel for how long it will take to sell your home). A good bare-bones equation:

   The price per square foot × your square footage = sales price.

(For example, say $100 is the average price per square foot for homes in your area × your home's 2,000 square feet = $200,000. But, as one real estate agent says, you have to factor in whether your home is prime ribs or hamburger.)

2. **Prep it:** When your home first hits the market is when it is hottest. Before putting the for sale sign in your yard, get it ready for display. The key to a swift sell is preparation. Keep your grass cut, shrubs trimmed, add a fresh colorful plant, power wash or paint the exterior (if needed) and create a sizzling presentation from the outside. Research shows that great curb appeal = more money when selling your home. If you entice buyers from the outside, they will want to see the inside. When it comes to your interior, appeal to the buyer's senses. Create love at first sight by adding a coat of fresh paint; de-cluttering; cleaning; taking extra furniture out of the room, for a spacious feel; and keeping the blinds open and lights on for a clean, cheerful, bright appearance. For a pleasant scent, have a candle burning or an apple pie warming in the oven at 200 degrees. If you have pets, deodorize your home in advance to get rid of the smell (consider deep carpeting cleaning). Avoid heavy potpourris and sprays. While the whole house is important, there are two rooms buyers really hone in on for cleanliness: the kitchen and bathroom(s).

   Also consider digging out your title and survey to help the buyers know as much as possible about your property before they buy it. Before a sale is complete, a buyer will do a title search to find out about any liens against the property. (You'll want to know if there are any liens you need to clear up *before* you sell. It prevents later problems, such as if a buyer decides to back out of the deal due to a certain lien against your home.) Buyers always want to know how much land they will get, so a survey can be a great tool. Share as much information with the buyer as you can; when all the "cards" are "on the table" between you and the buyer, the transaction goes smoother.

3. **Effective advertising on a budget:** It's not just about having a sign; it's about making your sign sell. Set up at least 20 pointer signs directing buyers to your home. Make sure your signs are at the main entrance(s) of the neighborhood. The sign in your yard should have an informational tube or brochure box where you can put fliers detailing information about your home.

   For newspaper ads, price, location, contact information and amenities are key pointers. Ask your newspaper for cost-effective packages for running more than one ad (it's cheaper than placing one ad at a time every week). See if they will place your ad online for free.

   Advertising is getting fun these days. New programs are popping up to help For Sale By Owners. Just look at the Assist-2-Sell programs that are helping sellers with marketing their homes, contracts, closings and more. The Home Finance Center in Florida is matching financially qualified buyers with For Sale By Owners, and many title companies are spurring programs to help you sell. Selling solo is a huge trend. Go with what fits your needs and budget. Buyers want to see your home, so hold open houses and do showings.

There are For Sale By Owner (FSBO) Websites and flat-fee listing programs that charge a fee to place your home on the Multiple Listing Service (MLS) to reach a large market of buyers. The MLS is a listing of all the homes for sale—it's where real estate agents go to find homes for their buyers. (For example, you can see the listing at www.Realtor.com.) Statistics show that the MLS sells about four out of five homes. Alternative options to posting your home on the MLS include FSBO flat-fee listing programs, discount real estate brokerages and online programs geared toward For Sale By Owners. If your home is on the MLS and an agent finds a buyer for your home, it would cost one commission (for the buyer's agent) instead of two, because you don't have an agent. One way to find flat-fee listing programs is online. Jennifer got her home on the MLS and it sold shortly thereafter.

There are so many options to help For Sale By Owners. There are Websites created specifically to help For Sale By Owners advertise their homes— you can place pictures, virtual tours, descriptions and more. (But find out how much traffic comes to the site before placing your ad there.) You can also use the Web address on your promotional fliers, so buyers can go there for more information.

One of your most effective marketing tools will be your flier—a flier featuring your home's features, amenities, number of rooms/bathrooms, pictures (interior and exterior images), price, location and additional details. This flier will be what buyers pick up from the information tube on your sign, at your open houses and showings.

Enjoy marketing your home; that charisma, energy and enthusiasm you show for your home will get the buyer excited about your home. Spark positive interest, and you will get a positive response.

4. **Scoring buyers, negotiating offers, and sealing the deal:** When a buyer presents an offer, look for a prequalification letter or preapproval (even better) for a loan. If they offer an ample earnest money deposit and down payment, they are ready to roll. But what if a buyer wants your home and doesn't know if he or she can afford it? Easy. Recommend they meet with a loan officer. Then you both will find out if the buyer can afford your home up front.

Always disclose defects or problems with the house up front; it prevents problems later. It is highly recommended to have a real estate attorney review the contract to protect your interests. (You should know that while Realtors write contracts, they can never give their clients legal advice.) It is always advisable to have someone protecting your rights.

5. **Steps to a hassle-free closing:** After the deal is signed, dated and agreed upon, the buyer will take care of getting financing for the home and setting up the whole house inspection, plus any other inspections. You will usually negotiate repairs with the buyer after the inspection. You or the buyer will set up the termite inspection. Contact a title company, escrow company, lawyer or real estate attorney to handle your closing.

"A seller doesn't have to do anything unless a buyer makes an issue of the survey or title commitment," explains Richard Barrett-Cuetara, a real estate attorney for Cowles & Thompson. "A smart seller will fix problems before putting their home up for sale." About 48 hours before closing, the buyer will take a final walk-through of the home to make sure it is in the same condition or better than when the deal was signed. Then, on closing day you get paid and the buyer gets the keys to your home. It is then officially recorded in the local government office.

Simple, huh?

Deciding to Sell

What should you consider when deciding to sell your own home?

Jennifer Wake and her husband decided to sell their home because the housing market was hot in their neighborhood, and they wanted to make money on the sale of their home. They did.

When you decide to sell, make sure you are financially qualified to purchase a new home, so after you sell your home, you can move into another one. Sometimes sellers get caught in a situation where they have sold their home, but are unable to purchase a new one. The first step is to meet with a loan officer to ensure your financial ability to purchase a new home.

Common reasons people decide to sell their homes are: life changes, career moves, a change in marital status, space needs (need a bigger or smaller home), high monthly payments, whether you have substantial equity in you home and whether the housing market is hot (a seller's market). But sometimes there are reasons to stay, such as tight finances, uncertainty of where you may want to move and a slow market.

10 Easy Steps to Selling Your Home

Buyers are so excited every time a new home hits the market. They are just as excited to buy your home as you are to sell it. The sooner your home sells after it hits the market, the better price you will get. The key is preparation before hammering the "for sale" sign in the yard. Following are checklists to help make the home-selling process easier on you. Let's get started!

STEP 1: Deciding to Sell

Meet with a mortgage officer. Get prequalified or preapproved for a loan, to make sure you are qualified to purchase another home.

✦ Call your lender to check your mortgage payoff amount.

Research homes you want to buy to find out the going prices.

Determine your time frame. Do you have time to wait for the best offer or do you need to sell quickly?

✦ Study how long it is taking to sell homes in your area, so you can estimate how long it will take you to sell.

Is it a seller's market? More buyers than sellers means houses sell quickly and sellers are getting close to asking prices. Sometimes sellers in this market get asking price or higher.

Is it a buyers market? More sellers than buyers means more seller concessions and longer selling time.

Consider how much it will cost you to move into a new home. Include down payment, loan costs, insurance, title work, etc. (A lender usually gives you a sheet of estimated costs when you meet with them for a prequalification or preapproval.)

STEP 2: Pricing It Right

Review the information in Chapter 2.

Find out how much your home is worth. Ask Realtors for a free Comparable Market Analysis (CMA) that will give you the pulse on the going price of area homes, get an appraisal or find out what area homes are selling for (see ads in your local newspaper or online at *www.Realtor.com*).

✦ Estimate your selling costs. Include attorney and closing agent fees, tax, prorate costs (property taxes, fuel tank, home owner association fees) and advertising costs. (See the "Seller's Estimate of Proceeds Worksheet" on page 35.)

Calculate a rough estimate of what you will make from the sale of your home. Just subtract your mortgage payoff from the estimated sale price. Then subtract your additional costs. Will your list price cover your costs to purchase another home?

✦ Buyers will also ask for personal possessions such as curtains, light fixtures and the stove. Establish what you are willing to give as a bargaining chip and hide what means a lot to you.

STEP 3: Preparing to Sell

✦ Many problems deal with the title and survey. Make sure you have a clear and marketable title insurance (free of liens), and be familiar with your survey.

✦ Consider curb appeal. Keep the grass cut, shrubs trimmed, flower beds mulched, trees pruned, sidewalks cleared and add flowers for color.

✦ Inside your home, apply a fresh coat of paint, de-clutter, clean, organize closets, take out the extra furniture, make sure windows sparkle and add some fresh flowers.

✦ Make repairs.

✦ Consider having a pre-inspection done. A home inspection before you put your house up for sale lets the buyer know up front what is wrong with the home—so no one is surprised when the buyer does a home inspection. (Home inspection is usually an area of conflict.) Sometimes by having a pre-inspection, a buyer will skip doing an inspection and make the contract process quicker. (See Chapter 11 about disclosures/disclaimers.)

✦ If your home was built before 1978, you need a lead paint disclosure form, which you can find at *www.hud.gov* or *www.epa.gov*.

STEP 4: Marketing Your Home on a Budget

✦ Review the information in Chapter 3.

✦ Get a quality "for sale" sign—it becomes a part of the curb appeal.

✦ Have directional signs, with your number, that easily direct buyers to your home.

✦ Savvy newspaper ads: buy package deals to save you money and see if they will post your ad online for free.

✦ Consider online advertising. More and more buyers are turning to the Internet.

✦ Utilize fee-for-service programs. If you need help with the contract or just need help marketing, for example, pay a flat fee only for the service you request.

✦ Get on the multiple listing service to reach buyers directly.

✦ Create a flier about your home to generate interest for buyers. It should include the address, price, photos, features of the home and your contact information. Put the fliers in a container on your sign and pass it out at showings and open houses.

✦ Other advertising options include running an ad in a home magazine or pamphlets (like those you see at the grocery store).

STEP 5: Getting Offers on Your Home
and Negotiating With Ease

✦ Get all offers in writing.

✦ Accept offer, counteroffer or reject offer.

✦ If you accept an offer, give the earnest money deposit to an attorney or closing agent.

✦ Make sure you have a copy of the fully executed contract.

STEP 6: Selecting a Closing Agent and Processing Paperwork

✦ Select an agent to handle your closing (a closing attorney, escrow company or title company).

✦ Give your agent a copy of the contract.

✦ The closing company arranges closing date and time.

✦ Deliver Home Owners Association (HOA) package to purchasers ASAP. Get buyers to sign acknowledgement of receipt. If you don't have an HOA, give the buyers a copy of covenants and restrictions, if applicable.

STEP 7: Inspections

✦ Whole-house inspection is set up by the buyer.

✦ Negotiate inspection repairs or credits in writing.

✦ Set up a termite inspection and well and septic inspections no more than 30 days ahead of closing.

✦ Buyers may have other inspections done.

✦ The buyer accepts the home, requests repairs, negotiates more or walks away if the inspection shows there is too much damage to the home.

STEP 8: Steps to a Hassle-Free Closing

✦ The buyer makes a formal application for a loan, and the mortgage is processed.

✦ Have utilities disconnected on the closing date.

✦ The mortgage company sets up an appraisal.

✦ The title search and survey should be going on behind the scenes.

✦ Clear out the home.

✦ Arrange for a final walk-through with the buyer.

✦ Deliver keys, deed if necessary, proof of paid utilities, sometimes proof of repairs and any information your closing agent requests.

STEP 9: Closing

✦ All paperwork is signed.

✦ The seller gets the proceeds.

✦ The buyer gets the keys.

STEP 10: After Closing

✦ Be aware of taxes (and tax breaks—see Chapter 17).

✦ If you haven't bought your home yet, review Chapter 19.

Chapter 2

The Price Tag: Finding the Right Price That Works

*"People are willing to pay top dollar for what they really need...
even more for what they really want."*
—Patrick Butler, VP of real estate operations
Home Financing Center

Anne Hunt will tell you she likes trees better than people. That is why she is reluctant to sell her hand-crafted home located on a resort island off the coast of Maine. Most go there to vacation at the four-seasons Rangeley Lakes Resort region. She calls it "home," surrounded by the breathtaking panoramic lakefront and mountain view, sandy beach, secluded coves and an eight-acre forest.

We haven't even talked about the house, yet. She always looks for homes with character so they are easy to sell later. When you enter the living room, your eyes immediately take notice of the cozy stone fireplace, high ceilings and amazing outdoor view.

So, how do you price beauty?

Anne started by calling several real estate agents to get price estimates on her home. You can get a free Comparable Market Analysis (CMA) from Realtors in your area. A CMA lets you know what similar homes sold for recently, how long they took to sell and the asking price of current homes. It gives you the maximum, minimum and average selling prices for the area, as well as price per square foot. (See pages 13–14 for sample calculation.) Experts say the average sells effectively. But, as Colorado Realtor Robert Walkowicz says, you have consider whether your home is "prime ribs or hamburger."

You can try this using the CMA's highest, average or lowest price per square foot going for your area. For example, if the maximum price per square foot was $119, the selling price for a 2,100-square-foot home would be $249,900; if the lowest was $76 per square foot, the price would be $159,600.

Some Realtors suggested high prices, trying to get Anne's listing. (Their tactic is to give you a un-sellable high price to get the listing and then, later, lower the price.) Others told her low prices so if they get to sell it, it would sell fast.

"I wanted to know what my home was worth—really, really worth," says Anne. For a few hundred dollars, she had an appraisal done to get a reasonably accurate value for her home. An appraisal is a representation of market value, because that is what properties have sold for in the market.

Ultimately, the asking price is in your hands.

"The market is not price driven," says multi-millionaire investor Ron LeGrand. He says it is about what the buyer wants, needs and is willing to pay.

Savvy Pricing

An old retail trick is also very common among top selling agents: price a home just under a larger round number, such as $349,000 instead of $350,000. It gives the feel of a discounted price.

What factors affect the price of your home?

Location: Do you live in a hot area? On Anne's island, there were only 28 homes. She had to wait a little longer to sell, as opposed to Karen Andrews, who lived in a neighborhood in Virginia where homes were selling like hot cakes and where it took her four weeks to sell.

Condition: Does the property look maintained? Does the outside of the home have a well-maintained lawn, trimmed shrubs and mulched flower beds? Is the inside clean and clutter-free?

Desirable amenities: *House Beautiful* editor-in-chief Mark Mayfield says amenities are important. He says to make sure appliances are in good shape—especially refrigerators, dishwashers, and ranges. Buyers check the appliances (especially in the kitchen). If it is a cosmetically bad appliance, consider replacing it—"it will come back to you in the resale," says Mayfield.

Wendy Tilton knows about selling. This New York University adjunct associate professor and Realtor-by-trade says that when you sell your home, you need to know the area competition, the average selling price and the time it is taking homes to sell (then you'll have an idea how long it will take you to sell). You also need to know your motivation: Are you pushed to sell, causing you to lower your price? Do you have time to wait for better offers and not give in to seller concessions (such as pitching in for a part of the buyer's closing costs)?

"People tend to be in too much of a hurry and take the lower price instead of waiting a few weeks and getting a higher price," says Thomas Davidoff, assistant professor at University of California, Berkeley. "People make the mistake of selling too low."

Patrick Butler runs a successful program matchmaking financially qualified buyers with For Sale By Owners in Florida. As president of the Home Financing Center, a mortgage company with a real estate division, he helps numerous FSBOs price, market and sell. He and other experts says there are several factors to consider when pricing your home:

Know the value of your property: See what homes in your area have sold for recently over the past three to six months. Call or e-mail three or four Realtors for a free CMA. Another option is getting an appraisal for a few hundred dollars. Other options include checking out your county assessor's office (or its Website)—it will show what your neighbor's house sold for (your neighbor said $161,000; the truth is $156,500). Many Websites are giving free CMAs (but some charge for them or try to pair you up with a Realtor, so be careful). To get a feel for your competition, go to area open houses, browse the newspaper and see how much competing homes are selling for. Take note if your home is much more expensive than 10 others nearby; a buyer may never consider an overpriced home, recommends NYU's Tilton. "You can't avoid the facts."

Know the time factor involved: Do you need to sell rapidly or do you have some time?

Available inventory: Are there many homes for sale and only a few buyers? This is a buyer's market. This means buyers have more negotiating power because sellers are not getting as many offers. On the flip side, are there only a few homes for sale and a lot of buyers vying for one home? This is a seller's market. In a seller's market, negotiating and pricing is in your favor.

How can you tell if it is a buyer's market or a seller's market? NYU's Tilton says you can tell when you look at a CMA; a seller's market is when property prices are up, selling quickly and spending few days on the market (DOM). It's a buyer's market if homes are on the market longer, pricing is lower and sellers are giving lots of concessions—a fair, good deal is what gets buyers in a slow market.

Tilton recommends looking at about six homes to see how many days they were for sale, concessions given and the difference between the asking price and sold price.

Negotiating needs. Who wants it more? Is the buyer's need to buy greater than your need to sell? Maybe the buyer needs to move into town quickly, versus the seller who has time to see what he can get for his home in a good market. Does the seller need to move fast because of a job?

Season for selling: The best times to sell are spring and fall. That is when most sellers are selling. (In fact, 45 percent of all moves happen between Labor Day and Memorial Day, according to U-Haul.) Slow periods tend to be midwinter and midsummer. "If you price right at market value or slightly below and put it up for sale in the spring, houses sell for higher prices in the spring and faster in the spring," says real estate investor Bryan Rundell. "No one wants to move in the winter. Houses, in a lot of cases, sell 10 percent below market value in the winter."

Fair Market Value

A buyer may fall in love with your home for the architecture, landscaping and amenities. But the fair market value takes into consideration other factors—factors the buyer is also considering when buying.	*At the same time, there are factors you can't control that affect the fair market value. The buyer is looking at everything that may affect their next move.*

Direct Factors on Fair Market Value

Community: Area services, conveniences, desirability of the area.

Schools: Quality of schools can be a huge asset.

Zoning and planning: Community development plans can be positive or negative.

Neighborhood and neighbors: Is it safe, attractive and in a good location? (To know if your home is located well, consider whether homes sell within a good time frame and for a good price, if the neighborhood is appealing and if people want to move into the area. These, along with the other factors that affect fair market value, all contribute to good location.) Are your neighbors nice? Are their yards well kept? Is the perception of your area good?

Transportation: Does your home have easy access to transportation? Is it close to the highway?

Indirect Factors on Fair Market Value

Disaster: Natural disasters, such as earthquakes, wildfires, hurricanes, tornados, etc., can lower property prices—especially if it is a reoccurring problem.

Economic changes: If the economy is good and rising, home prices often go up and increase sales. In a depressed economy, home prices and sales decrease.

Demographic changes: How is the area changing? You can find demographics of your area at *www.Realtor.com*.

Personal Perspective

"Depending on your local market and the condition/location of the home, I try to keep the list price at no more than 5 percent of the actual value of the home. The market in Florida has been really strong the last few years so I have been bumping that up to 10 percent in certain situations, but I rarely will list one over that."

—Ryan McCall, Broker-Associate
RE/MAX ACR Elite Group Inc.

Price to Sell: Techniques for Pricing Your Home

It is fast, effective and free: CMA. Call three or four Realtors for a Comparable Market Analysis. A CMA gives you a feel for the market and the going prices for homes. It compares your home to other similar homes that have sold recently.

CMA is data to simply help you establish your sale price, and it provides proof to buyers about how your sale price was established and why it is fair. When you look at a CMA, the important information to notice is:

+ How long it took the homes to sell ("Days on the Market" or DOM).
+ The difference between the asking price and the sold price.
+ Average, minimum and maximum sales prices.
+ Average, minimum and maximum of price per square foot.

Getting CMAs

We did an experiment: we sent four Realtors an e-mail asking for a CMA. Two never responded. One did not know how to do it. The fourth Realtor sent a CMA. Score: 1 out of 4. Make sure you look at several CMAs to get a feel for the market.

CMA Flaws to Avoid

It is important to get several CMAs from Realtors who specialize in your area (just notice the Realtor signs in your neighborhood and call them for a sample CMA—right off you know they are familiar with the area competition and pricing). Sometimes CMAs can have flaws, however, so get several to get a feel for the going prices.

Here are some flaws to look out for:

+ Sometimes, because Realtors will want to list your home, they will select high-priced homes in your area to show that your home could sell for a higher price.
+ Other Realtors will select homes that sold for low prices in your area in hopes that if you list with them the home will sell quickly.
+ Other Realtors may be inexperienced and the CMA could be incorrect or imbalanced.

CMA

When you ask a Realtor for a CMA, they will put one together in hopes that you will list your home with them. After they e-mail or bring a CMA to your home, expect them to ring you often to follow up and see if you will list your house with them. At the same time, keep in mind that from the moment you put your FSBO sign out you will get continuous calls from Realtors.

Price per Square Foot

Traditionally, the average price per square footage is the tried and true way of pricing your home. It's a good bare-bones starting point: Average price per square foot × your home's square footage = sale price. (Also keep in mind, location, amenities, and additional value when pricing.)

1. Look at the CMA and notice the average price per square footage. Use this figure, multiplied by your home's square footage for a basic sale price.

2. What if you don't have a CMA? Find out the sale prices of several homes in your area and divide by the total square footage to get the price per square foot. (For example, if a 1,950-square-foot home sold for $215,000, then $215,000 ÷ 1950 square feet = $110 per square foot.)

Hire an Appraiser, but the Thing Is…

If you want to find the value of your home, consider hiring a professional real estate appraiser for a few hundred dollars. Appraisals determine the price based on comparable homes that have sold and other information.

✦ **Pros:** Wendy Tilton has found appraisals to be right on target. She is a real estate broker and owner of Key Properties Consulting, a real estate education and investment consulting firm. Tilton says, in regard to working with appraisers for help pricing a home, "I have worked with some who are very good, and give the consumer a [price] range and explain what is going on in the market and in their neighborhood."

Nilla Roberts is a Peters, Cook & Company real estate agent with a background in appraising. She says, "I perform an analysis of the market, other properties that have sold and that are currently on the market. It is important that you discuss in detail your analysis with the homeowner so they understand the existing market and what is anticipated in the near future. Pricing the property within the market range is the key to making it attractive to buyers and other sales associates. This will also result in a shorter marketing time."

✦ **Cons:** Patrick Butler has an excellent example of the problem that can sometimes arise with appraisals. Suppose the appraiser says your home is worth $350,000. During the course of the week, there have been two sales— one house sold for $360,000 and another sold for $395,000. These sales improved the value of your property, and you could sell your house for more. With the appraisal, your house sells for the $350,000, "but you missed out on additional value," says Butler.

On the flip side, however, consider if a factory closes and 75 people lose their jobs and put their houses up for sale. Your house has appraised for $350,000, but now your home is competing against 75-plus other homes and there are only 15 buyers. "Value immediately drops based on supply and demand," says Butler.

While a Realtor's CMA can keep a "pulse on the market," Butler says an appraisal is only a "snapshot" of your home's value. An appraisal is particularly helpful if your home is unique (for example, if it has different architecture than the other homes nearby). If there aren't a lot of homes in your area, leaving you unable to gauge the going price, an appraisal also helps in this situation.

Did You Know?

When a buyer is going through the loan process, the lender gets an appraisal of the property done. That really isn't the time when you want to find out your home is worth $217,000 and you sold it for $207,000.

Appraisals are good if your home has acreage and if there aren't nearby homes/sales to compare it to. These independent appraisals for the sale may be higher or lower than appraisals for tax purposes. Usually appraisals for tax purposes reflect the lowest value of a home (it's usually not a good idea to price a home based on this). Study the market, know what homes are selling for and price your home.

County Assessor's Website or Office

When Karen Andrews wanted to sell her home, she went to the county assessor's Website to find out the sold prices of area homes. This is public information available to everyone at either the assessor's office or Website. (This is the same data Realtors use in a CMA, only now software makes it easier for them to show what area homes are selling for.)

Check out the Competition

Karen also looked at area homes with for sale signs, open houses and the newspaper to get a pulse on the going price. Then, using the price per square foot equation, she arrived at a price for her home.

Never Reveal Your Needs

If you are in dire need of selling, avoid telling potential buyers. Knowing you are in a pinch, they will offer a lower asking price to see how much they can get for as little as possible. The same is true when you go to buy a home, never let the seller know how much you love the home—they will try see how much you will pay for it.

Online and Private Companies

You can also get CMAs and estimates on your home's worth at scores of Websites. Some are free, others charges a fee, and some try to set you up with a Realtor. There are also private companies that provide CMAs for a price.

Word Choice

Experts say to avoid calling your price an "asking price" when talking with buyers—it sounds like an you're simply *asking* for this price and that it is not a price you *expect*.

Pricing and Negotiating Effectively

For advice on pricing and negotiating, we asked Realtor Robert Walkowicz, Certified Residential Specialist with The Group, Inc. Real Estate in Fort Collins, Colorado. He has some excellent advice.

Piper: Do you have advice/tips for pricing a home to sell effectively?

Robert: As odd as this may sound, no matter the price range, my best advice is to price your home right from the beginning and address any maintenance issues up front. Buyers compare homes and pick the best, period. Sellers are not always intimately familiar with the homes currently available. I have taken Sellers out to see similar homes so they can evaluate the competition for themselves. Be able to stand behind a market analysis with data and facts. Make sure you or your agent has a detailed written out marketing plan for your home.

Piper: What is the best tip during contract negotiations?

Robert: I feel negotiations should not be win/lose scenarios, but need to be win/win scenarios for all parties. I have a conversation with my customers when we first meet and ask them about their goals, objectives and a time table. When we begin to negotiate a contract, I like to remind the seller or buyer (depending on if I am the listing agent or selling agent) what they informed me their goals were before any emotional involvement in a contract. I feel this removes any ego or emotion that could get in the way of a good financial decision.

(See negotiating tips in Chapter 10.)

From the Buyer's Perspective

Panic pricing: A buyer falls in love with your home and is on the line about writing a contract. Next thing you know, another buyer walks in the door and falls in love too. Buyer #1 decides to write up a contract. Buyer #2 writes one, too. Both make competitive offers. To create this situation, set up showings for multiple buyers to see the house at the same time or during open houses when multiple buyers are viewing the home.

Pricing High	Pricing Low
What if you want to price your home high to see how much you can get? There is a difference between inching up your asking price and all-out overpricing.	*Next, let's say you price your home too low. You would be surprised how many homes are underpriced. When a buyer goes through the loan process, the lender gets an appraiser to do an appraisal—that's not the time to find out your home is worth $217,000 and it sold for $207,000.*
✦ Buyers will spot an overpriced home and not even consider it, especially if there is another house nearby that is just as nice. (Try to avoid this in a slow market.)	✦ If you are strapped, need to sell quickly and opt to price low—sit down with a mortgage officer or your attorney and find out what seller's costs you will be paying at closing (any loan pay-off amounts and so forth) to make sure your low cost covers your expenses.
✦ You renovated the kitchen, you added a Jacuzzi and the bathroom floors are in marble—great. But the buyer will oftentimes not be willing to pay for your renovations. (But these perks help your home stand out.)	✦ Some price low in hopes of creating a bidding frenzy with multiple offers that will drive the price up. This is called "Below-market pricing." Your property should be in high demand to use this tactic—a brisk market helps. Be sure to advertise your bargain price.
✦ You start off with a high price. It's been sitting and no offer. You lower the price. Still, no offers. You lower it again. Meanwhile, buyers notice your home has been on the market for a really long time and start wondering what's wrong with it. The longer your home sits, the more likely you are to get lower offers.	✦ Sometimes if you price your home too low for the area, people will think either "What a steal!" or "Honey, what do you think is wrong with that home?"
✦ "Price right at market value or slightly below market value. Most try get more for it, but it's a risky strategy," says real estate investor Bryan Rundell.	

Sell Fast With Incentives

There are incentives that can really help sell your home. Following is a checklist. If any apply to you, check it off and use it as a negotiating point and advertise it when selling your home.

✦ **Home warranty:** If you don't offer it, often a buyer will ask for it. A home warranty policy covers unexpected repairs in the home. (When you go to buy a home, be sure to ask for one, too.) Home warranties cost several hundred dollars (many times $300 to $400)—usually this isn't an out-of-pocket expense, but one that is covered at closing.

✦ **Pre-inspection:** A home inspection before you put your house up for sale can be beneficial to you and the buyer. A pre-inspection tells you what is wrong with your home and what needs to be fixed. Either you can make the repairs before you put your home on the market, or you can tell the buyer the problems up front. Sometimes if you have a pre-inspection, buyers will skip doing a home inspection and the closing process goes more swiftly. Most of all, you won't be caught off guard by any surprises when the buyer does have a home inspection done. One of the biggest deal-breakers is when, after the home inspection, buyers find out problems and start negotiating. A pre-inspection helps ensure a smoother process. (Ask your lawyer about disclosure laws in your area. See Chapter 11.)

✦ **Fast closing:** If you are able to close quickly or are flexible with the closing date, let buyers know. This is a nice advantage.

✦ **Be flexible about move-in arrangements:** If the buyer really needs a place to store their stuff during this process, offering storage space can be an incentive.

✦ **Decorating allowance:** You know the house could really use some fresh coats of paint and new carpeting in the main hallway near the living room. Because you don't have the time to make these changes, you can offer some funds at closing to go towards decorating and so on.

✦ **Offer to help with closing costs (without losing out):** A mortgage officer can help you with this aspect (where the sales prices can be bumped up to cover some of the closing costs—yet not get the lender in trouble—and you still get what you were asking for).

✦ **Seller financing:** Seller financing appeals to buyers who need to really stretch their finances. You can use seller financing as an investment, for example offering buyers a lease option (see Chapter 9 for turning customers into buyers). A mortgage officer will be able to help you with ways you can financially help a buyer while still winning all the way around as a seller. (Check out Chapter 8 for more on how a mortgage officer can help you sell your home.)

Seller's Expenses

While your home is for sale you are paying insurance, property tax and other costs. If you already purchased another home, these costs can add up.

How Much Cash Will You Make From the Sale of Your Home?

When you have a rough estimate on your sales price, you can determine how much money you will walk away with at the end of the sale. (It is especially helpful to know how much you will have when you go to purchase your new home). From your estimated sales price, subtract the following costs:

Possible Expenses	Costs
Mortgage payoff on your present loan(s)	$ _____
Attorney's fees /title company fees	$ _____
Unpaid property taxes/ Tax proration	$ _____
Any prepayment penalty on mortgage	$ _____
Broker's commission (if the buyer has a Realtor)	$ _____

Local rules dictate whether buyers or sellers pay for these next items. You can ask your closing agent—attorney, title agent or escrow agent—who typically pays for the following:

Check Which Costs Apply to You	Costs
❑ Title insurance premium.	$ _____
❑ Transfer taxes.	$ _____
❑ Survey fees.	$ _____
❑ Inspections, termite repairs, etc.	$ _____
❑ Recording fees.	$ _____
❑ Home protection plan.	$ _____
❑ Natural hazard disclosure report.	$ _____
❑ Homeowner Association transfer fees and document preparation.	$ _____
❑ Home warranty.	$ _____
❑ Miscellaneous.	$ _____

You and the buyer will agree on arrangements for closing costs. The attorney, escrow agent or title company you are working with for closing will help you determine your final closing costs.

Making Sure Your Sale Price Covers Your Expenses

Your expenses will vary depending on your location and situation of the sale. Following are common expenses associated with the sale:

✦ **Termite inspection fee:** Sellers usually have to do a termite inspection at the request of a lender.

✦ **Tax proration:** You will just be covering taxes for the part of the year you owned the home.

✦ **Recording fees:** These cover recording the transfer of the deed, mortgage status and various releases.

✦ **Legal fees:** These include the cost of an attorney or title insurance company used for services, representation or closing.

✦ **Loan points.**

✦ **Mortgage prepayment penalty.**

✦ **Revenue taxes.**

✦ **City certification:** Some areas require that a home is up to code before it is sold. In these areas, you would pay for city certification to cover the cost of an inspector coming to your home.

✦ **Real estate commissions:** If the buyer is represented by a Realtor, there is a brokerage fee (usually based on a percentage of the price of the home).

Following is a Seller's Estimate of Proceeds Worksheet that will help you determine how much you will make from the sale of your home.

Seller's Estimate of Proceeds Worksheet

Provided courtesy Nicholas & Co. Mortgage

SALE PRICE $ _____

PRORATIONS OF TAXES, INSURANCE & ESCROW ACCOUNT $ _____

ESTIMATED GROSS PROCEEDS DUE SELLER $ _____

SELLING COSTS:

Mortgage or Land Contract	$ _____
Balance	$ _____
Home Equity Loan/2nd Mortgage	$ _____
Title Policy	$ _____

Transfer Tax: :$7.50   County: $1.10

$8.60 x $_____ =	$ _____
Mortgage Discount (Points)	$ _____
Mortgage Costs Paid by Seller	$ _____
Recording Discharge of Mortgage and/or Death Certificate	$ ____50.00____
Special Assessment	$ _____
FHAIVA Termite Inspection	$ ____45.00____
Delinquent Taxes	$ _____
Estimated Repairs	$ _____
Home Warranty	
345.00 $375.00	$ _____
Document Preparation	$ _____
Well/Septic Inspection	$ _____
Water Bill	$ _____
Occupancy	$ _____

$ _____
TOTAL

ESTIMATED NET PROCEEDS DUE SELLER $ _____

Plus

Water Bill	$ _____
Occupancy	$ _____

_____
TOTAL

Chapter 3

Getting Buyers to Come to You: Effective Advertising on a Budget

"There are thousands of houses advertised in a weekend.
What will make them come to you?"

—Mort Goldstrom, VP of advertising
Newspaper Association of America

Johanna Bilodeau was eavesdropping on a conversation when she heard about the "Hobbit House." Envision *Lord of the Rings* architecture meets New Hampshire. Tucked into the woods with a grass-covered roof and large inviting windows, the entire home was built by a man who later began losing his eyesight and had to sell it. It was his artistic creation, and he wanted to ensure the next person who bought it would love it as much as he did. He found his match when Johanna's jaw dropped and she took off her shoes to run her feet through the moss outside with delight.

The For Sale By Owner had advertised online with pictures, ran ads in the newspaper and was on the Multiple Listing Service. But a local resident who heard the home was for sale and Johanna's perked ears, curiously wanting to know more, were what spurred the sale.

Johanna is now the proud owner of the Hobbit House.

There are numerous ways to advertise your home: signs, newspaper ads, Multiple Listing Service (MLS), word of mouth, open houses and showings, just to name a few. And your neighbor? Tell him too; he may know a friend or family member who wants to move into the area. But the key is using these options in an effective way to actually get buyers in the door.

Tell me, what made you fall in love with your home?

Now, tell buyers.

Selling on a Budget

One of the top selling real estate agents in the country says he never sold a house—a house sells itself. It's like falling in love. A buyer will walk through your door and just know your home is the one. Well, to ever get that buyer to walk through the door, you have to let them know the door is open. Following are cost-effective options to advertise your home.

Make Your Sign Sell for You

Many people sell their home with signs alone, says Ron LeGrand, who is one of the world's leading experts at selling homes fast. He recommends putting up 20 pointer (directional) signs to drive traffic to your home. Ron says you get three percent more calls from signs than from an ad in the newspaper. Here are some pointers:

✦ **Attach a brochure box or information tube to your sign:** Then you have a place to put fliers, information sheets, brochures or packets detailing information about your home. The information sheets should include pictures of the home, address, square footage, amenities, details about the home, number of bedrooms and bathrooms, the school district and your contact information—you know your home best, so give interested buyers a reason to find out more and to want to see the inside after picking up your flier. People passing by can grab a flier instantly and contact you for more information. Your sign will keep advertising, even when you're not there.

✦ **Put your phone number on your signs.**

✦ **Place a directional sign at every entrance and road going into your neighborhood.** This is also great with open house signs; you want as many people passing by as possible to see that your home is for sale.

✦ **Make sure your signs point people easily to your home:** Think of directional signs as a cookie trail to your home. Make sure your directional signs have your address, so people know where they are headed. Sometimes a phone number on these signs also helps, in case a person needs additional directions, especially if you live in a hard-to-find location. (Check neighborhood, community or local government restrictions on signs.)

✦ **Make sure your "For Sale" sign is attractive:** The sign becomes a part of the curb appeal of your home. In addition to the overall appearance of your home, the sign in your yard becomes a representation of you; make it neat and professional.

Writing Effective Ads

What do you say to sell your home? Sell with few words. Make your ad sizzle with to-the-point details: location, sale price, number of rooms, highlighted special features and your phone number. Mort Goldstrom, vice president of advertising for the Newspaper Association of America, says it is important to include the following in your ad:

Fantastic Rancher!!! - $349,000

Fantastic Rancher on 3.2 acres, 5 BRs, 3 Baths, Fabulous Living Room, Wet-Bar & Wine Rack, Eat-in-Kitchen, 2 Car Garage. Great Moldings. Don't Miss This One! **$349,000** Call Mark Anderson. 555-1234

- ✦ **Location, area, address and price.**

- ✦ **Type of housing:** Is it a house, condominium or townhouse? Then, elaborate: for instance, a colonial style traditional home. "All you need is one person to absolutely love your home," says Mort. "The less information you have, the *more* calls you are going to get from people that have no real interest and the *fewer* calls you will get from people who want more information."

- ✦ **Highlight important features in your home:** How many bedrooms and bathrooms? Is there an eat-in-kitchen, a finished basement or a two-car garage? If anything has been remodeled or renovated, let the potential buyer know.

- ✦ **Amenities:** If one home talks about amenities, it draws more response than an ad that doesn't. (Include nice features, for example: A patio, fireplace, new kitchen. You get the idea.) "The more information, the better," says Mort. For example, say you saw two ads for the same car. One ad says there is a 1968 Mustang convertible for sale for $73,000, with low miles. Another ad for a 1968 Mustang convertible says that it is $75,000, with an AM/FM radio/cassette and air, in mint condition. Even though it's a higher price, the reader feels they are getting a better deal on the second. "The more descriptive you are, the more potential buyers are attracted to the home," says Mort. "The slightly higher cost of a few more words in an ad is money well spent to be descriptive."

> "The more descriptive you are, the more you are attracted to the home. The little more cost on a few more words in an ad is money well spent to be descriptive."
>
> -Mort Goldstrom

- ✦ **Include a headline:** The location determines where the ad runs, but it is not a headline. "You need to make your ad stand out from the others in a positive way. Do that with the single best feature of the house," says Mort. Ask yourself: What is unique about my home? What feature made me select this home above all others?

When Mort sold his home, his headline was "32 Oak Trees." The ad stood out because the headline was unusual, he admits. "While some might be turned off at the prospect of raking all those leaves (not to mention the acorns!), they would be just as unlikely to purchase the home after seeing all those trees. But for someone seeking privacy and natural surrounding, I had painted a picture of their dream home in just three words."

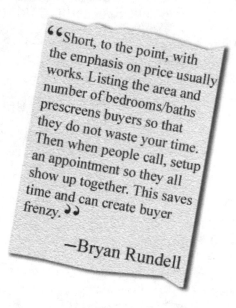

"Short, to the point, with the emphasis on price usually works. Listing the area and number of bedrooms/baths prescreens buyers so that they do not waste your time. Then when people call, setup an appointment so they all show up together. This saves time and can create buyer frenzy."

—Bryan Rundell

Lenexa Area

Nice 3bd/2ba
Home Priced Below Market
$149,500
Call 555-0006

Shawnee Area

Motivated Seller
Home Below Market
4bd/3ba $197,500, call 555-0007

West End

Must See, 3bd/1ba,
New gas furnace, fresh paint,
new carpet. FSBO $152,000
Call 555-0023

Should You Use Abbreviations?

When Mort was moving to South Carolina from Florida, he saw a lot of ads said the home had a "FROG" (for example, "4 BR, 3 BA and a FROG"). He didn't know what it meant and "I didn't want a FROG in my home," says Mort. He later found out FROG was the abbreviation for "Finished Room Over Garage." When it comes to abbreviations, he says to rely on the newspaper person working on your ad to know what are common abbreviations for your area. It's important that readers understand what your ad means. Avoid a lot of abbreviations. Remember, people are moving into your city from other areas and may not be familiar with the abbreviations in your town. Ask yourself, "Is the abbreviation common?" Mort tends to enjoy ads that read more like a story and tell you about you about the home. For example, it was your grandmother's home and you renovated the garage.

Mort says, "There are thousands of houses advertised in a weekend. What will make them come to you? It's how the ad is written."

Brightidea

Make Your Ad Pop

Adding a picture of your house makes an ad pop, says Mort. Most newspapers will accept a picture or digital image (usually in a JPEG or TIFF format). Some newspapers will even take pictures of your home. Adding an image can cost a good deal more. To get someone to glance at your ad faster, you can add decorative features such as: **Bold headlines**, *stars* or *italics*. "But, if you're trying to be careful with your budget, the most important thing is what you say," says Mort.

Newspapers Offer Added Edge: Posting Your House Online

Many newspapers across the country will post your newspaper ad online, in addition to running it in the newspaper. Sometimes there will be an additional charge, but some papers will post it online for free. Ask your local paper. If you do post your ad online, Mort says it is important to include an image or no one will look at it in an online format. Also, if you do opt to advertise your home on the Internet, consider your local newspaper's Website. Why? When people are moving into your town from another city, one of the first places they will look for homes is in the local paper—online and off.

Best Days to Run Ads in the Newspaper: Cost-Effective Advertising

"Don't assume you will run your ad once and in one day it will sell," says Mort, who has seen homes that sell overnight and others that take 90 days. He suggests asking your local newspaper about packages for running an ad on a couple of days, a few weekends, etc. at a lower price than running an ad once, then running another ad, one-by-one. "Newspaper packages are more cost effective," says Mort. After your ad runs, look at how it compares to other ads and modify it if you feel you need to. Traditionally, the best days to run the ads are on Saturdays and Sundays. "Normally, Sunday has the heaviest real estate ads. Sometimes Saturdays or Fridays have many ads, too," because those are the days people have more time to look at homes, he says. But, look at the days real estate ads are heaviest in your area and run your ad then. As Mort says, "Fish where the fish are. If all the house ads are running Sunday run your home on Sunday. Don't run your house on Tuesday if there are no other houses."

Laws Regarding Ads

When you are writing your ads, keep in mind the Fair Housing Laws that protect against discrimination in advertisements regarding race, color, national origin, religion, sex, handicaps and familial status. (For more details, visit *www.hud.gov*.) Mort says, for example, you can't say your home is near a church—it suggests you're discriminating against someone who doesn't attend church. Or, you can't say, "Perfect for a retired couple." In short, Mort says, "Be careful."

Other Publications

When you walk into the grocery store, you always see specialty real estate magazines, fliers, pamphlets and direct mail fliers you can advertise in. It is like writing an ad for a newspaper, just a different avenue for getting the word out.

Responding Effectively to Calls From Ads

When you get phone calls from your ads, answer the phone promptly, says Bryan Rundell, coauthor of the *Rogue Real Estate Investor Collection*. If you get messages, promptly return calls. When buyers want to know information, (1) they want to know it now and (2) you want to talk to them when they are excited about your property. "Then when people call, setup an appointment so they all show up together. This saves time and can create a buyer frenzy," says Bryan. If you have three or four people interested in dropping by—have them all come at the same time to see your home. Then it saves time for you and it creates pressure—competition to buy if several show interest in the home.

Internet Marketing and the Multiple Listing Service

Advertising your home online has more space for words and pictures than a traditional ad in a newspaper or magazine. The Internet is just another form of exposure, another way to show off your home. It's a great tool to use on fliers: *For more pictures and information on 19375 Riverside Avenue, visit www._____.com.* Following are five types of real estate Websites you can use to advertise your home:

1. Newspaper Websites

Statistics say that 80 percent of buyers live in your county or surrounding areas. The first place most buyers turn to is the area real estate ads found in the paper and online. This is also the first place a buyer moving into the area looks for information. Some newspapers will place your ad online for free when you buy ad space; others will charge a fee.

2. Free

You can post your home online for free at a number of Websites—check out *www.freelistingservice.com.*

3. Less than $30

Some real estate Websites are designed to appeal to local buyers and let you post a description and up to 10 photos of your home.

4. Less than $200

Often sites in this range let you post unlimited pictures. Many times you can have a virtual tour added (a virtual tour is simply a series of pictures), and residents in all the states can see your ad.

5. Flat-fee listing Websites

There are real estate service Websites that can post your home on the Multiple Listing Service (MLS) for a flat fee to advertise to real estate agents working with buyers. The MLS sells four out of five homes and about 85 percent of buyers work with Realtors.

Say a real estate agent sees your home on the MLS, finds a buyer and you accept this buyer's offer to purchase the home. You would typically pay a flat fee for it to be posted on the MLS, plus commission of the buyer's agent (usually 3 percent). If you find your own buyer, you don't pay a commission to a real estate agent.

Here's how it works: In traditional real estate transactions, the seller has an agent and the buyer has an agent, who traditionally charge 3 percent each (claiming a total of 6 percent of your sale price). The flat fee listing services cut one agent out—the seller's. Instead of paying a real estate agent to list your home on MLS (and work to sell it), you would pay a listing service a flat fee, often ranging from $200 to $600, to post your home on MLS. When an agent representing a buyer offers to buy your home, after seeing it on the MLS, you then pay *one* commission to the buyer's real estate agent. But these fees would only be charged to you at closing, so they don't come out of pocket up front. Some discount brokerages also offer to post your home on the MLS, with additional services for a flat fee (which we will discuss next).

Compare flat-fee listing services to see what services they offer and what they charge. Just do an Internet search for "flat fee listing" as starting point to find a service that works for you. The following chart shows examples of how much you could save selling your home through a flat-fee listing.

Selling Price	Traditional Commission for 2 agents (6%)	Flat Fee ($500) + Commission for 1 agent (3%)	Total Savings
$80,000	$4,800	$2,900	$1,900
$125,000	$7,500	$4,250	$3,250
$250,000	$15,000	$8,000	$7,000
$500,000	$30,000	$15,500	$14,500
$700,000	$42,000	$21,500	$20,500

What to Look For

Look for a flat-fee listing program that advertises your home using color photos, information about your house (such as square footage, number of rooms, heating, etc.) and the commission (3 percent, on average) for the buyer's agent. The commission is listed in the MLS ad, so you never have to deal with an agent negotiating the commission with you.

When you use a program that puts your home on the Multiple Listing Service, make sure it provides a variety of services. Following is a list of options that a good service will make available to you (some services will be covered under the flat fee, and others will have additional charges—it just depends on the program you select):

❑ **Help with paperwork and disclosures/disclaimers:** Help writing the contract, paperwork and disclosures/disclaimers in compliance with state and national laws.

❑ **Help with pricing your home:** A good service will give you a comparable market analysis that tells you recent house sales in your area and helps you with pricing your home.

❑ **Multiple Website exposure:** Your home should show up on multiple sites, especially *www.Realtor.com*.

❑ **Magazine ads:** Some also place an ad for your home in a magazine.
❑ **Key Lockbox:** You store your keys in a secure box that only authorized real estate agents can open, to show buyers your home.
❑ **Signs.**

Also ask about the flat-fee listing program before you join:

✦ Can I cancel without a fee? (Some charge a cancellation fee.)
✦ Will my house be put in the area and national MLS?
✦ How will my home be marketed? (Websites, magazines,newspapers, pamphlets, etc.)
✦ Will my house be listed on *www.Realtor.com*? (The largest listing of homes available on the Internet.)
✦ Exactly what other services will I get? (Find out the details before you pay.)

The Other Ways to Be Listed on the MLS

In addition, there are additional cost-effective avenues for getting your home listed on the Multiple Listing Service. You can ask local real estate agents if they can list your home on the MLS for a flat fee. Or you can try a discount brokerage. These programs offer a discounted price or flat fee for services to help you sell your home. In turn, you handle other aspects of selling the house. For example, for a fee you pay the discount broker, you will get your home listed on the MLS and in their home magazine, marketing (or advertising), and they usually help you with the sales contract and closing. In turn, you chip in on selling your home by doing the showings, open houses, dealing with buyers and so forth. The fees vary and so do the services. You can find discount agents in your area. Two leading national discount brokerages are Assist-2-Sell and Help-U-Sell. There are also local discount brokerages or agents offering their services at a discount to all their clients. Interview several discount agents before you select one; know their services, fees and what the ultimate end cost will be for you. It is also important to note that usually a discount brokerage doesn't charge fees up front, but rather gathers their profit at the closing, after the home is sold. Make sure they only charge you if your home sells, and read the agreement carefully. But of course, it varies from company to company. Go with the service you like the most.

Creating an Internet Ad

Most buyers turn to the Internet first when house-hunting. Having a Web address on your fliers, ads and promotional materials is another tool to help you sell your home. You can have your house posted online with your newspaper ad, For Sale By Owner Websites specializing in advertising homes, e-mail, message boards or you can create your own Website. Think of it as an extra space to share more information about your home. When creating your Internet ad, it is just like creating any other ad: pictures, compelling writing and your contact information. Make sure your ad includes the following:

✦ Pictures in JPEG or GIF format. Select quality interior and exterior pictures.

✦ Great text that really sells your home.

✦ Number of bedrooms and bathrooms; a listing of living room, kitchen, home office, master bedroom, special features, and so on; and room dimensions, if available.

✦ Details: Square footage, acreage, year the home was built, utility and tax costs.

✦ Area schools and local information you feel is important to add.

Create Your Own Website to Advertise Your Home

All the time, agents create Websites to show off the homes they are selling. You can do it, too. You can create a Website just for your home. Then, put your Web address on your promotional fliers, signs and ads. There are vast numbers of resources for creating a site; a good way to begin is simply by doing an Internet search for "web hosting" or "free web hosting."

Help Tailored to Your Needs

Assist-2-Sell (*www.assist2sell.com*) has creative programs to help you sell your home, depending on your needs. Say you have a buyer—now all you need is help with the contract, paperwork and closing. Assist-2-Sell's "Paperwork Only" marketing program takes care of this for you.

But if you need help marketing, try Assist-2-Sell's popular "Direct-to-buyer" program that takes care of marketing your home through local media advertising, Internet listings, signs, brochure boxes and publicity in an in-house publication.

If you want to be in the MLS, plus get all of the previously mentioned services, the cost is less than a traditional Realtor, because they sell your home for a flat fee plus the commission for the buyer's agent (if the buyer has an agent). With discount brokerages, you get an agent to show your home, free advertising, Internet marketing and prequalification of buyers, plus they handle all the paperwork and there are no upfront or hidden fees. Help-U-Sell is another discount brokerage offering similar services.

Showings

From your advertising, you are sure to get calls. Buyers can look at ads in the newspaper, online and in magazines, but nothing beats stepping into a home and knowing if it is truly "the one." You will spend a lot of time showing your home to interested callers. (And you will know your advertising is paying off.)

Experts say to evaluate early on whether a buyer is a match or not, so you don't waste their time and your time. Listen to people's needs; consider what they are looking for in a home and if your home is a fit. But don't feel forced to push a home on anyone or spend a lot of time with someone if you know it isn't a fit during a showing. There will always be other buyers.

When you sell solo, you have more control over when prospective buyers drop by—you'll be scheduling when they do. You may, however, get the occasional call from a buyer driving by who would love to stop in the next five minutes, so it's always important to keep your home shipshape, because you never know when the right buyer will drop in.

Here are a few key pointers for showing your home: keep all the lights on, have a clean-smelling home (avoid strong sprays and potpourri) and give your pets a vacation at a friend's house (some buyers don't like pets). If you get a second showing, the buyer is very interested. Make sure the house is top-notch. (For more tips, review Chapter 5 and Chapter 7.)

Will Realtors Working With Buyers Be Showing Your Home?

If you are allowing Realtors with buyers ("buyer's agents") to show your home, one option is to get a lockbox that securely stores your keys, so they can show your house during the daytime, even while you are at work. Only real estate agents can open the lockbox with their "security key." But make sure they call first before showing your home and make sure they give you feedback on what their buyer thought of your home after they have shown it. You can get a lockbox at your local real estate association store or online.

Power of Word of Mouth

Mike McNulty sold the Hobbit House he made for his mother. He first used a Realtor for six months and only had five showings, which he conducted personally, because he knew the intimate details of the home better than the Realtor. Then he opted to sell it himself. He advertised in the local newspaper, 10 other newspapers and online at *www.Isoldmyhouse.com* (800 hits), but he still can't get over the fact he sold his home by word of mouth. His buyer, Johanna, overheard her brother's friend talking about the Hobbit House. Next thing Mike knew, he got a phone call. Johanna was at his home the next day—she hadn't slept the entire night hoping he wouldn't sell the Hobbit House.

In real estate, they say to contact everyone in your "sphere of influence"—everyone you know. Let everyone know you are selling your home.

"I spent a lot on advertising, but it was still cheaper than a Realtor," he says. "Word of mouth is the way to go." Tell your friends, family, neighbors, coworkers, church, organization members, golfing buddies and folks you run into during the day that your house is for sale—you get the idea. Also send out fliers to nearby neighborhoods with homes priced slightly lower than yours. Many times people "move up" in house price the next time they buy, and they many buy within the same general area, so make sure area neighborhoods know your home is for sale. They also may know someone who would be interested, especially if your home is located in a desirable location.

Creative Marketing

There are creative ways to really sell your home. What sets your home apart is really (1) how it looks (yes, home selling is shallow)—it's all about appearance and (2) how you market. The best agents are the most creative ones. Following are some of their creative tactics you can use. Create virtual tour CDs or online tours that show pictures of the inside and outside of the home (they can be a series of photographs or 360-degree views of each room). Contact relocation programs (for people from outside the area looking for a place to live), human resource departments or businesses to let them know your home is for sale, in case they have clients moving into the area. E-mail advertising is cost-effective and efficient—from sharing photos with interested buyers, announcing open houses, to answering questions fast and efficiently. Use your e-mail as a tool. Get creative and, as always, have fun. It will reflect in the energy and charisma you show when selling your home. Use follow-up calls and thank-you cards after showing your home to potential buyers.

Home Brochures/Information Packets/Fliers

At the end of the day when a buyer has looked at five homes and it's all muddled together—you want yours to stand out. As the buyer sits down in front of the fireplace with their loved one and discusses what they looked at, you want them to be holding the flier of your home in their hand. You want them to read it, look at the interior and exterior photos and remember that your home had a great patio, lush lawn, cozy study and eat-in-kitchen. And wow, your home really was nice! Let them think, "Maybe we should see it again." Your contact information is on the flier, so they can call you if they would love to see your home again.

The information sheet is one of the most important aspects of selling your home. You will put it in your information tube attached to your sign and pass it out during showings and open houses. You can pass out your fliers to interested buyers and neighbors, post them on community bulletin boards, place them in apartment lobbies and so on. Your information sheet can be designed as a flier, brochure or several-page packet/booklet (whichever design works best for you). Be sure to include important features:

✦ Picture(s) of your home.

✦ Address.

✦ Contact info.

✦ Sale price.

✦ Number of rooms, bathrooms, kitchen, other rooms, special features (garage, eat-in-kitchen, walk-in closets, etc.).

✦ Square footage.

✦ School information, location and any details you feel are important.

✦ Improvements, renovations and any remodeling aspects of the home.

CHARMING RANCHER

[Include a catchy headline or the price if it is a great selling point]

```
┌─────────────────────────┐   ┌─────────────────────────┐
│                         │   │                         │
│                         │   │                         │
│      INSERT IMAGE       │   │      INSERT IMAGE       │
│ [Include exterior and   │   │ [Include exterior and   │
│   interior photos]      │   │   interior photos]      │
│                         │   │                         │
│                         │   │                         │
└─────────────────────────┘   └─────────────────────────┘
```

14357 Starlight Lane
Richmond, Virginia 23293

DESCRIPTION HERE: Always include the basics. Your address, contact information, location, price, features, number of rooms/bathrooms, amenities, schools, etc. Add life, be colorful and tell the buyer what you would want to know if you were looking for a home. If you are selling your home at a great price, make sure to include your price in large numbers and bold.

✂ Describe your home so it sells—jot down what you want to advertise:

_____
_____
_____
_____
_____
_____

✉ CONTACT INFORMATION: You want the buyer to call you for a showing.

☞ BROCHURES/HOME PACKETS: You can do several page pamphlets showing more photos of your home, sizes of each room, more detailed information, (some even include the disclosure/disclaimer statement). Think about what sets your home apart and special features that are really appealing about your house. Also consider doing your fliers, brochures or packets in color.

Chapter 4

Making Your House "Picture Perfect": How to Take Professional Pictures of Your Home

*"You aren't taking pictures, you are making invitations to a home.
A picture is worth a 1,000 invitations."*
—William W. DuBois, chair
School of Photographic Arts & Sciences, RIT

When William DuBois walks into a home, this architectural photographer always wonders: *How would I live in this house?* And he captures that essence in his photographs. It's not about the rooms; it's about visually expressing a way of life, a lifestyle.

Photograph the way you live. Take pictures of the outdoor patio where you would have coffee with a loved one at sunrise or that cozy room where you curl up to read a book. Or take a vignette of the beautiful fireplace that warms you up on a cold night. "Create mood settings," says DuBois.

DuBois creates the lived-in look by strategically placing a few single items in the right place. It gives the added character to the perfect room. A pen and envelope on the desk in your home office, a vase of fresh flowers on a table, a folded blanket placed across the bed or a folded hand towel on a bathroom counter all create the lived-in feel.

"The goal is to get the person to care and feel warm," says DuBois, administrative chair at the School of Photographic Arts and Sciences at the Rochester Institute of Technology in New York. "You aren't taking pictures, you are making invitations to a home. A picture is worth a 1,000 invitations."

Pictures are one of the most important aspects of advertising your home. Use pictures of your home on your fliers, online, in newspaper and magazine ads. The picture is meant to draw buyers in. We went to the experts for advice on how to take sensational pictures that will entice a buyer to see more.

Inviting You in…Wanting More

Jim McHugh photographs amazing architecture and specializes in photographing portraits of celebrities such as Keanu Reeves, Anthony Hopkins, Clint Eastwood, Tina Turner and Martin Sheen, just to name a few. Growing up in California's "Glamorous Hollywood" in the 50s and 60s, he became a widely acclaimed photographer. Now based in Los Angeles, McHugh photographs for *Architectural Digest* (for its LA and France editions, too), *Met Home* and *The London Sunday Times*, among others. He's also having an exhibition at the British Architectural Association in London.

What can we do to take better pictures of our home? First, Jim McHugh walks through a home, snapping test Polaroid shots from a variety of angles to see at what angles the room looks best (digital cameras also work great for this exercise, because you can take a lot of pictures without the film expense). He says the entrance often has the best view of the room, because the design is from that standpoint. McHugh recommends thinking about what time of day the rooms are most attractive—for example, the dining room lit in candlelight at twilight, for a romantic mood, or the living room when it is sunny and beautiful in the morning. "Shoot rooms in their best light and select a day with good weather so the light coming through the windows is nice," says McHugh.

Make sure the rooms are clean and de-cluttered and think about props. "Think about when you see pictures in *Architectural Digest*," says McHugh. The dining room tables are always set. Why? It doesn't look so empty; it looks better when you have props. Select props like decorative throw pillows, vases, flower or artwork (borrow artwork from a gallery or an artistic friend). "It makes a difference," says McHugh. "Make sure you have someone to help you to move furniture, get props and make sure the time of day is best suited for each situation."

From wide-angle shots to up-close vignettes to show off architectural details, he says "shoot lots of film, don't spare on that. Once it's done, it's done. It's better to have a lot to choose from."

Detailing a Room

When William W. DuBois takes photographs, he pays attention to the following details:

+ Sinks and faucets need a polish so they don't look dull.
+ Eliminate footprints in the carpet. Take a clean never-used garage broom and brush the nap of the carpet toward the camera. It gives the richest and deepest color of the carpet and removes footprints and vacuum wheel marks.
+ Wash the windows.
+ Clean up, as if you are about to have a huge party and want to impress your friends.
+ When photographing tight spaces, such as the bathroom, use the mirror to show off as much of the room as possible. But, also keep in mind what the mirror is reflecting. (Is the toilet lid down?)

Creating the Image:
The House Everybody Wants

Following are great tips from the experts for taking great pictures of your home. We share how to remove distractions, tips for great lighting, details to look for when photographing a room and more!

✦ **Remove distractions.** The New York Institute of Photography says there are three distractions in a photo: Too much clutter, bad interior lighting (the worst are florescent lights) and photographing a room without aligning vertical and horizontal lines (envision a picture with crooked walls).

✦ **Pay attention to lighting.** Architectural photographer Mike Butler has a good rule of thumb: rooms that have a lot of pastels, color or light look better photographed in the daylight. Rooms that are more wood-heavy, brown, maroon and other dark colors look better shot in the evening. Most of all, experts recommend watching for the best time of day, when light graces the rooms you want to photograph.

✦ **Create warm illumination.** Create mood with lighting. For warm lighting, many experts say to photograph in the morning, late afternoon or twilight. "For 'warm' lighting, take the picture within the first half hour of sunrise and the last half hour of sunset," says DuBois. "For diffused lighting that won't have harsh shadows no matter what angle you photograph, shoot on an overcast day. Cloudy days can be an asset from time to time."

✦ **Avoid overexposure.** Shooting photos while directly facing a window full of bright light can sometimes create exposure problems.

✦ **Be selective.** Photograph the strongest rooms in the house, select the most captivating architectural details and don't feel compelled to show all the photos you took—select the pictures that show off the rooms best.

✦ **Prepare for the photo.** Adding props can really add to a room, says Florida-based architectural photographer Mike Butler. A wonderful dining room looks even better with plants, table settings and candles. Or in the bedroom, add a breakfast tray. Also, don't be afraid to take items and furniture out of the room. If you don't like the table—take it out. Are there too many chairs? Take the chairs out. Prepare for the photo: Add props, clean and clear the space.

✦ **Experiment with angles.** Take pictures of the inside and outside of the home from a variety of angles to see how it shows best. You want the viewer to get a feeling for the home and want to see more. *Los Angeles Times Magazine* home design editor Barbara Thornburg say to take at least two angles of the room your are photographing to get an overall feel for the room.

✦ **Details, details, details.** What often separates *good* from *great* is attention to detail. When Thornburg sets up a room for a photo shoot, she pays attention to details. She has a keen eye for hiding cords, making sure tables aren't dusty, grouping collectables together and taking extra items out for a clean, edited environment. "We all have too much stuff; take it out. Be disciplined," she says. "Still photography is not very forgiving, it has to be perfect."

Photo courtesy Mike Butler Architectural Photography. *(top)*

Private residence in Los Angeles, photo courtesy Jim McHugh Photography, Ron Wilson Interior Design. *(bottom)*

Evoke Emotion With Your Photos

When photographer Lisa Kereszi takes photos for herself, she works alone and by instinct. She loves to record places as she finds them. Her photos of interiors, people and places are striking, captivating and moving. She teaches at Yale University and is a faculty member at the International Center of Photography. Her photos have been featured in books, galleries, museums and magazines (*New York Times Magazine*, *The New Yorker*, *Jane*—the list goes on). She has a love for photography and it shows.

Piper: How do you evoke emotion when photographing a still room?

Lisa: Pay attention to the little details; things you might not think are that interesting can turn out to look very surprising and telling in the final product. Also think about the history of the space and try to keep in mind that you are recording the traces of time passing.

Piper: When you go to take a photograph, what do you notice first?

Lisa: The corners. The way light describes something.

Piper: How do you use lighting effectively in a photo?

Lisa: Remember that what you are essentially recording is reflective light. So, if the light is dull or too even overall, you won't have the same effect as you would if the light were dramatic or directed. This is not to say that dramatic is always good, but appropriate for certain situations.

Piper: What are important elements for a great image?

Lisa: It just has to click—have that certain something special—like something I haven't seen that way before. You should also be able to see telling details.

Piper: Is there anything you would like to add that you feel is important?

Lisa: When I photograph interiors for a magazine like *Wallpaper** or *House and Garden*, I am working for someone else, with a crew, and am attempting to do a very different thing with the pictures than with my artwork. In these cases, I am trying to make a room look as appealing or welcoming or pretty as possible. For magazines like those, I always work with a stylist who comes bearing hundreds of dollars worth of flowers, a vacuum, Windex and mainly, years of experience making rooms look perfect. I usually follow their lead. In those cases, I am like the cinematographer, and he or she is the director. So, if you are trying to make your home look great for pictures—add flowers, pay attention to the folds of the drapes and the position of the pillows, and clean up a bit! Also, put the lamps on dimmers so you can control the light better.

Photographing the Exterior

Do you want a tight shot because the yard isn't that great? Or do you want a wide angle shot to show off your beautiful landscaping? When photographing the exterior of your home, experiment with angles to make your home look most appealing.

When people shoot the outside of the home, they often get too close to the house, it fills the frame, and "it can be too literal," says Mike Butler. For example, if your home is in Colorado on a ridge—take a picture of the house in relationship to the ridge. If you live in great environment, it's important—show it off!

On the other side, if you're landscape isn't that great, take a tight close-up shot of your home. If there are certain aspects you don't want to show, take the picture at dusk.

Exterior Lighting Tips

Light tip #1: If you photograph the house straight on and the sun is coming up behind you, you get a "frontal light that has no depth or feeling," says Butler. He says to avoid backlight, where you are in front of the house and the sun is behind the house. Light from the side is best; it emphasizes the bricks and color and gives a three-dimensional feeling. If your house is facing south, 11 a.m. and 4 p.m. are great times—but not if it is facing southwest or northwest.

Light tip #2: "Look for as bright a day as you can get," says William DuBois. As you point your camera at the home, the sunlight should not be directly over your shoulder. The sunlight should be to the right or left of you. If the light is at a 45-degree angle from the front of the home, shooting from the opposite angle would be good says DuBois. "Let the sun create texture."

Photo courtesy W.W. DuBois/Images & Ideas.

Angles of Interest

William DuBois gives us a couple of pointers:

+ Low angles eliminate the ground level and focuses on the house.
+ High angles show the rolling plains of grass to the doorway.

Your House = Sweet Temptation

Photographer and American University assistant professor in the Visual Media Division, Libby Cullen, shares how to take a quality photo. She also teaches at The Art League School, Gallaudet University, The Smithsonian and, recently, George Mason.

Piper: What are some great photography tips for taking a quality picture?

Libby: Know your equipment very well—your lenses, interaction between aperture and shutter speed. Learn to see, not what you think is there.

Piper: When you shoot a photo how do you evoke emotion—especially when shooting a still image, such as a home or room?

Libby: You can create a mood through lighting and color when shooting an interior. Hard versus soft lighting creates a different mood.

Piper: When taking outdoor photos, versus indoor photos, what should you consider?

Libby: You must always consider the time of day that is best to photograph an interior or exterior. Through observation, determine the time that renders the space the most favorably.

Showing off the Interior

The art of photographing your home is showing off the strongest rooms. Highlight the living room, dining room, kitchen, master bedroom suite or that amazing home theater you love.

+ **Show how a home transitions from one room to the next.** Mike Butler says it is important to show the layout of the home. Take pictures that show the room flowing from another and transitioning to the next one. As you take a picture of the living room, let the viewer catch a glimpse of the living room flowing into the kitchen. Help the viewer get a sense of how the house is laid out, how it feels, how it flows. And when you get pictures of the living room and kitchen side by side, you get an overall sense of how the house is on the inside. "The viewer has no background knowledge of your homes, they are seeing it for the first time," says Butler. You must take pictures that show "not only how it looks to you, but how it feels. Find a way to make the viewer feel."

✦ **Make your home look spacious.** To create spaciousness, use a wide-angle lens. A standard lens makes the image feel smaller, says architectural photographer Greg Wilson. Experts say if you photograph the room in the daylight, you see the room plus the outdoors, creating a more spacious visual. A room will feel smaller if you take the picture when it's dark outside and the view only stays in the room. If there are items outside that you don't want buyers to see, take the photo in the evening to hide them.

✦ **Light up the inside.** Open the blinds to let in the natural light (make sure the windows are clean)—it helps expand the room, as opposed to a darkness coming through the window that makes the space more confined, says DuBois. Turn on the interior lights to make the room as bright as possible. "Have a little glow in the light fixtures so it doesn't look like you're shooting a dead room," says DuBois. "It twinkles."

✦ **Highlight strong features of a room.** Avoid taking pictures head-on. Pay attention to strong focal points. If there is a fireplace in the study, photograph it at an angle that includes it in the picture of the room. "Go for the strongest architectural aspects," says Thornburg.

✦ **Perfect your techniques.** If you have a digital camera, you can take several angles of the room and "stitch" the image together to show a complete room. Thornburg also suggests taking a series of shots or Polaroid images of the entire room and placing the images side by side to get a perspective of the whole room.

Private residence in Los Angeles, photo courtesy Jim McHugh Photography, Ron Wilson Interior Design.

Did You Know?

A wide-angle lens will help take in as much of the room as possible.

✦ Zoom point-and-shoot cameras max wide angle setting is 35mm.

✦ Point-and-shoot cameras see 35mm to 38mm.

—New York Institute of Photography

Focusing on the Fine Details

"Don't forget to show special details of the home," says DuBois—"Customized touches in a home that are overlooked as a buyer walks through a home quickly." The inlaid tile floor at the entryway or the special trim around the window can go unnoticed, but can be singled out in a close-up shot to highlight, savor and point out to the buyer in a photograph.

Vignettes give detailed close-ups of special features in your home: The fireplace, window treatments or great crown molding—you get the idea.

To create an intimate image, photographer Jim McHugh recommends photographing at a level that seems as if you are sitting in a chair—not standing. For example, if you are photographing the living room, rather than stand there, think about sitting viewing the area; take the camera to a chair's height where you would sit (as you would sit naturally in that room).

Digital Photography 101

Digital cameras make it easier to take a lot of pictures, save them to your computer and use them instantly. You can easily add the images to your fliers, post pictures online for your internet ads, e-mail images to an interested buyer or send a picture off to go along with your ad in the newspaper or home magazine. Following are a few tips for using your digital camera and images.

✦ **Refresher:** Take time to understand how your digital camera works, as well as the computer program that came with it, says Butler. The 30 minutes it takes to refresh on the features your camera has can really improve your photos and it's "well worth it."

✦ **Experiment with exposures:** There is a range of exposures on a digital camera. Butler recommends taking multiple shots using different exposures: A little brighter, darker or close to normal. Then, when you look at the images on your computer screen, see what exposure lends well to colors that really "pop."

✦ **Lighting:** Is the same for film or digital, says DuBois.

✦ **Be selective:** Digital photography and the Internet are making it easier to post as many pictures as you want, to your heart's content. "Too many photographs may kill the enthusiasm," says DuBois. "Select photographs to entice the viewer to see more."

✦ **Cutting and cropping your image artfully:** Cropping your images is important. If you have a long horizontal home, cropping the image long and horizontal makes the home look longer and spread out, says DuBois. Providing a square is also a unique format for a home. If you are selling a townhouse or a condominium—a three-story narrow home—do not crop it narrow and vertical; it makes you feel like you have many steps.

"Cropping is important relative to how one feels inside a home, and you also want to leave enough room in the frame for a house to breath and grow. If you crop too close to the sky, it's a stifling view," says DuBois. "Remember, the first impression is a lasting impression."

✦ **Size of the image:** Make the photographs large enough on screen for the viewer to see the home. If the file is too large to download, viewers may not patiently wait to see it. Move in on a subject and fill the frame with what you want to show your viewer.

✦ **Saving images:** Save work-in-progress images as TIFF files, so they stay at maximum quality. (You can always have the original to go back to, like a film negative.) For e-mailing or posting the picture on the Internet, save a copy as a JPEG.

✦ **High-resolution image:** Resolution is measured in dots-per-inch (dpi) or pixels per inch. For printing images, you would want a high resolution (Hewlett-Packard recommends looking for a "photo-capable printer that has a high resolution, say 4800 x 1200 dpi"). If you are e-mailing it, lower resolution is better so the file downloads faster and a person can see it faster.

Mike Butler on Good Photography

✦ Use a tripod at all times.

✦ Turn the flash off to get a bright foreground and a dark background.

✦ There are two kinds of light: Daylight and incandescent light (primary residential lighting at night). Without the correct white balance of the digital camera, at night the image will tend to turn out orange; in the day, the image will turn out blue. Use the settings on your camera to adjust the white balance for the same light.

Click-Worthy Photography Sites

For some great photography tips, check out these Websites:

✦ **New York Institute of Photography:** *www.nyip.com.*

✦ **Nikon:** *www.nikon.com.*

✦ **Kodak:** *www.kodak.com.*

✦ **National Press Photo Association:** *www.nppa.org.*

✦ **Hewlett-Packard:** *www.hp.com* (digital photography tips).

To see examples of great photographs, check out sites of photographers highlighted and interviewed in this chapter:

✦ **Mike Butler:** *www.mike-butler.com.*

✦ **William W. DuBois:** *www.rit.edu/~wwdpph.*

✦ **Jim McHugh:** *www.jimmchugh.com.*

✦ **Lisa Kereszi:** *www.lisakereszi.com.*

✦ **Greg Wilson:** *www.gregwilsonphoto.com.*

From Pictures to Presentation

Are you going to put pictures on your flier? Are you going to e-mail them or post them online? Here are a few techniques, adapted from Hewlett-Packard, on how to make your pictures look top-notch.

✦ **Saving your image:** For printing your image, save your image as a TIFF. For e-mailing or posting your image online, save it as a JPEG (which downloads faster).

✦ **Quality resolution:** Resolution is in pixels or dots per inch (dpi). The photo should be at least 240 dpi for smaller images (4 x 6 inches or smaller) and 300 dpi for larger pictures (5 x 7 inches or larger).

✦ **Printer perks:** To avoid pixilated images with jagged edges, select a printer with at least four colors and 600 x 600 DPI. Make sure to set the preferences on your printer to the highest print quality setting.

✦ **Paper settings:** Controls the amount of ink deposited on the paper. Make sure you're using the right setting for the type of paper you're using—the setting for plain paper uses the most ink; settings for photo paper or glossing film use the least.

Using Pictures for Your Promotional Materials and Fliers

When you put your pictures on your fliers, select images that show the house well. Usually include an exterior image of the home. If you have space, select images you feel are a great representation of the interior. If you have a flier, usually one compelling image works well. If you opt to do a packet that includes more images and gives more details about individual rooms and aspects of the home, selectively choose photos that represent the house well.

Posting Images Online

If you are advertising your home on a Website, you will have an opportunity to use many images. But remember DuBois' advice not to "kill the enthusiasm" by posting too many. You want to leave viewers curious to see more when they look at the pictures on your promotional fliers and ads. There are also free Websites that allow you to post pictures of your home online and announce it is for sale. (Check out *www.freelistingservice.com.*) You can also do an Internet search to find more free sites where you can post your pictures online. If you post your home online, include the Web address on your promotional materials. (Review Chapter 3 for more information about posting pictures online.)

E-mailing Images to Buyers

How many times have you received images of your friends' new babies? Or pictures of a great party? It is so much fun to get pictures. Do you love to see what you really want to buy? If you get a call from a buyer who grabbed your flier while passing your home and who wondered if you would mind e-mailing images of the house, go for it. Use e-mail as a marketing tool and have fun with it!

More Than Anything...

Enjoy taking pictures of your beautiful home, play with it and experiment. So often, we are used to taking pictures of those we love, places we relished visiting and important moments in our life. We don't often take pictures of still objects, and many times we don't even think of our home in pictures. So visualize your home in a nostalgic way and bring viewers into a cozy way of life you shared and enjoyed in this home—a home you hope they enjoy, too.

Chapter 5

Preparing Your Home Before the "For Sale" Sign Goes up: How to Make Your Home Irresistible to Buyers

"When you come into a home, I think there's a need to know who's living there has a sense of pride and loved living there."
—Larry Bilotti, executive editor
Country Living Magazine

Your house is hottest when it's first on the market. That's when you get the most potential buyers. It's a new home and people want to see it. This chapter focuses on helping you prepare your home *before* putting the "for sale" sign in the yard.

We interviewed the best experts across the country. Can you guess their top tips? Repaint, de-clutter, clean, organize, create spaciousness, don't overdo it on the potpourri and bring light into your home for a clean, cheerful and appealing first impression.

In addition, you should bring the buyer home. Add that fresh bowl of apples to the kitchen table, a stack of books for flair, draw attention to the cozy fireplace by sparking a flame, light a candle, add life with real flowers and add a couple of decorative pillows to give your home an irresistible charm.

"Make the house look as good as you can without going into debt to improve it," says *Trading Spaces* television show interior designer Hildi Santo-Tomas. "You're entertaining people in your home who may want to buy it."

We all don't have a lot of time—or money. We went to the experts for the easiest and most cost-effective ways to improve our homes before we sell. *Better Homes and Gardens*, *Trading Spaces*, *Los Angeles Times*, *Country Living*, DIY, *House Beautiful* and the American Society of Interior Designers gave us some great advice.

Before Putting Your Home up for Sale, Gather These Documents

Louis Guttmann, real estate attorney with the Attorneys' Title Insurance Fund, in Florida, gives us insight about preparing for the sale, to avoid delays later. The biggest concerns that come up between signing a contract and closing are problems with the survey and title. "Prior to selling the property, it's important to show the property accurately and represent things accurately to prevent problems later," says Guttman. If you present everything up front, a buyer can never come back later and say, "You never told me...." Guttmann offers tips on how to be prepared in advance to avoid stumbles later.

✦ **Survey:** Pull out your old survey or think about having a survey done. Know your property. Are there easements? Is the fence slightly off the property line?

✦ **Title insurance policy:** Be familiar with your title. Is your home part of a home association? Title insurance expert Bob Anastasi, CEO of Odona Technology, says also to check your title for any liens against it and clear/fix it before you sell your home so this problem with the title doesn't come up later and potentially delay your closing. Another option is having a title search done.

✦ **Pre-inspection:** A home inspection before selling your home gives you an evaluation of the physical property. It gives you a chance to make repairs or let sellers be aware of problems with the home up front. If you do a pre-inspection, you will need to disclose to buyers what the inspector found. It's always recommended that you contact your attorney about disclosure laws and how they apply to information from a pre-listing inspection.

✦ **Disclosure:** Many states require sellers to let buyers know of any problems with the home or issues that could affect the buyer's decision to purchase the home. Ask your attorney about disclosure/disclaimer laws and requirements in your area. (See Chapter 11.)

✦ **Real estate attorney:** Develop contact with a local real estate attorney who is familiar with local traditions and rules. Find a lawyer by word of mouth.

Five Easy Tips to Prepare Your Home Instantly

Larry Bilotti, executive editor of *Country Living*, is searching for the home of his dreams. It has to meet his requirements for price range, space, number of bedrooms and bathrooms, and the location is critical. This New Yorker also has a passion for charming, older homes and considers the possibility of their potential as an investment. He also says, "When you come into a home, I think there's a need to know who's living there has a sense of pride and loved living there."

We asked a number of buyers what made them select their homes, and they said what Bilotti says: "Your insides know when you've found the home...when you walk in and see the potential it holds as the house of your dreams. A home is a big investment for everybody."

When a buyer walks in, they want to be able to see themselves in the home. You want the home to be as appealing as possible the moment they open the newly painted front door. In the following sections are the five top tips experts say can spruce up your home instantly.

Tip #1: Most Bang for Your Buck—Paint

At the top of every expert's list is paint, paint and yes, paint. Paint is a quick fix. Add a fresh coat to walls in neutral tones (white, off-white, tan) that can allow someone to move right in. Fresh paint makes rooms look clean, crisp and bright, and neutral tones make it more appealing to more people. Turn-offs include multicolored walls, handprints, crayon markings and worn walls. And buyers don't want to see the walls scratched because of pets. It's hard to sell a home in that condition at the price you're asking, because people want to get what they pay for. *Trading Spaces'* Hildi Santo-Tomas says, "Colors are personal. When you sell your house, it's not the time to go experiment with paint and appearances." (Save that striking red paint for your new home.)

The Art of Paint

American Society of Interior Designers (ASID) fellow BJ Peterson, of Peterson Arce Design Group, shares an artistic, easy-to-do approach to paint.

♦ **Accentuating or hiding molding:** If you have an older home with great molding, paint the molding a color that contrasts with the walls, so it stands out. On the contrary, if the molding is hideous and you want to hide it, paint it the same color as the walls so it blends in.

♦ **Having continuity with color:** If rooms are painted different colors that are appealing to the eye, to have continuity throughout the home, paint the molding the same color. In a contemporary home with an open floor plan, you can paint one wall a strong color (an accent wall) and paint the rest of the walls a lighter, neutral color for a dramatic effect.

♦ **Out with the old:** "The old thought of paint is: paint it neutral, to appeal to everyone," says Peterson, but adds that there is an openness to color these days. You can make your home more unique if you use color, but opt to use an interior designer for advice, she says. ASID member Laurie Smith also suggests thinking about the location of your home when using color. For example, she saw a home in Chicago with very bold colors that were appealing for a city-setting that may have seemed out of place in the suburbs.

Hot Tip

Wallpaper or Not?

House Beautiful editor-in-chief Mark Mayfield says the worst mistake people make is horrible wallpaper. When buyers walk in and see wallpaper they detest, they think, "I don't have the energy to rip off all that wallpaper. People don't like wallpaper." He says if you have wallpaper, make sure it is a calm pattern.

Tip #2: Clean, De-Clutter and Organize With Ease

Karen Andrews is the mother of two and works at home. When her home went up for sale, she picked up all the toys and organized her scattered work papers. As many potential buyers walked through her house, she quickly learned, "People look *everywhere.*" Experts say to make sure the home is clean at all times. Stash away family photos, degrees, trophies, accessories and other memorabilia. "We want people to be able to picture themselves in the home. If personal possessions are everywhere, the home just screams, 'this is Bob and Mary's home.' If Bob and Mary want to move on, they need to remove personal items," says Nancy Krueger, who specializes in staging homes for sale.

De-clutter. "It sounds like a simple thing, but it's important," says *Trading Spaces* Santo-Tomas. Organize: Look at book shelves, extra stuff and scattered newspapers. Reorganize it. Are those extra books making the shelves bend? Box away some of them, so it clears some space and give a neater appearance.

One of the biggest problems is the scattered collectibles and treasures we accumulate. *Los Angeles Times Magazine* home design editor Barbara Thornburg says to group similar items together. For example, you have glass items scattered across the room— a paperweight, a vase and figurine—on the fireplace, table and counter, arrange those glass items together on the same table instead.

Clear storage areas and counter spaces. Naturally, when clearing out the house, you put it in your closets, garage and attic. But the buyer wants to see the storage space in these areas. Renting storage space while your home is for sale is helpful. Or you can try an approach like homeowner Lia. When she put her Connecticut house up for sale, she had a garage sale. She vowed that anything that didn't sell she would give away to charity and not bring back into her home. It worked!

Tip #3: Lighten up

Keep blinds and curtains open so you can see the outside and let the light in. "You need to create a home to impress buyers," says Hildi Santo-Tomas. When people walk into a dark home and it's all closed up, that is how they remember the house. Turning on the lights and opening the blinds is "something very simple, but it makes it more vibrant." says Santo-Tomas. You want your home to be bright, clean and cheerful. BJ

Peterson recommends that with an indirect overhead light, adjust it for a soft ambient lighting. Or turn on a lamp light, to soften the area with mood lighting.

Photo courtesy Justin McDonald.

Tip #4: Scent of a Home

"If you can smell it, you can't sell it," says Realtor Nancy Krueger. "No unpleasant pet odors, no smoking odors—they are a repellent to most buyers." Mildew is also a turnoff. Deep-clean carpets and flooring so it's odor free, especially if you have pets. *Trading Spaces'* Santo-Tomas is the number-one fan of pets, in fact, she has one of her own. But she says no one wants to see a litter box. If buyers see litter hanging out and traces of pet hair, they will be afraid they'll "never be able to get rid of that smell." Strong potpourris or sprays used to mask odors can also be offensive to a buyer. *Talk2DIY* cohost Lynda Lyday recommends creating a pleasant aroma using apple pie or other baked goods, gentle potpourri, a pleasant candle and a clean smelling house.

Tip #5: Creating Spaciousness

Hildi Santo-Tomas goes into homes across America lending her interior design skills on TLC's *Trading Spaces*. When she walks into a home and looks at the arrangement of the furniture, she asks, "Why is this here?" The common response is: "We moved in 10 years ago and its been there ever since." Hildi says, "Wherever it lands is wherever it stays." So, her key tip is to take everything out of the room; start with a blank space and four walls—then only bring back into the room what is important to you. Experts say the least amount of furniture in the room makes the room appear larger. "Don't have too much furniture in the rooms. If it's hard to maneuver around a lot of furniture, it won't feel like a comfortable home," says award-winning interior designer Marcello Luzi. "Too much furniture just makes it feel smaller."

To create spaciousness, leave the basic necessities in the room. Take everything else out, says BJ Peterson of Peterson Arce Design Group. "If it's in the living room, don't take out all the seating. Take out an extra table or a lamp that's too big so the room still looks usable, or else it won't show well."

LA Times editor Barbara Thornburg, *Better Homes and Gardens* editor-in-chief Karol DeWulf Nickell and award-wining interior designer Marcello Luzi of Weixler-Peterson-Luzi Interior Designers in Philadelphia, Pennsylvania, offer this advice:

✦ Smaller scale furniture makes rooms feel bigger. Larger scale furniture makes rooms feel smaller. So, if you're trying to make a small room seem big or a big room feel cozy, follow this principle.

✦ Add a mirror to the wall to expand the space. Be careful of it's reflection—no one wants to see the ceiling or a dark hallway.

✦ Sometimes people with a very small children's room can paint a mural scene that vicually extends the space.

Creating a Clutter-Free S.P.A.C.E.

By Julie Morgenstern, columnist for *O, The Oprah Magazine* and founder of Julie Morgenstern's Professional Organizers

Ready to de-clutter your home in preparation for showing, but don't know where to start? Whether cleaning out a closet, kitchen cabinet or garage, follow Julie's S.P.A.C.E. formula to make the task manageable, methodical and rewarding. The key to succeeding with the S.P.A.C.E. formula is to do *every one of* the steps and, most importantly, to do them *in order.* Attack and complete one room at a time for the biggest sense of accomplishment and success.

Sort: No matter what you are organizing, from papers to clothes to sports equipment, start by grouping similar items to see what you have. Clear a space on the floor, begin in one corner, and circle the room, putting each item into a category. Resist the urge to focus on throwing things out right away—it's much easier to decide what to keep and what to toss once you have some perspective on how much you've accumulated in each category.

Sort
Purge
Assign a home
Containerize
Equalize

Purge: Now, going pile by pile, review the contents, asking yourself of each item: "Do I use this? Do I love this?" If you answer yes to either question, keep it. If no, out it goes. Most of us only use about 20 percent of everything we own. That is, we wear the same 20 percent of our clothing, refer back to the same 20 percent of our files, and listen to the same 20 percent of our CDs over and over again. Still, purging is the toughest step. To make it easier, keep the following in mind:

➡ **Toss the "no-brainers":** items that are obviously in such bad shape and so irrelevant to your current life that you'd never dream of using them—for example, dried-up pens; stained, torn or pilled clothing; and rusty safety pins.

➥ **Adopt-a-charity or friend.** Give away items you bought long ago, but have never actually used—no matter how much you spent on them! It's much easier to part with things if they're going to a person or organization you care about.

➥ **Focus on the payoff.** Realtors say a de-cluttered home fetches a much higher price than a cluttered one. If you aren't ready to toss or giveaway an unused item, send it to storage for now.

Assign a home: Decide precisely *where* you're going to store each category of keepers. Be specific—which shelf, which drawer, which section of the rod, which side of the bed? Keep frequency of use, accessibility, and logical sequencing in mind. Workout wear might make sense next to bathing suits; dress shirts next to blazers.

Containerize: Containers allow you to personalize and beautify your system. By waiting until this stage to go shopping, you'll be sure to get the exact containers you need. Make a list, measure the spaces you containers must fit into, and take your tape measure to the store. Label containers to make it easy for you and your family to remember what goes where.

Here are some must-haves for your closet.

➥ **Shelf dividers:** Prevents stacks of sweaters, jeans on top shelf from falling over.

➥ **Wooden/acrylic hangers:** These are better than wire hangers; it will help preserve the shape of your clothes.

➥ **Hooks:** If you put them inside your closet door, they work great for ties, scarves, belts, etc.

➥ **Stacking shoe racks:** Great to store shoes under short-hanging garments.

Equalize: Once your system is in place, design a simple maintenance program. Make it a policy that you put everything away before leaving a room or before going to bed. The real bonus of de-cluttering now is that you can move into your new home completely organized!

Make Your Home Sizzle

Lynn Bernstein, Ethan Allen designer and color specialist from New York, gave us insight to special, simple touches to really give your home a graceful feel.

✦ A lighter paint makes rooms appear larger. Darker colors make rooms appear smaller.

✦ Use accessories in groups. Use groups of three in varying heights in the design concept: heaven (tallest accessories), man (middle), earth (small).

✦ In corner spaces, you can spruce it up with a tree, topiary or stand.

✦ Add nice touches. Two sconces on either side of a large painting over the sofa usually look good. On the dining table, display a floral centerpiece with candles on either side. By simply changing the colors of the candles, you can change the tabletop. You can change the colors of the candles for fall, spring, holidays and so on.

✦ Many feel overhead lighting covers it, but turn on tabletop lamps. Overhead light provides lighting, but lamps control the mood of the room. A room should have five sources of light, including windows and fireplaces.

✦ If you are going to get window treatments, just go with nice fabric. "Less is more."

✦ If you are selecting a color for the wall: Paint an area on the wall first—not the whole wall. Notice if there are any changes you may not be happy with. You'll have to live with it in the day and night, so see if you like it first.

✦ A mirror in a small place makes it feel more spacious. Effective places to hang a mirror are over the console in the entryway (it gives the appearance of a larger entryway) or opposite a window (to bring the outdoors inside).

✦ If you are painting two colors in a dining room with a chair rail, use the darker color on top and lighter color on the bottom. It's more appealing. And for a nice touch, you can paint the chair rail white or off white.

✦ If you have red paint in your home, make sure it is in an inviting room where there will be lively conversation. Red increases your blood pressure.

✦ Blues and greens lower blood pressure and make you feel more restful. These are good colors for the bedroom.

✦ When choosing a paint color, place a sample of your coordinating wood or fabric on top of the paint chip to see if there is a good contrast between the two. The paint color should be darker or lighter than your sample—so there is a contrast—to be most effective. If there isn't a contrast, it will have too much of a blended look.

One Seller's Story

We went inside one seller's home to help prepare it before her first open house. Jenny Morgan, owner of the Ethan Allen store in Richmond, Virginia, gave us interior design tips for improving the look and feel of a home. It was a beautiful afternoon and upon entering My Linh Tran's home, it was perfect. The dining room table was elegantly set, the living room with white furniture was graced in sunlight and the rooms were clutter-free. But with a skilled eye, Jenny Morgan gave us insider's tips:

✦ **Appeal to the senses:** Jenny Morgan says it's important to appeal to the senses. When a buyer walks in the front door, let them smell the aroma of an apple pie baking at 200 degrees or see and smell an attractive candle. If it is a cold day, make sure the home feels warm so buyers know the heat is working; if it's warm, keep the house cool. What you hear is also important. For example, when we entered My Linh's home, she had the music just right—not too loud or objectionable, just easy listening. "It's important because we're affected in our home emotionally; most women buy based on emotions," says Morgan. And a husband will always ask, "Honey, what did you think about that house?"

✦ **Living room:** With the spacious windows, Morgan recommended raising the blinds to let in as much light as possible. Also know that prospective buyers may ask for ("convey") the draperies or window treatments, chandeliers, etc. in your home. If there is anything in your home with "sentimental value, strip it out," because buyers may ask for it, says Morgan. As well, keep in mind that plants bring the outdoors in.

✦ **Master bedroom:** My Linh had a striking red patterned bedspread (patterns appeal to women, solid colors appeal to men, says Morgan). My Linh was debating using a white curtain or a deep purple one she loved. Jenny recommended the light, airy, graceful curtain that let in a lot of light. Check to make sure all lights work (the brighter the light, the better), and make sure you have the right type of bulb for your lamps. Plants will bring the outdoors in for bedrooms too.

✦ **Bathroom:** "Create a spa feeling in the bathroom," says Morgan. Add decorative towels, soaps, a shower curtain and, if you don't have a closet, add a towel closet. Make repairs. If the bathroom is missing a couple of tiles, that's something a buyer will use to try to mark down the sale price, because they will have to repair it.

✦ **Getting rid of furniture feet prints in the carpet:** Pull the carpet pieces up and, when your carpets are cleaned, those impressions won't be as noticeable.

✦ **Rugs:** Remove rugs because, buyers always wonder, "What's under there?"

Last-Minute Detail Checklist

Owner of the Ethan Allen store in Richmond, Jenny Morgan, critiqued the living room. She recommended a checklist for removing last-minute items when taking a critical eye to your own home. For a more polished look, remove the following:

❑ Sofa covers.

❑ Personal items.

❑ Magazines and newspapers.

❑ Remote controls.

❑ Extra video tapes.

❑ Bags.

Also be sure to fluff up sofa cushions and pillows and turn on all lights for a cheerful, bright appearance.

Rooms That Draw Attention

Mark Mayfield, editor-in-chief of *House Beautiful*, bought a home because he fell in love with the kitchen; it had a cozy fireplace, cobblestone floors and a nice farm table with Windsor chairs. "Kitchens draw a lot of attention because people spend a lot of time in them," says Mayfield. People will check the appliances in your kitchen—make sure they are in good shape and not falling apart. People notice it. In a kitchen, people pay attention to appliances such as the refrigerator, dishwasher and range. If it's really a cosmetically bad appliance, consider replacing it. It will come back to you in the resale, says Mayfield.

The two most important rooms are the kitchen and bathroom—make sure they're clean!

The master bedroom is also a hot room. Invest in new bedding or a new headboard and make sure the room is painted in a neutral color. "Amazingly, people don't do anything because they think, 'I'm leaving this house and don't want to spend money on it,' but it will help in the resale value," says Mayfield.

When it comes to the living room, make sure it looks spacious and the walls are painted. Make sure all the electronic components (TV, VCR, CDs, speakers, etc.) are organized.

Making Your Home Cozy, Warm and Inviting to Buyers

House Beautiful editor-in-chief Mark Mayfield and *LA Times* editor Barbara Thornburg share suggestions to make the buyer feel right at home the moment they step in the door.

+ **Keep fresh flowers in the house.** Do not use silk flowers or fake flowers. "I love real flowers; I hate fake flowers. If you have something like fresh flowers in a room, it makes it warmer. A candy dish like my grandma use to have or a channel throw over the sofa that you envision yourself curling up in makes the room warm and cozy," says Thornburg.

+ **Add nice touches.** Put out a bowl of fresh apples. Avoid empty bowls.

+ **Organize books:** Make sure there are books on the bookshelves—straight, not scattered. It lets the buyer feel that "intelligent people live in this house, and it makes an unconscious difference when they walk in the house and it looks like it's well taken care of by educated people," says Mayfield. For an added touch, place four books on the coffee table, with one orchid in a vase. It's simple, yet elegant. Use decorator arts books, photograph books or decorating books; books tell a lot about you, and this makes a difference.

+ **Create a spark.** If you have a fireplace in the home, burn a few logs to give that great lived in feel.

✦ **Remember details when showing your home or having an open house.**
Put out fresh towels and guest soaps and put up a new shower curtain.
Set the table with pretty dishes and candles.

The Art of "Staging"

Staging helps rearrange furniture you have to improve the way your home looks. It helps rearrange a room to downplay negative features and it helps improve a vacant home.

"Staging is the process of preparing your home to be sold. It is no longer your home now, but a commodity you tend to market. Home buyers are attracted to what they see, not by what may be," says Market Ready Redesign's Elisabeth Campbell-Westlind. "It is making it as appealing as possible to the new buyer and allowing them to imagine themselves moving into your home with their own belongings, and to inspire them." Campbell-Westlind, along with Nancy Krueger of In Order of Appearance, give us some tips on staging.

Piper: How would you describe staging, what is it, how is it effective?

Nancy: Home staging is usually, with the exception of a vacant home, using the homeowner's own furnishings, pictures, rugs and other items in rearranging rooms, possibly moving things from one room to another, editing out items or adding items so that these rooms look as attractive, warm, and inviting as possible to a prospective buyer. You will note that when builders put their models on display to buyers, they have interior decorators come in and fill them with wonderful things, they don't leave them empty. It is a marketing tool; you must also appeal to the emotions. Buying a home is a very emotional process, part of the pull of one specific home over another is they way the people feel when they are in the home. The goal of staging is to neutralize the home.

Another part of staging is to rearrange things in rooms to downplay negative features and highlight positive ones. Negative things can be anything from an oddly placed window, a view of a brick wall from a window, or a room that is too small or peculiar in dimension.

Piper: If you have a home that is bare, what can you do to help it show better?

Nancy: Vacant homes can be dealt with by either picking out furniture to be rented for the property while it is listed or doing what are called *vignettes*. A vignette is a little bit of something in each room that makes a statement, in the family room by the fireplace a leather chair, a footrest, a table next to the chair with a lamp, possibly a book and a pair of glasses on the table, or a wineglass and a bottle of wine, or a lovely cup and saucer and pretty napkin next to an upholstered rocker in a feminine setting.

Piper: What tips do you have for folks selling their homes?

Nancy: My tips for folks selling are clean, clean, clean—not only on the inside, but the outside too: trimmed shrubs and trees, attractive plants, no peeling paint and no junky cars parked in the driveway. Empty a third of the items in each closet. Pack away your seasonal clothing. Remove personal items such as pictures and diplomas. Pack away all collections.

There is no set rule for where furniture should be, but it is not especially attractive lining the walls in a room. One of the things you should not do is obstruct doorways with large bulky items. For example, when entering the bedroom doorway, the wall on your immediate right should not have an armoire or dresser on it that is close to the doorway, like a roadblock. You need rooms to flow.

Piper: If a seller hires someone to stage their home, what should they look for in a quality company?

Elisabeth: Referrals are the best to way to hire any contractor or con-sultant. Ask your friends and family, real estate agents, or decorators. Once you have found a redesign specialist, ask them for referrals. Speak with their past clients. They should have a portfolio of their work and testimonials from past clients. A good stager or redesigner should also have an intimate understanding of the real estate process.

Piper: Is there anything you feel is important that we should add?

Elisabeth: Staging is an investment in your property. Just like any other investment, it requires a little bit of spending on the front end—and if you do it yourself, some creativity and effort! But there is no question that it will pay off in the end, bringing you a faster sale and a higher price.

Sell Buyers on Your Home's Great Features

What do you love about your home? Share it with the buyer. "A good kitchen and enough bathrooms mean everything," says Mayfield. He says there are features people love about homes, too. For example, fireplaces. "People love fireplaces and it's great to come home to on a cold night," says Mayfield. "Fireplaces are just fantastic, it adds warmth literally to a home. It's a cozy place to come home to." Also, a lot of windows are a plus. Other good selling points are rooms that are practical and functional, such as a kitchen with hearty cabinet space or a master bedroom with a bathroom attached to it ("people want to pamper themselves," says Mayfield).

Thornburg agrees. She says that a kitchen with the latest appliances, a home theater room, or a great bathroom space are attractive features. Experts don't recommend doing expensive home improvement projects to sell your home, but say that you should point out what is great about it. Thornburg says to point out the architectural details of your home that are appealing, such as if you have great crown molding, ornate ceilings or wonderful architecture.

"You want to look for something unique; I like all types of architecture—older homes are charming and nostalgic," says Thornburg. In fact, she fell in love with her 1887 Eastlake Victorian home because it was extremely warm and because of the special features: the great wraparound porch, quality carpentry work, the fireplaces with Victorian tiles, deep crown molding and even the Victorian hinges. She thought it was "beautiful—it was the architecture."

Accentuate what is appealing about your home. "No matter how big or small, there are features in a home that make it unique—find out what these things are and play these features up," says *Country Living* magazine executive editor Larry Bilotti. "Do what you can to make it as appealing as it can be. It will help sell your home."

Brightidea

Top 10 Cost-Effective Ways to Prep Your Home

Before you put a "For Sale" sign in your yard, take a look at it with fresh eyes. Editor-in-chief of *Better Homes and Gardens* magazine, Karol Nickell DeWulf, has the most cost-effective ways to improve your home before you sell it. Here are some tips that will go a long way:

1. De-clutter and clean, thin out closets, clear out the garage, make rooms look like they're ready to be photographed.
2. Stash away family photos—most people like to picture themselves there.
3. Deep-clean carpeting and flooring so that it's odor-free, fluffy and/or shiny.
4. If possible, paint walls in neutral tones that can allow someone to move right in.
5. Add new hardware to kitchen cabinets or doors.
6. Hire an inspector to point out any problems you need to fix in advance.
7. Have the kitchen and refrigerator spotless; people want to picture themselves cooking there (not eating leftovers).
8. Have the house freshly painted or spray washed to have it looking mildew-free and spiffy.
9. Spruce up the yard by planting perennials and adding containers with herbs or flowers. If possible, start fertilizing the lawn a few months before selling your home.
10. Keep the dog or cats at bay by leaving them at a kennel or at a friend's house.

Last-Minute Checklist

- [ ] **Living areas:** Arrange furniture for a spacious environment. "Examine how much furniture you have in a room," says executive editor of *Country Living* Larry Bilotti. Also, pay attention to the "traffic flow from room to room." Make sure your home is easy to navigate. Dust, vacuum and touch-up walls with paint.

- [ ] **Bedrooms:** Make beds, put away clothes and clear out closets to show off space.

- [ ] **Bathrooms:** Cleanliness is a top priority to buyers. Clear counters, drawers and cabinets (space, space, space.) Mirrors, windows, vanity, faucets, appliances and soap dishes need to sparkle. Caulk any areas, if needed. Don't forget to tackle moldy shower curtains, soapy residue in the tub, dirt in the sliding shower door and worn bath mats. Consider adding fresh towels, guest soaps and flowers, as well as a new shower curtain and bath mat. (Tip: Lower the toilet seat when showing your home.)

- [ ] **Kitchen:** Buyers love working, clean or new kitchen appliances. Clean the stove, cabinets, refrigerator and make sure dishes are all washed. Replace stained or corroded reflector plates. Buyers often look at the kitchen exhaust hood (is it clean?). Clear off counter tops to show space.

- [ ] **Garage, attic, sheds, closets and counters:** Clear out all storage areas to show off space. At first glance, you want buyers to feel that they will have plenty of space to store their clutter. If your garage is unfinished, install wallboard or shelves so it looks clean, tidy and ready to move into.

- [ ] **Lights:** Indoor and outdoor lights should be working. A lot of light gives a welcoming and clean appearance to your home. Replace burnt-out bulbs, electrical sockets that don't work and broken/outdated fixtures. Steer away from fluorescent lighting and use mood lighting lamps, says American Society of Interior Designers member BJ Peterson.

- [ ] **Fresh paint:** The number-one tip by all home design experts and Realtors is that nothing beats a fresh coat of paint to give the home a clean, bright and appealing feel. It's also the cheapest way to update a home, and "you get the biggest bang for your buck," says *LA Times Magazine* home design editor Barbara Thornburg.

- [ ] **Repairs:** Cohost of *Talk2DIY* Lynda Lyday is a home improvement guru who recommends repairing leaky faucets, broken plumbing fixtures and clogged drains. Fix doors that have trouble opening. Double-check that toilets flush and windows and doors open/close easily. Heating and air-conditioning systems also need a quick check.

- [ ] **Windows:** When you open your blinds to bring as much light into the home as possible and show off the beautiful view outdoors, make sure your windows sparkle. Are the window treatments clean? Sometimes they get neglected or dusty.

- [ ] **Details, details, details:** A clean water heater or water softener, a polished door knob or a shiny doorbell are tiny details that count.

- [ ] **Most of all:** Keep your home clean and show-ready at all times.

Chapter 6

Sell Your Home at First Glance: Perk It to Perfection

*"The first impression is the most important in life;
you want the visitor to feel like they have come home."*

—John Byrd, spokesman
Outdoor Living

A buyer stood looking at two homes for sale that sat side by side. Do you know what sold one house over the other? The buyer said, "My wife really likes the way the outside of this home was taken care of."

The bushes were neatly trimmed, the flowers were blooming in the hanging baskets and the grass was cut—this is known as curb appeal. The home's exterior is the first thing you see. Most buyers first drive by your house to determine if they want to see the inside. You want them to want it from first glance.

Curb appeal is one of the most important aspects of selling your home. Statistics prove a home with great curb appeal = more money.

Curb Appeal 101

When one buyer was searching for a home, he always said: "I think the outside of a home is a reflection of how they keep the inside." If any of the houses he looked at had an unkempt or overgrown yard, there was never any interest to see the interior of the house. Instead, he moved on to the next home.

When your home is on the market, it's on display. A few quick rules of thumb: cut the lawn, trim shrubs, de-weed, mulch flower beds, prune trees and rake leaves. Make sure the backyard appears suitable for entertaining and relaxing.

Evaluate your home. Notice if your deck, patio or porch needs a new coat of stain. Check if steps or walkways need to be repaired, and if fences, gates or railings need to be fixed. Look at the entrance of your home: Is there peeling paint on the doors or windows? Does the house look like it could use a fresh coat of paint? What about the siding and trim? Most of all, is it welcoming?

"Ignoring little things will lead to lower offers and longer market time," says Colby Sambrotto, chief operating officer of ForSaleByOwner.com.

Following, you will find a handy checklist you can use when preparing your home's exterior. We tackle how to improve your curb appeal instantly, lawn-care quick fixes, backyard tips and tricks, evening yard appeal, paint tips, easy finishing touches and how to show off storage space in garages and sheds.

There are important features to your home's presence, including windows, doors, gutters, siding, trim and the roof—just to name a few. Follow these tips to perk it to perfection.

The Curb-Appeal Checklist: Best House Forward

❑ **Windows:** Clean windows and replace torn screens. If the screens are really bad, take them off.

❑ **Shutters:** Simply sand the shutters and add a coat of fresh house exterior paint. (If possible, take the shutters off the house before you sand them.)

❑ **Gutters:** If it's been a while, clean your gutters and make sure they are aligned. If your gutter or downspout is broken, replace it.

❑ **Doors:** Check for chipped or worn paint. (Tip: Repaint the door, polish the doorknobs and make sure the front door and screen doors don't squeak—WD-40 works great on rusty hinges.) A fresh welcome mat is inviting.

❑ **Damage:** Check walkways, sidewalks, foundation and steps for crumbling and cracking. Sweep the entrance.

❑ **Roof:** Loose, worn or damaged shingles can be replaced or repaired. Remove tree branches, leaves and moss.

❑ **Siding and trim:** Repaint, repair or pressure-wash siding. Consider adding paint to highlight features of your home: Trim work, railing, shutters, gutters and downspouts. Check caulking.

❑ **Brick:** Fasten any loose bricks and fill any cracks.

❑ **Chimney:** Inspect and clean.

❑ **Porch, deck and patio:** Repair broken boards. If it is dingy, pressure-wash it. Make sure outdoor furniture is clean. If you don't have any, borrow some pieces from a friend to increase appeal.

❑ **Railings:** Porch railings can get wobbly and be an eyesore. Just tighten a few bolts. (Most porch railings are held by lag bolts, a large screw with a bolt head type. If they are loose, just tighten them. If the railings are screwed into the brick of a home and become broken or worn, replace them.)

❑ **Fences:** Paint or stain if needed and repair broken hinges. Replace any missing stakes, posts or slats.

❑ **Mold & mildew:** Check the house, sidewalks, roof, driveway and foundation along the ground for mold or mildew. Get rid of it.

❑ **Garden tools, toys and old cars:** Make sure these items are stored somewhere else while your home is for sale.

❑ **Driveways:** Make sure the driveway is tidy and not cluttered with vehicles. Clean up oil spots or stains. For an asphalt driveway, reseal. Keep the garage door closed.

❑ **Front entry:** Paint the front door, polish door handles and door knockers, make sure porch lights/front yard lighting works and replace a dingy mailbox or broken doorbell. A new mat or flowers are welcoming.

❑ **Swimming pool:** Make sure this area is clean and secure. Adjust chemicals so it sparkles.

❑ **Air conditioners:** Fix poor draining. Replace or paint rusted exposed metal that can be an eyesore.

❑ **Address numbers:** Make sure address numbers are readable. If they are old or dingy, replace them. The buyer is guaranteed to be looking for your house by number or writing the number down to remember its address—make sure the numbers are visually appealing.

❑ **Front and backyard beauty:** Keep your lawn cut, watered and tidy.

Quick Fixes for Lawn Care

The lawn is a really important part of the appeal of your home and sometimes may need a bit of help. We turned to Ashton Ritchie, agronomist for Scotts Company—the grass seed people—to show us some fixes to get your lawn in lush form. He recommends mowing your grass at a higher setting and water deeply to grow deeper roots. To maintain growth, lawns need about an inch of water a week. According to Scotts, lawns that are free of problems receive four or five feedings with fertilizer annually.

✦ **For greener grass and no weeds:** Try Weed And Feed. It makes your grass greener and gets rid of weeds. It also helps fill in bare spots in your lawn. Use the Weed And Feed in the daytime, in 60 to 80 degree temperature, spring, fall or late winter. Follow directions on the product you select. Weeds need to be actively living to be able to kill the root system. For best results, do it about a month before you sell your home.

✦ **Getting rid of weeds in shrub beds:** Use Roundup for weeds. Spray the Roundup on the leaf of the plant you want to get rid of; it doesn't hurt the soil. It's effective to use on cracks in walkways and driveways. Be careful not to use near flowers or plants you want to keep, because if they come in contact with the Roundup, they will wither away too. (Tip: Replace dead shrubs, plants and trees. Trim overgrown shrubs and trim dead branches in trees and shrubs.)

✦ **Sprucing up the outdoors:** Plant flowers. Flowers add color and they are inviting. If you don't have time to plant flowers, buy containers, pots or hanging baskets and place flowers in them to give a nice look to your porch.

✦ **Patching lawns:** Small dead spots in your lawn can be filled in three ways:

  ✧ You can let the lawn heal itself.

  ✧ Patch it with sod that can be found at a local nursery. Select sod that's close to color and type of your lawn. Or you can cut a patch from an out-of-sight area in your yard and place it in the dead spot.

  ✧ Reseed dead areas.

✦ **Edging and trimming:** Grooming the lawn's edges and along sidewalks by cutting them vertically (edging) and trimming stray high grass gives the lawn a finished look. Lawn-care experts edge first before cutting the lawn, because the lawn mower collects the edging clippings or mulches them into the lawn.

Scotts Sharp Lawn-Care Tips

✦ Don't mow a wet lawn: It leads to uneven cuts and invited fungus.

✦ Don't lightly sprinkle your yard: It promotes shallow roots.

✦ Avoid sharp turns with your mower—sidewalks and driveways can be used.

✦ Mow in different directions (diagonal, horizontal, vertical) to prevent leaning blades.

For quick answers to your lawn questions you can call 1-800-543-TURF or e-mail the experts at *www.scotts.com*. Another site with healthy tips is *www.ahahome.com*.

Making Your House Outshine the Rest

From the Emmy-award winning show, *This Old House*, landscape contractor Roger Cook shares what we can do to improve our curb appeal instantly; how to stand out from other homes; and how to make our home look the best, depending on the season.

Piper: How can you improve your curb appeal instantly?

Roger: Right away, easy fixes for your yard include mulching beds, fertilizing the grass and having perennials. Make sure your shrubs are pruned, take them out if they are dead or overgrown. Mature plantings block windows or destroy the body of the home. Notice if your walkways or driveways are cracked, irregular or bumpy. Seal coat your driveway or power-wash your walkways. You can do it instantly and you can do it yourself.

Piper: What if you have more time to plan your yard before you sell your home?

Roger: If you are planning to sell your home in six months to a year from now, landscaping gives more return on your money. Rip out the old landscaping and create a new lawn. Add a new walkway, if possible. Put in lighting. For example, put lights along the driveway that leads to the house.

Piper: What can you do to stand out from other homes?

Roger: Pay attention to the time of year you are selling your home. Good elements are perennials, pots filled with color and hanging baskets that brightens the area. If you are selling your home in the spring, plant bulbs in the fall. It will be pretty in the spring and stand out from other homes in the area. When buyers see your "for sale" sign in the yard, they will say, "Ugh" or "Wow" when they drive by.

Piper: Do you have tips for selling my home in the winter?

Roger: In the winter, point your money and attention to hard-scaping—fix a walkway, shovel the driveway of snow and ice—clean it from a safety standpoint. Also, by having a clear path, the buyer never thinks about having to shovel it and it doesn't detract them from living in the home.

Ask for Estimates

Sometimes, roofs, HVAC (heating, ventilation and air conditioning), and other items come up as concerns for buyers. A proactive way to combat these worries is easy. You can ask roofers, HVAC experts and electricians for help. For example, a common concern is old roofs. A buyer often wants to know how many years it has left and how much it would cost to replace or repair. Just have a roofer come out to take a look. Find out how many years your roof has left and the price tag for replacement or repairs. Then, when a buyer expresses concerns, you can present the roof expert's estimate and report. If you have it done, disclose the problems and the repair costs with buyer. Address everything upfront with the buyer.

Create a Welcoming Entrance	Easy Landscaping Tips
Jessie Mack Burns has a natural knack for landscaping. The host of DIY's show Weekend Landscaping, *shares some feel-good tips. "A cheery landscape, yard and entrance says, 'Welcome home, come on up.'"* ✦ **Appeal to the senses:** In your plant pots on the front porch, add silver herbs for great foliage. When the wind blows the herb (for example, chamomile), it has a pleasant aroma and gives a calming feeling right from the entrance of your home. It also provides something for the buyer to look at as they wait for you to open the door.	✧ **Add quick punches of color:** Use hanging baskets, containers planted with flowers or garden vegetables (it's easy to plant and easy to take with you when you move), shrub beds or repaint your patio. ✧ **Jessie Mack Burn's favorite go-together colors for plants:** Blues and yellows; white and pale pinks; hues of reds and magenta. "Contrast colors work well." Use warm colors in the fall and cool colors in the summer. ✧ **Recycle landscape:** Don't toss it, move it. If you are tweaking your yard, and want to move something because it doesn't fit, see how it looks somewhere else.

Desert Landscape

Jessie Mack Burns has seen trends in gravel-lawns and pop-colored tumbled glass—even a riverbed using colored glass or rock. "You don't have to be limited anymore," she says. "So, you can use anything your heart desires." For plants, she recommends succulents that hold moisture well, such as water-efficient shrubs, cactus, silver dollar plant and plants native to the area. Boulders (particularly "surface boulders") with plants close to them accent the landscape. Another creative idea is adding granite in natural beige or desert gold to your yard or grouping plants. Burns says, "Simple says so much more; don't overdo it."

Brightidea

Driveway, Garage and Shed

Sometimes, we forget about the driveway, garage and shed that is a part of the home. Don't use the garage as storage. "Does it have a garage?" is a commonly asked question. For example, during an open house one Sunday afternoon, folks wandered in one-by-one. "Oh, the garage is close to the kitchen, so I'll be able to bring the grocery's in pretty easily," said Vivian. She opened the garage door, "Hmmm, it looks a little small." The seller made the mistake a lot of sellers make: They use their garage as storage.

The idea is for the garage to look as large as possible. Clean out and clear out the garage. Rent a storage unit for a little while, store your excess items and vehicles at a friend's or hold a yard sale to get rid of unnecessary clutter. Repaint the door and if it's an automatic door, make sure it is working properly. De-clutter attics and sheds. Envision yourself as the buyer—does it look spacious to you? Make sure any cobwebs, dust, dirt, stains and grease spots are removed from the garage.

If You Have a Garage That Faces the Street

In many instances, a garage facing the street can be unappealing to buyers. *Outdoor Living* spokesman John Byrd says a remedy for this deterrent is to hang an arbor with brackets over the garage and add vines over the garage doors to help bring the garden to the house. (It's also a happy medium for couples; many husbands are against attaching vines to the home's brick or stucco, but many wives like vines. By growing the vines on the arbor, it doesn't cause damage to the structure, says Byrd.)

Driveway Woes

Reseal asphalt or get rid of weeds if it's a gravel driveway. But don't feel compelled to redo it completely; you may never recover the money you spend. No buyer will repay you for work done on your home. If the driveway needs major repair, it may be preferable to offer the buyer an allowance. If you have a gravel driveway, Byrd says pea gravel (the khaki/brown gravel) gives a beautiful look of refinement and age.

- ✦ Clean up oil spots or grease on concrete surfaces
- ✦ Ensure that your garage door opens with ease and make sure the automatic door opener works too.
- ✦ Try not to obstruct the view of your home by having the driveway filled with cars, trucks, RVs, campers or boats.

"Shed" the Old Look

Two common problems sheds share are (1) it hasn't been painted in years and time has worn its wrinkle in the cracked paint and (2) the shed is packed with old forgotten clutter. To a prospective buyer the shed looks like an eyesore that will need to be repainted and cleaned out. (And how much do we all really like to do that?) Spare the buyer the visual. In advance, splash a new coat of paint on your shed and haul out the clutter. You'll feel better about it and the buyer will be excited about actually having a shed.

Freshen up: Paint

Jennifer Wake repainted the exterior of her home, shutters and trim. She lived in the home for about five years and it took its share of wear and tear. She spent extra on expensive paint and in the end feels the investment was well worth it.

Experts recommend painting highlight features of your home, such as shutters, doors, railings, trim and downspouts. If necessary, they recommend power-washing the exterior or adding a fresh coat of paint. If you paint the exterior of your home or hire someone else to do it, make sure the color you select matches the color scheme of the neighborhood. Interior design experts recommend having three colors on the exterior of your home. (For example, color can be used on the home, trim, door and shutters.) Also be aware of any painting restrictions in your area.

6 Easy Curb Appeal Tips and Tricks

John Byrd is also an exterior designer for John Byrd Garden Design in Charlotte, North Carolina, specializing in residential design work. This pro gives us tricks of the trade to wow your front yard (and even some essential tips for your next home.) He says it is really important to "make it look like you live at the home."

1. **Keep the front yard simple to read for drive-by buyers:** Don't let your front yard be muddled. Select your plant choices. Have mass plantings of the same plants and then have a unique plant that stands out, such as a Japanese maple, River Birch or Crepe Myrtle. For example, in Byrd's yard, he has a beautifully manicured lawn, a mass of packasandra and boxwood. In one corner of the yard is a striking Japanese maple that is spotlighted at night.

2. **Focus your budget toward "hard-scape" (such as steps and walkways):** Concrete walkways are the least appealing. Go for stone or a brick walkway. Byrd has square and rectangular blue stones sitting on the lawn. (The stones were attached by a bit of mortar.) When he cuts the lawn, he can mow right over the stones, and this style cut the cost of the walkway by about 80 percent. (Concrete is what causes the cost of walkways to be expensive.)

3. **For resale value:** Adding pots and benches are an added bonus for you because it increases the curb appeal when your home is for sale. You can find the seating in any price range, from store-bought treasures to flea markets and yard sales. Make sure the seating matches the architecture. If the house is elegant, go with more refined seating—although it is easier to find seating for cottage homes. But you can take the pots and benches with you when you sell your home and move into your next one. You may also negotiate it in the contract if the buyer asks to keep it.

4. **If you're landscape is bare:** Cherry trees and river birch tress grow fairly quickly if the front of your home is bare. You can also add hardwoods to your yard, such as maple and oaks. Byrd says, like a forest, you can create a front lawn with trees that grow quickly and trees you can have for the long run.

5. **Front yards look inviting because there's a little shade:** Frame the house with two trees. It's a nice touch to have a frame of green around the home and trees are great for the environment.

6. **Tastefully set up a fountain:** Place a small fountain near the front door; the sound of running water is soothing. For example, if you live in a town home, you can place the fountain with bushes near the front or have a

wall fountain placed off the garage. If you have a larger, more formal home, you can add a large fountain.

Outdoor Lighting

Sometimes, the only time buyers have to look at homes is in the evening after work. If they drive by at dusk or in the evening, you want the house to show just as nicely. Great outdoor lighting can really enhance your home's evening curb appeal.

✦ Make sure your outdoor lighting is in working order.

✦ Low-voltage lighting, for use in landscaping elements or along sidewalks or a driveway, is easy and effective.

✦ Solar outdoor lights are easy to install, but only work if they receive full sunlight.

✦ Install a new light fixture on the front porch or a nice street lamp.

✦ Any lighting you can see outside through the front windows is sweet.

Backyard Beauty

Byrd also offers suggestions on how to make a small home appear larger by utilizing the backyard, what to do if your property is small, how to block out unwanted sound and how to make your backyard look ready for entertaining. He has the following advice for the backyard:

✦ **If your home is small, extend the home by creating an optical illusion:** Have an outdoor terrace with a fireplace. (You can use a portable fireplace.) The look of a fireplace viewed from indoors mimics the interior and makes the home look larger.

✦ **If your property is small:** Add a fence, brick wall, or evergreen planting of shrubs for a green buffer (although it is preferable to do this when you move into a home).

✦ **Back porch:** If you have unappealing views off your back porch, one trick is using fabrics, such as outdoor drapes on the porch. This is popular in coastal areas.

✦ **To block out unwanted sound:** If your neighbor's dog barks a lot or you're close to a roadway and get a lot of noise in your backyard, a fountain is very important. The sound of the water is soothing and blocks out other noises. For example, get a Koi pond for Japanese goldfish or a small gurgling kern in a concrete basin that you can unplug and take with you.

✦ **To extend your property and for entertaining and enjoyment:** At the very edge of your property, add an arbor or gazebo far back in the backyard. It extends the domain and creates a mini-escape.

✦ **What about pools?** A lot of people feel a pool would attract more buyers. But, you don't need a pool. In fact it can be a deterrent because of its high maintenance, cleaning and safety concerns. If you do have a pool, make sure it is sparkling clean.

Finishing Touches

Country Living Gardener vice president and publisher, Marjorie Gage, has excellent advice for polishing your home to perfection. Give your home these last-minute touches:

✦ **Window boxes:** Bring color to the windows so it is beautiful to look at from the outside and inside.

✦ **Path to your door:** Have a path that leads you to the door. If you have a grassy lawn, add simple stepping-stones. Create a path for buyers to follow to your home's entrance.

✦ **Hide:** This is a time to stash away the gnomes and pink flamingos. If you still have icicle lights on your front porch, take them down.

✦ **Mood lighting:** Lighting is appealing in a garden. Solar lights are nice to light up a pathway. For bulbs outdoors, use a soft light (instead of a harsh light). "So people feel safe, it's well lit and it's not glaring," says Gage. In the backyard, sensor lights are easy to hook-up.

✦ **Two flowerpots for symmetry on the porch:** Fill them with flowers to add on either side of the porch. It is easy to do and you can easily take them with you when you move.

✦ **Making trash cans look good:** Use a garden trellis as a shed for trashcans and recycling boxes.

✦ **Most of all, neatness counts:** Look organized and it will look like there is more storage space. For example, invest in a nice hose holder. Wind up the hose; it looks better than being in a big pile in the yard. Gage says, "The better organized it is, the more it gives the feeling of spaciousness."

Chapter 7

Successful Open Houses:
Show, Tell and Sell

"People buy houses on emotions. They drive through a neighborhood they like and see an open house sign. It's a powerful way to get buyers."
—Mary LaMeres-Pomin, cofounder
Assist-2-Sell

Open House

make them feel welcome

image: justin
photo: mike butler

Buyers *want* to see your home.

"You can't buy it if you can't see it," says Mary LaMeres-Pomin, cofounder of Assist-2-Sell. "Believe it or not, houses have feelings. You walk into an open house and within a minute, it feels like home."

The best way to get potential buyers to see your home is to hold an "Open House." It announces that your home is now on the market and up for sale. Here are a few practical tips to having a successful open house: clean as if you're having a party for friends; have a good open house sign; and pass out an information sheet that describes your home, so the buyer remembers your house long after a Sunday of house hunting.

People like to explore a house in different ways. Offer to give buyers a tour, some of them like you to carry them through the process and tell them all the details. Others want to be left alone—give them space. Let buyers shop a home in a way that is comfortable for them.

"It's that simple. People want to see it," says LaMeres-Pomin. "Put your open house sign out there and go on with your life. You never know who will drop by."

Your home is on display to catch the interest of potential buyers. Following are checklists to help you advertise your open house. In addition, we share what to do before, during and after your showing. With all the homes buyers will be seeing— *Better Homes and Gardens* editor-in-chief Karol DeWulf Nickell gives us tips on how to make your castle memorable.

5 Ways to Make Buyers Remember Your Home

When buyers go house-shopping on Sunday, they plan on seeing several open houses—only spending about 10 to 20 minutes per house, unless, they really fall in love with your home. DeWulf Nickell offers five creative ways to make your home outshine the rest:

1. **Play sentimental music at a soft level.** "One person told me that she and her husband bought their first house with Billie Holiday jazz music playing in the background," says Nickell. "When they listed a few years later, they sold it the very first day. The person who bought it asked for the name of the CD. Later, when they sold another house, Billie brought them luck, too."

2. **Serve freshly baked cookies.** Not store bought, to show you go the extra mile.

3. **Have the home smelling clean:** Avoid using strong potpourri or room deodorizers, which make most people want to leave. (If there is a problem with odor, such as carpeting that smells like a "dog," clean or replace it. Take care of that way in advance.)

4. **Arrange simple bouquets in various rooms.** However, avoid having too many aromatic floral arrangements (think allergies).

5. **Offer typed-up information sheets.** It should detail all of your home's features and upgrades. The flier should share the number of bedrooms,

bathrooms, special features, price, pictures and your contact information. (Check out Chapter 3 for how to set up an information sheet.)

Preparation for the Open House: Show and Sell

Preparing a house for sale is like giving a gift. It is all in the packaging and presentation. For a moment, think of yourself as the buyer: You spot the open house sign. From the moment your eyes glance across the front lawn, you know if you want to see the inside of not. Sometimes, we get immune to the way our home looks. Here are a few tips to get your home ready inside and out:

✦ **Clean and de-clutter:** Sure, you've been staring at that extra sofa for two years now. It has almost become as immovable as the walls. Take a close look at the rooms; remove extra furniture (interior designers suggest taking 2/3 out) and cut back on the accessories—plus that unorganized stack of newspapers in the corner.

✦ **Depersonalize your home:** We know you are proud of the trophy you won from last year's bowling tournament and the time you graduated from college. And, how can you get rid of the cute pictures of your puppy? But you want buyers to be able to visualize themselves in your home, so pack away the sentimental items that identify the home as yours—the trophies, degrees and pictures. It makes a home too personal for a buyer to see themselves there.

✦ **Ready to move-in:** You want buyers to feel like they can move right in. No one likes to do a lot of work or cleaning. To help it look like it's move-in-ready, paint or clean the walls; make rooms look spacious; and make sure the garage, attic and closets are also cleared out, to show off storage space. Make sure rooms are clutter-free and store extra furniture elsewhere so the rooms look bigger (only leave functional furniture, take out the rest, says California interior designer BJ Peterson.) Make sure bathrooms and kitchens are spotless.

✦ **Curb appeal:** You know what a great yard looks like. Keep it neat and tidy, cut the grass, trim shrubs, sweep walkways, rake leaves and add a container of flowers for color. Tend to chipped or flaking paint. Clear away yard equipment, toys and old cars. Remember the overall appearance of the outside is what buyers judge if they want to see the inside.

✦ **Pay attention to details:** People pay attention to the little things because they feel it is an indication of the bigger picture. Let the buyer know you take care of the house. Take care of the details; fix the leaking faucet, clean windows, polish floors, repair loose door knobs or steps, make sure the toilet seat is down and wash all the dishes.

✦ **Weather-proof it:** If it is raining, make sure you have a place buyers can put their umbrellas and coats upon entrance. If you are selling your home in winter and it's snowing, shovel and salt the sidewalk, driveway and porch. Have a mat at the entrance.

For a Sensational Open House:

✦ Water your lawn 30 minutes before an open house so the lawn sparkles.

✦ Warm some vanilla for a pleasant aroma.

✦ Baking cookies or a cake also gives a welcoming aroma.

✦ Turn on all lights and open the blinds or drapes for a bright, clean appearance.

✦ Make sure the temperature is comfortable.

✦ Fresh flowers offer a splash of color.

✦ A new welcome mat, shower curtain, fresh towels and nice guest soaps are all nice touches.

✦ Refreshments are always welcome.

✦ Set the dining table with pretty dishes and candles.

✦ If you have a fireplace, show it off with a cozy fire.

✦ Place information materials about your home (flier, booklet, etc.) on the kitchen table.

✦ Replace faded mailboxes, light fixtures or address numbers.

The Open House

Are you ready? Put your "open house" sign in the front yard and directional signs at every entrance to your neighborhood. When you hold an open house, you are inviting the public in for a few hours, typically anytime Sunday between noon and 5 p.m. Share the grand tour, as you would entertain a friend at your home for the first time. Throw open your door and get ready to invite in your potential buyers.

✦ **Visible signs:** Make sure your signs are legible, tidy and professional. Include your phone number and/or address. A bit of red is eye-catching; it makes your sign visible. Put signs at every entrance to your neighborhood to direct buyers to your home.

✦ **Sign-in sheets:** When buyers enter your home, just ask them to sign in with their name, number, e-mail and address, as well as how they found out about your house. The sign-in sheet has multiple purposes: you can follow up with them about interest in your home (what they did and didn't like), and it helps you know the effectiveness of your advertising. Did they find out about your open house because of the sign or the ad in the paper? When they sign in, personally jot down a description of who they are, their car and the license plate number. This is a safety measure and it helps you remember who is who when you follow up with the potential buyers. (See the sample sign-in sheet at the end of the chapter, on page 98)

✦ **Make the following information available:** Utility costs, down payment estimates, closing costs, monthly costs, taxes, insurance and sample financing information. If you did a home inspection before putting your house up for sale, let them see that this information is available.

+ **Information to justify your sale price:** Have information on how much surrounding homes have sold for in the area. Get a comparable market analysis (CMA) that shows the price other homes have sold for in the area over the past few months or year and includes details about the homes that are currently listed, sold and pending. It would be great to show to justify your sale price. You can get a CMA from a Realtor or online.

+ **Folks are also interested in area details:** What is the school district? Are there area parks, shopping centers, services, transportation, local zoning ordinances and any construction expected that might affect the property? Think about questions they may ask you and be prepared and answer simply.

+ **Contract handy:** Make sure you have a contract handy in case you find a buyer, or else know who you would like to handle your contract before your show your home to buyers. Then you are prepared when a buyer wants to buy your home.

+ **Buyers come in ready to look:** Offer to give them the tour or invite them to look around alone. Listen to buyers needs and tailor your tour toward their interests. For example, maybe they tell you how they have a baby on the way and you can casually point out a room that would be great for a nursery.

+ **Questions, anyone?** At the end of the open house, ask if they have any questions you can answer.

+ **Pass out your information sheet:** Give the buyer the information sheet at the end of the tour after they have looked at the home. Don't give it to them before or else they will read the sheet instead of looking at the actual home.

During Your Open House

If you have little children or pets, let them stay with friends or family while you hold your open house, because you want the attention on the home.

What Do You Do When...?

Louis Guttmann is a real estate attorney for the Attorneys' Title Insurance Fund based in Florida. We asked him what to do if a buyer shows at the open house with a Realtor and wants to buy your home.

Piper: What do you do if a buyer shows up at your open house and wants to buy your home? Do you write the contract or do you get someone else to? What do you do if you and the buyer do not have real estate agents?

Louis: If you have reached an agreement on the basic terms, you can also agree to have an attorney prepare a residential contract with the terms, which are customary to the area for residential transactions.

Piper: What do you do when a buyer comes with their agent to your open house? The buyer wants to purchase your home, but you do not want to deal with a Realtor. What do you do? What are your options?

Louis: Make it clear that the Realtor is not representing you and that you are not going to pay any commission to the Realtor. The buyer can employ a Realtor to represent them as the buyer's agent (and the Realtor looks solely to the buyer for payment).

When Talking to Buyers:
What to Say, What Not to Say…

You are going to come across numerous buyers during your open house and showings. Nolo (*www.nolo.com*) has several tips on what to say and what not to say when dealing with potential buyers.

- Don't share personal information that they could use against you when you are negotiating a contract or sale price. For example, avoid telling buyers you are anxious to sell because you are starting a new job soon. They may end up pitching a low price because they know you need to move soon.

- Listen to the buyers' needs. For example, the buyer shares how much they love entertaining. In a subtle way, you can share a light pitch, pointing out the great kitchen with great appliances or the spacious living room and dining room.

- Avoid over-praising. Sometimes too much praise can seem phony. Also avoid expressing disagreements about personal taste.

- Be cordial. Try to not overwhelm buyers with too much enthusiasm. Think about it as when you are walking through the mall and you have people calling loudly to you to see their product, compared to the salesperson that greets you simply, lets you look around, remains polite and sometimes lightly asks you if you need any help.

Following up With Potential Buyers

After your open house, call the folks on your sign-in sheet. Find out what they did and didn't like about the home. Ron LeGrand is a multi-millionaire investor—who has a knack for selling houses fast—and author of *Quick Turn Real Estate Millionaire*. He says one of the most important steps to selling your home is follow-up. Find out if buyers are interested or not in the house. Be a proactive seller. He says it is kind of like if a guy keeps waiting for a girl to ask him out, he may never be asked out. Selling is the same. If you wait for a buyer to call you, they may never call you. Contact prospects, energize them and follow up about their interest in your home.

+ Follow up with buyers to get feedback about your home.
+ Make changes to your home to improve it, based on the feedback.
+ Get ready for any second showings from interested buyers.
+ Prepare for your next open house.

Advertising Your Open House

The goal is attracting buyers, making a good first impression and advertising effectively. Always remember, a buyer is as excited to see your home as you are to sell it. Every Sunday, there are hundreds of buyers that pick-up a newspaper to see who is holding an open house. The look for every open house. You want to be right where your target audience can see you; place newspaper ads, post visible signs, alert friends, tell neighbors, invite coworkers and get the word out.

+ **Signs, signs, signs:** Savvy Realtors put "open house" signs at every neighborhood entrance to drive traffic to their home. Put signs at main roads to direct traffic into your neighborhood. Make sure your directional signs point folks easily to your home (so they don't get lost and frustrated). Last, but not least, make sure the sign in your yard is very visible.

+ **Newspaper ads:** Place your ad in the newspaper the day of the open house. Call the newspaper in your area and find out their ad deadlines to be sure to get your ad in on time.

+ **Invite your neighbors:** Neighbors may have a friend or family member that wants to move into the area. Hand out invitations or brochures with information on your open house: time, date, address, contact information and that there will be refreshments. Keep it simple. For example:

> You're invited to our open house!
> We are selling our home and will be holding an open house
> Sunday from 2 to 5 p.m.
> at 1042 Baker Street.
> We'd love you to drop by. Refreshments will be served.
> —Rich & Liz Parker 756-9315 parker@addyouremailaddress.com

+ **Warm call or e-mail:** Let friends, acquaintances and coworkers know you're holding your open house and would love them to drop by if they're in the area.

+ **Contact "move-up" neighborhoods:** Drop off fliers, call or knock on doors in surrounding "move-up" neighborhoods where homes are priced about 20% less than your home. Many people move within the same area where they are currently living.

+ **Mortgage officer or your attorney:** If you are working with a mortgage officer or attorney that has clients looking for homes—send them an invitation to your open house that they can pass on to their clients.

Virtual Tours

A popular trend is online virtual tours that show off your home. If you advertise your home on a Website, many offer you the option to provide a virtual tour, which is usually a series of pictures or 360-views of rooms throughout the home. When displaying images of your home, avoid having expensive valuables in the image that would attract robbers to your home.

Keep Safety in Mind

It's best to hold an open house with another person. But if you hold it solo, let others know you will be having your open house. Keep your cell phone charged and by your side at all times. If you have small children, have them stay with a friend or relative. Experts recommend not walking into small, closed spaces (such as bathrooms, walk-in closets, etc.) with potential buyers. Let buyers lead and you follow behind—never turn your back to your prospect. Based in Boston, Massachusetts, real estate safety expert., Robert Siciliano says to avoid abandoning your prospects while new folks are walking in and never feel shy about asking people to stay if a new arrival makes you uneasy. He says if someone comes into your home who makes you feel really uneasy, practice your 911 call and be ready to press dial. Also, store away any valuables, jewelry or prescriptions while your home is on display.

Insider Secrets: Winning Open House

What can you do before, after and during an open house to make it successful? Realtor Joanna Parker-Lentz of Re/Max Village Square in Short Hills, New Jersey, shares insight to how she makes an open house work for her.

> "We go through the home with a fine-tooth comb with our sellers and decide how to prepare the home for the open house. It is important that a home is ready for showings. A first impression is always the most important one. We make sure to eliminate any unwanted odors—no one likes a stinky house.

> "During an open house, we take clients through the house individually and devote time to their specific questions about the home, neighborhood, schools, commute and anything else that comes up. We have each person sign in and fill out a brief questionnaire so that we have a record of who has come in and what their home-buying needs might be."

Cooking up a Sensational Open House: Grandma's Secret Recipes

Want your open house to have a cozy feel? Nothing sooths the heart more than the aroma of freshly baked goods and refreshments that not only tickle the taste buds, but make your house smell great too. What better than easy-to-make lunch box cookies or mouth-watering lemon bars? It's a treat for the taste buds. Long-time connoisseur Hilda Toguchi shares her delicious recipes for lemon bars and lunch box cookies.

Lunch Box Cookies

Ingredients:

1 cup shortening

1 cup brown sugar

1/2 cup sugar

2 eggs

2 Tbs. milk

1 tsp. vanilla extract

2 cups flour

1 tsp. baking soda

1 tsp. salt

1/2 cup chopped walnuts

3 Almond Joy bars (or any candy bar of your choice)—refrigerated and dice coarsely

Directions:

Cream together shortening and sugars. Add eggs, milk and vanilla and mix thoroughly. Combine dry ingredients and gradually add to egg mixture, mixing well after each addition. When dough is mixed, stir in nuts and candy. Drop by Tablespoon 2" apart on ungreased cookie sheet. Bake at 350 degrees for 15–20 minutes or until lightly brown. Yields 48 cookies.

Out-of-This-World Lemon Bars

Crust:

>   2 cups sifted flour
>   1/2 cup powdered sugar
>   2 sticks margarine (room temperature)

Directions:

> Cut dry ingredients into softened margarine, as if making a pie crust, and form into a ball. Lightly and evenly press into a 9 x 13 lightly greased pan. Bake at 350° for approximately 20 minutes. Watch until it is lightly brown. Be careful not to burn.

Filling:

>   4 eggs slightly beaten
>   1 1/2 cup sugar (combine until sugar dissolves) then add:
>   4 Tbs. flour
>   1 tsp. baking powder
>   1/3 cup + a little more lemon juice (from approximately 4 lemons)

Directions:

> Mix together using a hand mixer. Slowly pour mixture into baked crust. Bake at 350° for about 25 minutes until nicely browned. *Note: When it's still warm in the pan, go around the edge with a plastic knife. If it is cold, it will stick to the pan.* When it's cooled, sprinkle with powdered sugar and cut into squares.

Brightidea

Quick 'n' Tasty Treats

✦ You can also bake your favorite chocolate chip cookies. They have a wonderful comforting aroma and are a delicious treat for visitors.

✦ Heating apple cider on the stove makes for a pleasant aroma and refreshment.

✦ Spruce up powder lemonade. Make powder lemonade or pour a bottle of already-made lemonade. To spruce it up and make it look more formal, add a lemon slice or mint sprig for garnishes.

Summer Classic: Lemonade

What is better than a glass of cold lemonade on a summer's day? Give your open house a welcoming, inviting feel with classic refreshment.

Ingredients:

1 cup sugar
1/3 cup lemon juice
1 pint water
Lemon slices, mint sprigs for garnishes

Directions:

Boil 1 cup of sugar and 1 cup of water for 12 minutes to make syrup. Add the lemon juice, let it cool and then dilute it with water. Add garnishes, such as lemon slices or a mint sprig. (The lemon syrup can also be bottled for later use.)

Welcome to Our Open House
Sign-in sheet

Name	Phone Number	E-mail	Address	How did you hear about the open house?

PART TWO

FOR SALE BY OWNER

Sell Like a Pro

Chapter 8

Making Sure the Buyer Is Financially Qualified to Buy: How Mortgage Officers Can Help You Sell

"I've learned you get a lot of interest, but what you want is serious interest."
—Karen, a For Sale By Owner

Sure, it's common sense: You want a buyer who can afford your home. But, surprisingly, this is the one of the biggest challenges sellers face—finding a buyer with purchasing power. Countrywide Home Loans senior vice president Doug Perry says, to think of it like this: You're the seller. Someone comes at you with an offer below your asking price, but they have paperwork to prove they can afford your home. Versus another buyer that makes an offer, but hasn't been approved for a loan and isn't sure if he can purchase your home. Which offer would you go with?

Perry says there are three types of qualifications to look for when a buyer comes to you with an offer or interest in your home—an approval (loan commitment), preapproval or prequalification. It's like a paperwork stamp of approval that lets you know the buyer has met with a mortgage officer and can likely afford your home—and it makes for a smoother transaction.

The Best Kind of Buyers

Like anything, there is a difference between a buyer that is approved, preapproved or prequalified. (The strongest buyers are ones that are approved or preapproved.)

Pre-qualification: A prequalification is an estimate of what a buyer can afford. The loan officer tells the buyer, "You can *probably* afford a house for X amount of dollars," says Bryan Sheeran, vice president of Investors Savings Bank in Millburn, New Jersey. Prequalification is informal. The buyer and loan officer have a 10-minute chat about the buyer's income, debts, credit and employment. Before you know it, the buyer has a prequalification letter to give to sellers when he goes to make an offer on a house he likes.

It's fast, it's noncommittal, it's free—which is what makes this option popular. However, it also has loopholes.

Because the information isn't set in stone—the buyer's credit hasn't been checked and his employment and income haven't been verified—there are a number of reasons a buyer may not be approved for a loan. And if they can't qualify for a loan, they can't buy your home. Then the contract falls through, and you have to try to sell your home again.

"It's common to give a prequalification letter, but there are endless loopholes for a buyer to get out of the contract," says Brian Shulman, president of MBA Mortgage Corporation. "Instead of just a prequalification letter, ask to also see the buyer's bank statements or savings statements to show adequate funds for down payment and closing costs."

If you have two buyers, one has a prequalification letter and another has a preapproval, and they are asking to buy it for the same price, the stronger buyer is the one with the preapproval. The following entry explains why.

Preapproval (better): A preapproval means the buyer made a formal loan application and knows exactly how much he can afford. The buyer gave the loan officer their W2s and pay stubs, a credit report was pulled, employment was checked and funds were approved by the lender; in other words, information was verified. If a buyer "walks in with a preapproval to pay for the house, it's more dramatic, more impressive, more approval" than a prequalification, says Sheeran.

Approval/loan commitment (best): A loan commitment is an actual underwritten loan, says Stephen Katz, senior loan officer at Homebridge Mortgage Bankers. "This is as good as it gets." (Unless, a buyer makes an offer in cash, but that doesn't happen often.)

How Mortgage Officers Can Help You Sell

Mortgage officers can be one of your greatest friends in selling your home. How do you ask them to help you? Simple. Tell them you are selling your own house and ask if they would mind meeting with potential buyers to see if they can afford it. Many mortgage officers agree to help because it is a way of drumming up clients. At the same time, you have a friend on your side to help you sell your home. There are several ways loan officers can help you:

✦ If a buyer doesn't know if he can afford your home, it's not a problem. Ask a mortgage officer to meet with the buyer (the loan officer can preapprove or prequalify buyers for you). Send the buyer to your expert.

✦ If you want to know what you will have to pay at closing, the mortgage officer can tell you what your closing costs will be.

✦ You can make buying your house look affordable. If you want a monthly breakdown of how much your home will cost, plus more great financial breakdowns, ask your mortgage expert for a "mortgage qualification worksheet" that you can pass out to buyers.

✦ If the buyer can't cover closing costs, there are concessions. You can offer to pay a portion of closing; the loan officer can bump up the asking price to cover it. It gets the buyer in the backdoor and you still win.

Can the Buyer Afford Your Home?

The scenario seems perfect. The buyer knocks on your door, falls in love with your home and wants to buy it. There is one problem: the buyer hasn't met with a loan officer and doesn't know if he can afford your house. Not a problem. There is a simple solution. Countrywide Home Loans senior vice president Doug Perry suggests:

✦ You can recommend that the buyer meet with a mortgage officer.

✦ Establish a relationship with a mortgage officer when you go to sell your home. Then you have an expert to direct buyers to get preapproved or prequalified, and you will know if the buyer can afford your home.

Most common horror story: Ken got an offer on his house. The contract was signed and, close to closing, they found out the buyer couldn't afford the home. The loan wasn't approved. So Ken had to put his house on the market and sell it again.

When Jennifer Wake was selling her home, she found out there were a lot of window-shoppers. To narrow the list down to the serious buyers, she asked, "Are you prequalified or preapproved?"

If they were qualified, she let them inside for a showing. If they weren't qualified, Wake directed them to a mortgage officer.

Finding a Loan Officer

How do you find a mortgage officer to help you? Easy. You can visit local lenders in your area, search online or call mortgage officers. Let them know you are selling your home yourself and you would love their help meeting with buyers that haven't been financially qualified.

Prescreening Buyers

As a good rule of thumb, Ron LeGrand, author of *How to be a Quick Turn Real Estate Millionaire,* says there is a way to screen potential buyers before they ever come to your home. Use a special phone line to take incoming calls about your home. Here's a creative option: You can use a 24-hour answering service that asks potential buyers a handful of questions. Ask the following questions to know if the buyer is serious or not:

1. What monthly payments are you comfortable with?
2. Can you make a down payment and how much?
3. Is your credit good, fair or ugly?

If callers have a down payment and fair credit, they are good prospects to call, says LeGrand. If they don't have these elements—if the callers have ugly credit and can't afford a down payment—they are "suspect." Prescreening prospects saves you from spending a lot of time with unserious buyers and more time with those who are serious buyers.

For prospects who pass the test, thank them for their inquiry and move forward from there.

Free Service

Did you know that most mortgage officers will prequalify buyers for free? Preapproval doesn't have out-of-pocket costs up front, but it may have costs associated at closing for pulling the credit report, etc.

Finding a Mortgage Officer to Help You

What should you look for in a loan officer?

Gibran Nicholas of Nicholas & Co. has advice on how to select a mortgage officer. He says to look for an individual who really "takes a consultation approach when working with you and can give sound advice."

- ✦ **Referrals:** Ask friends, family and coworkers for referrals of a professional they had a good experience with.
- ✦ **When you select a mortgage officer:** Make sure they can *preapprove* buyers, not just prequalify them.
- ✦ **Get familiar with the mortgage process:** Know about preapprovals and prequalifications (as discussed previously). Be aware that a seller pays closing costs and the less contingencies in a contract, the better.
- ✦ **When you interview the loan officer:** Nicholas recommends asking the loan officer questions, such as *Why do interest rates fluctuate?* and *What is the difference between ARMs and Balloon loans?* "Listen for intelligent answers that show the officer knows what he's talking about," says Nicholas.

Selling Tip

Bryan Sheeran explains that, while you can suggest a mortgage officer to a buyer, the buyer has the right to select who he or she wants to use.

How Much Your Home Will Cost Per Month: Easy Financial Breakdown for Buyers

Tantalizing details. Buyers love details. The number one detail is money. How much does your home cost? How much does that mean per month over 30 years or 15 years?

How much will it cost with a down payment of 10 percent versus 20 percent? These are the bare bones we all want to know. We never buy anything without knowing all the details and how it fits into our budget. When you purchase a car, you want to know all the financial details. You want to know if it will fit in your budget. The same is true of a home. Give buyers the financial details.

"When a car dealership tells you X monthly payment, it helps you visualize buying that car. If you have a breakdown of monthly payments for the home instead of a lump sum, it helps the buyer visualize buying it," says Nicholas. "The buyer thinks, 'I can buy this home for $3,000 to $4,000 a month.'"

But where do you get this financial breakdown on your home? Turn to the mortgage officer working with you. Ask for a "Mortgage qualification worksheet." It is a flier that lets buyers know, in general, the loan amount and price per month with varying down payment amounts. It gives a general overview and, at the same time, provides the mortgage officer's information so, if buyers have more financial questions, they can contact the loan officer directly. And it's all free.

Brightidea

Great idea #1

You have a buyer who loves your home, but needs to meet with a mortgage officer to see if they can qualify. On the spot, a potential buyer can go online or call a mortgage lender to get preapproved or prequalified. Many established lenders provide Websites, phone service or area branches that can instantly work with a buyer on the spot for a fast, efficient process.

Great idea #2

You have an open house. Invite the mortgage lender you are working with to attend the open house with you, so buyers that express interest—but haven't been financially qualified—can meet with a loan officer on the spot. However, you have to ensure the loan officer you will have traffic at your open house, so that it is worth their time to come.

Closing Costs

You want to know how much you will pay at closing? This is an area in which you can turn to a mortgage officer for advice and guidance. They can guide you through seller-paid closing costs, says Gibran. (For a list of common seller's closing costs, check out Chapter 2.)

Hot Tip

Be Wary

Gibran Nicholas warns that there are "contingencies" the seller should be cautious of. In the contract, when a buyer says the contract is contingent on whether the buyer is approved for financing in X amount of days, the offer is not as strong as someone else's offer that is not contingent on that. On another note, talk your mortgage officer about seller financing options.

Helping With Closing Costs—You Ultimately Win

It is a trend for the seller to contribute toward closing costs for the buyer. The seller offers to help with closing. The selling price gets bumped up slightly (so the lender is still okay), and a portion of the closing costs are covered. It's like a backdoor to get the buyer in the house. It's called a *seller's concession*.

For example, Shulman explained that closing costs tend to range from 3 to 5 percent of the purchase price, depending on state and county localities, because transfer and recordation tax differs.

For most conventional loans—if less than 20 percent is being put down on the house—the seller is allowed to contribute 3 percent toward closing costs (also known as a 3-percent concession). If more than 20 percent is being put down on the house, sellers are allowed a 6 percent concession.

Today, many don't have a lot of savings and it is harder to come up with closing costs. But this tactic is helping sellers help buyers—but you ultimately win.

Making Sure the Transaction Goes Smoothly to Closing

After the purchase contract is signed and it's a "go," you want to keep track of how the loan is going so that you have the closing done on time, says Countrywide expert Perry. "Make sure the loan is progressing so that you can close on the agreed-upon date." Here's what you should do:

+ Check in with the buyer's lender. Ask, "Are there any problems? How is the loan going?" The lender can let you know if it is coming along smoothly or if there are a few bumps. (But, a lender can't disclose personal information about the buyer. For example, the lender can't tell you there are issues with the loan because of the buyer's income.)

+ Check on the appraisal.

+ Check on the title search.

Be Aware

Brian Shulman, president of MBA Mortgage Corporation, says that a seller should be aware that buyers with an FHA (Federal Housing Administration) loan will have to go through a stringent FHA inspection—it is a more critical inspection than a typical one if a buyer had a conventional loan.

What Can Affect Approval of the Loan?

Brian Shulman says there are several scenarios in which a loan may get denied—and that may affect a deal:

- ✦ **Appraisal can affect the loan.**
- ✦ **Credit:** Another reason a loan can get denied is poor credit. "If a seller is smart, they will ask for bank statements," says Shulman.
- ✦ **Debt-to-income ratio:** Say the buyer's car breaks down. Instead of fixing the car, he or she buys a new one. Well, with this new debt, the buyer may no longer be able to afford/qualify for the loan, so the loan doesn't go through to purchase a home.
- ✦ **Loss of a job.**
- ✦ **Employment change:** The buyer has worked three years for a company, but during a check, it turns out he was fired last week. This affects a loan approval.
- ✦ **Serious problems with the house:** If an inspection shows there are serious problems with the home, the buyer can walk away from the deal completely. The seller and buyer shake hands and the deal is off. (In cases of minor damage that can be fixed, many times buyers and sellers negotiate repairs or the seller contributes money [credit] toward repairs at closing.)

Outside of the loan:

- ✦ Select a closing agent, be it an escrow company, title company, attorney, etc. Sometimes, if you don't know who to select, lenders can help you find a closing agent, title company or attorney you can use.
- ✦ Make sure the contract you have is sound.

Advice You Should Know

Q&A with mortgage guru and popular radio cohost of the "The Real Estate and Finance Hour," Norman Bour, is based in California.

Piper: How can a mortgage officer help a For Sale By Owner sell his or her home?

Norm: Individuals who sell "by owner" are exposing themselves to many liabilities, the least of which is not having experience in making sure that the intended buyer is qualified to buy their home. Many potential buyers out there are "tire kickers"—many have the intent to purchase, but not the ability,others just like to play the game.

Piper: What are problems that can affect a closing that can be avoided?

Norm: There are two stressful periods in the home purchasing timeline: at the beginning when the negotiation is under way and the emotions run high (which is one of the advantages of having a Realtor as a buffer), and at the end, when the logistics are falling into place. I estimate that 25–50 percent of purchase transactions do not close on time due to various factors. Remove the Realtor from that equation and you increase your odds dramatically.

Piper: What are common contingencies that sellers should be aware of when reading an offer from a buyer?

Norm: Certainly the contingency of *qualifying* for the loan, plus the "customary" timelines for inspections, etc.

Piper: How would you describe "seller concessions"?

Norm: If a buyer knows they can buy a home for $300,000, many times they will offer more than that price (as long as it will appraise), and receive that difference in the form of a "seller credit." That $10,000 they are financing in the loan is now available to them as cash back, to defray their closing costs or cover moving expenses, fix up costs, etc.

Chapter 9

Turning Potential Customers Into Buyers: Negotiating the Deal and Writing the Contract

"If it's not in writing, it's not binding."
—Tom Hayes, real estate attorney
R.T. Hayes & Associates

You list your home. List price: $205,500.

Buyer makes an offer. A buyer falls madly in love. He makes an offer to buy your home. Your adrenaline is rushing. His purchase offer is $203,500, plus a $1,000 earnest money deposit. The contract depends on two common contingencies: approval of the home inspection and financing. Get the offer in writing.

You can accept, reject or counteroffer. Pretty basic, right? As the seller, you find out two things: (1) the buyer has a prequalification letter or preapproval for a loan (better), and (2) he's serious, because he put down an earnest money deposit. Instead of rejecting the offer—you counteroffer. You want $204,500. Write it on the contract, initial the changes and give it back to the buyer. Give them a deadline to respond.

Negotiating begins. The buyer will accept, reject or counteroffer again. Counteroffers mostly deal with price, move-in date and scheduling inspections sooner. Sometimes buyers want to buy the home based on selling their home—if this happens, protect yourself with a *kick-out clause*. "A so-called kick-out clause in the contract will allow you to consider other offers if the buyer isn't able to sell within a certain period of time," says ForSaleByOwner.com. Another option to protect yourself is a *first right of refusal*, which lets your home stay on the market. If you get a better offer, you can ask the buyer if they want to go through with the purchase or you can accept the better offer. Have a real estate lawyer look at your contract to protect your interests. Get all counteroffers and contingencies to the contract in writing. As North Carolina real estate attorney Tom Hayes says, "If it's not in writing, it's not binding."

It's a deal. When you and the buyer reach an agreement, initial all changes and date and sign final documents. You now have a legally binding contract.

Just one more thing, if there is a contingency. The buyer may make the sale of the home dependent on the inspection or appraisal. The inspection happens one to two weeks after the signed contract. If there are major defects, the buyer may counteroffer again, to try to lower the price; request repairs; or walk away from the sale. Negotiate and find a happy medium that works for you and the buyer. We are all human, we give and take in every situation everyday; it's just that we don't often think about it.

What is the key to turning an interested prospect into a buyer? "Listen to what they want, answer their questions and, when they believe you have found the right property, ask them if they would like to write a contract," says real estate broker Nilla Lauberts. When it comes to dealing with buyers, she says, "be yourself; learn body language, it speaks louder then words. Most importantly, be honest. When asking them to write a contract, think whether this is a house you would want to buy."

In this chapter, we will share what to look for in an offer, what to do if you get multiple offers, what's in a contract, negotiating tips, contingencies to look out for and how the process works. The end of the chapter goes over contract terms and common contingencies ("escape clauses").

Evaluating the Offer

It's human nature: the buyer will see how little they can offer, and sellers will want to see how much they can get—unless you throw fear in the mix. If buyers see scores of other buyers vying for your home, they will offer sale price or higher. If the seller is not getting many offers and the home has been on the market for months, he or she may, out of fear of not selling, accept a lower offer.

It is an interesting mix of circumstance and, sometimes, a gamble on the unknown. Will there be a better offer tomorrow or no offer? Will the buyer bite a higher price or walk away?

So, like every other decision in life, you base your decisions on the facts, gut instinct and your position.

When you get an offer from a buyer (insist on a written contract) and remember time is of the essence. The offer has an expiration date. For as you sit at your kitchen table debating to accept, reject or counter the offer—the buyer has the right to withdraw their offer before you act on it.

When you get your first offer, you will feel your adrenaline rush. It pulses through your veins with excitement and negotiating begins. A serious buyer will offer a price that is fair market value, an earnest money deposit, a contract that isn't filled with a lot of contingencies (escape clauses) and should be prequalified or preapproved (even better) for a loan.

With a clear mind and hopeful heart, knowing what you want yet understanding give-and-take and reason, give the offer a good look:

✦ **Can the buyer afford your home?** A quality offer should come with the buyer's prequalification letter or preapproval letter. The leading reason sales fall apart is that the buyer cannot afford the home. A prequalification is an estimate of what the buyer can afford. A preapproval for a loan is even better—the buyer met with a loan officer and turned in proof of employment, pay stubs, bank statements and W2 forms. The loan officer looked at their credit and gave them their loan options. A cash offer is the best you can get, but it does not happen often. You want a financially sound buyer.

If the buyer cannot afford the home and is not approved for the loan, he or she can walk away from the deal and get the earnest money deposit back. Then you end up back at square one: Finding another buyer and your home has spent quality time off the market. Make sure buyers are prequalified or preapproved.

✦ **What is going on in the market?** Are homes selling quickly or slowly? Are there many homes on the market and few buyers? Are there few homes for sale and many buyers?

✦ **What if you want a higher price?** You can counteroffer. Never be insulted by a low price—a lot of times buyers use that tactic because they expect a seller to counteroffer, they may be testing the seller or it may be all they can afford. Experts say your highest prices and fair market value offers come when your home first hits the market. The longer your house sits for sale, the lower the offers. But sometimes sellers who wait for a higher price get what they are looking for; depending on how much time you have to wait, how quickly you need to sell and the options that are presented to you.

✦ **More than the price tag:** Be wary of too many contingencies. Think of a contingency as a loophole to get out of a contract—it is really a tool that protects the buyer. For example, the buyer will not purchase the house unless they are satisfied with the home inspection, unless certain financing is met or based on other terms.

✦ **The contract should include key points:**
  ✧ Address and legal description (available from tax records).
  ✧ Financing terms: Purchase price, type of loan, down payment, loan amount, terms, assumption clause.
  ✧ Desired closing date.
  ✧ Personal property that conveys with the sale of the home, such as the curtains, some fixtures, appliances, etc.
  ✧ Contingencies.

(For a full list of contract terms, see the end of this chapter.)

What If Contracts Give You Cold Feet?

Not to worry. You have numerous options for assistance when selling your home. For example, you can have your real estate attorney review the contract (and you can make the sale of your home "contingent upon the acceptance of your attorney"—just make sure to write that in the contract). Sometimes attorneys will prepare the offer and final contract for everyone involved. Or you can check out programs such as Assist-2-Sell's (*www.assist2sell.com*) new program that handles the contract through closing for you. Many title companies will also now handle the contract through closing for you. You have many options. Know that you are not alone and that this support on your side can provide relief and comfort in your contract process.

Contract Writing 101

The offer from a buyer can vary from a verbal offer to a contract written by the buyer's Realtor. Insist the offer is a written contract. Most verbal agreements will not hold up in court. You an also purchase standard real estate contracts from title companies, office supply stores or legal bookstores. You can find contracts that deal with your locality at your local board of Realtors association or local bar association (these associations usually have a real estate store where you can purchase these contracts). Keep blank contracts on hand while selling your home. If you ever have questions while going through the process, contact your attorney for advice.

Accept, Reject or Counteroffer

As a seller, you can accept, reject or counteroffer any offer you receive.

Accept: When you accept the offer, you sign it.

Reject: You don't sign the offer.

Counteroffer: Most often, after the initial offer, the seller usually counteroffers. The counteroffer should be in writing with all agreed-upon changes to the contract initialed by all parties. You may go back and forth on counteroffers several times until you come to an agreement or walk away from the deal. If you both come to an agreement and sign, date and initial the contract and any changes, and if it's an official contract, it's sold. (Of course, if there are contingencies, it is subject to those contingencies.)

Earnest money deposit: A serious offer will come with an earnest money deposit (sometimes called, "good faith money"). The deposit is about 5 percent to 10 percent of the sale price and usually goes toward the down payment. (Depending on the buyer's ability, it may be $500 to $1,000, more or less, depending on the sale price, and the buyer's ability. You can also do contracts with no earnest money deposits.)

Earnest money should be enough to be a loss to the buyer and fair to the seller if the buyer walks away from the deal. In most cases, the buyer gets the earnest money deposit back unless it states otherwise in the contract. A neutral party holds the earnest money deposit. Your attorney can be the escrow agent in the transaction and hold the money and documents for the closing (or you can get other escrow agents to hold the deposit). The deposit is not made out to you.

The earnest money is deposited after the acceptance of an offer.

You Get an Offer, but...

What if you want your attorney to look at your contract before selling your home, but he isn't available? The Attorney's Title Insurance Fund says you can sign with a contingency that says the deal is "subject to my attorney's approval."

The Art of Negotiating

Getting an offer is the easy part. Getting what you want is the art of negotiating. You will negotiate with the buyer over the price, personal property (such as light fixtures or curtains), move-in dates and contingencies. Negotiating is not only about a price tag.

There are a few tips to keep in mind:

✦ **Don't reveal your motivation.** Try to avoid telling the buyer how much you need to sell your home because you got a new job in another city. The buyer will turn around and try see how low of a price they can get because they know you are in a pinch—it is human nature. At the same time, you will want to know their motivation for buying—maybe they really need to move—and you will see how much they will pay.

✦ **Play ball, counteroffer, be fair.** You and the buyer are at the two opposite ends of the spectrum. The buyer wants to buy your home for $199,000. You want $205,000. The farther apart you are on settling price, anticipate a longer negotiating period. Counteroffer, try to achieve fairness and evaluate the offer and your selling situation. A buyer that has a sizeable down payment and large deposit is a serious buyer.

✦ **Do you need to sell fast or do you have time to wait for better?** As soon as your home hits the market, there is an automatic buzz. It is like a new model car hitting the market or a new fashion—people want it. You will get initial bids, usually at fair market value for what homes are selling for in the area. But what if you want to hold out for a higher offer? Traditionally, the longer a home sits on the market, the lower the bids that follow. Sometimes sellers do get lucky and get a higher price when the right buyer comes along.

✦ **Know your market.** Look at how quickly homes are selling in your area. Are they selling slowly? That means you may get fewer offers. Are they selling like hot cakes because there are only a few homes and many buyers? Who has the ball? If it is a hot seller's market, you may get multiple offers.

✦ **Handle multiple offers.** If you are in an active market, come up with an order for receiving more than one offer at a time. Whatever you do, do not accept more than one offer—if both buyers accept, you will owe a home to two people.

✦ **Do not rush.** Take the time to get offers in writing. Consider the terms, contingencies and offers carefully. Never feel rushed.

✦ **Decide early on the lowest offer you will take.** But this information is only for you. Never tell anyone the lowest price you will accept for your home.

✦ **Get everything in writing.** There is no guarantee with verbal agreements.

✦ **Always be pleasant.** Having a pleasant demeanor is a very important aspect of selling. You can disagree with a buyer, but you can always maintain your demeanor and composure and negotiate calmly, getting your idea across and listening to the buyer.

Can a Buyer Withdraw an Offer?

Hot Tip

Yes—at any time before you accept an offer, a buyer can withdraw it. Vice versa, this is true for you, as well. Sellers can withdraw a counteroffer before the buyer accepts it.

What Should I Consider When Looking at an Offer?

Real estate agent Ginny Leamy has a few key pointers when it comes to price and negotiating:

Bright idea

✦ Price within 5 percent of the target sale price.

✦ Don't be insulted if the buyer pitches a low price.

✦ Stay calm and don't let the negotiating get personal; it is business.

✦ There is more to negotiate than the price—consider personal property, closing and possession dates, loan approval, earnest money, home sale/close contingencies, attorney approval, home inspections, and so on.

✦ Don't consider an offer until you have done a net sheet subtracting the costs to sell. They could total 8 to 11 percent, including mortgages and home equity loans, title and closing fees, state and county revenue tax, local revenue tax, local inspection fees, marketing fees, processing fees, survey, termite, lead, paint/mold/etc. inspections, home inspections, attorneys fees, property tax escrow and special assessments. These are crucial to figure in for your bottom line. (See a full list in Chapter 2.)

✦ Consider a rent back to make possession work.

✦ Know your bottom line before you begin to negotiate. Work toward a number bother parties will be happy with. Both sides need to be satisfied to "get the deal done."

(See your legal rights as a seller in Chapter 14.)

Understanding People's Personalities

Negotiating is not just a price tag, technical terms or legal jargon. It also has a very human heart. Remember that we are dealing with personal pocketbooks, the future of our families, the place we call "home," stress, hope, peace and dreams. We sometimes get so driven by numbers, minute details and legal clutter—that we forget there is another person on the other side. While nontraditional, it is important to know the characters you may encounter in the negotiating process. It not only makes you a better negotiator, it makes you a more successful seller. (And it is always the best feeling to feel good about a transaction.) Like investor Ron LeGrand says, "You want to be a pleasant person to deal with."

There are four special categories most of us relate to when it comes to negotiating. Which one describes you and which one is your buyer?

Personality Types	To Work With This Type
The friend everyone loves—the talker, social-savvy and personable: Wonderful people skills, personable, friendly, team player and good humor are characteristics of this personality type. They usually like to make impulsive decisions, not always swayed by facts.	Negotiations are best when they are good-natured, light-hearted and genuine. The best settings in which to negotiate are social settings, such as lunch.
The steady, peaceful diplomat: These folks are peaceful, relaxed, patient and really want the best situation for everyone. They usually like to avoid conflict and take their time when making decisions.	Try to avoid hard sells. Be patient and take your time. Ensure you will do what you promise, and show that you genuinely care.
The dominator we all know: They believe in winning, being in control, love challenges and the bottom line. These people value facts, details and materials that provide information that helps them make a decision. They are great listeners and like negotiations to move forward quickly.	This is usually the person with an organized desk and who usually asks early on for a price tag. Avoid attacking their view. If you have differing views or positions, support your view with clear logical facts. Be direct, work toward the goal and give them the feeling of winning.
The perfectionist: These are your cautious buyers. They want to know every detail, proof, data, and documents.	Provide information, be direct and give many details. They will usually focus on one point—most often, price—and they will want to win this issue.

The key to a good negotiation is when you feel like you have a good deal and the other person feels like it is a good deal, too.

Profile of a Buyer

On your journey, you will come across a variety of buyers. You will encounter the first-time homebuyer—often soon-to-be married couples (commonly accompanied by their parents), single people, college grads, former town home owners or apartment dwellers. Sometimes first-time homebuyers don't have enough saved up for a down payment or have trouble with financing. A lot of first time homeowners also go with FHA loans. According to Brian Schulman of MBA Mortgage Corporation, an FHA buyer gets a stringent FHA inspection—a stricter inspection than if the buyer had a conventional loan with a typical inspection. On the flip side, first time homebuyers are some of the most exciting, rewarding folks to work with, because they are so excited about owning a home.

Did you know many people move within the same area they are currently living in? That's why it is so important to market to nearby neighborhoods that are similar to the price of your neighborhood and neighborhoods priced a bit below ("move up neighborhoods"). Traditionally, buyers "move up" when they buy their next home. So, target those move-up buyers. These buyers will usually have funds from the sale of their home to purchase your home. Just watch out for contingencies that make the sale of your house contingent on the sale of their house. (An option to protect you in this situation is a first right of refusal—your home stays on the market and if you get a better offer— the buyer can move forward with the purchase or you can take the better offer.)

You will also come across out-of-towners moving into the area, who will want to know everything about what is nearby, the type of schools, closest shopping centers, etc. They usually have a lot of questions about the area, in addition to asking about the home.

NBC12 business analyst Randy Cost says there are also retirement-age buyers looking to move into smaller homes. But there are others who, for financial reasons, need to move into a smaller home and may be suffering from financial difficulties. Listen to people's needs and tie in how your home fits what they are looking for in a home.

You will come across folks who are easy to work with and willing to negotiate in order to get the home. At the same time, you will have others who see that your home is a For Sale By Owner and will try to get as much of a "deal" as possible. Stand by what you want in the sale of your home and always trust your gut instinct when dealing with people.

Disclosure/Disclaimer

Confess everything. According to the Attorneys' Title Insurance Fund, sample defects that you should tell the buyer about include: damage to the property due to fire, sink holes, floods, etc. Share problems with major systems in your home, such as the foundations, HVAC, siding, plumbing and so forth. Disclose problems with critters and termites. Also reveal additions made without building permits, environmental hazards (lead-based paint for houses built before 1978) and contaminated water/soil. Owners of condominiums and properties in subdivisions have to give the buyer covenants, conditions, restrictions and fees/bylaws established by the Homeowners Association. If you don't disclose defects you know about, the buyer can sue you for fraud, says The Fund.

Be aware if your state requires seller disclosure. Some require sellers to fill out a questionnaire, while other states allow verbal disclosures. In addition, some federal and local laws also require disclosures. For example, according to federal law, if your home is built before 1978 you have to disclose known lead-based paint hazards. (See more on this in Chapter 11.) Check out your local, state and federal laws regarding disclosure in your area.

It's a Deal When...

When you and the buyer reach an agreement, initial all changes, date and sign final documents—you have a legally binding contract.

Moving Forward With the Deal: Financing

Most deals depend on the buyer's ability to get a loan to purchase the home. That makes sense, right? They will have a period to receive written approval for a loan. Unless the deal does not need a loan. Does the buyer have a prepurchase loan commitment? If the deal falls apart, the buyer is usually entitled to their earnest money deposit and you start again. Alternatively, if it moves forward, your next hurtle is the inspection.

The Home Inspection

The buyer will usually have a home inspection, unless they waived their right to an inspection or say you already did a pre-inspection. For the most part, the sale usually depends on the inspection. If there is damage, the buyer will want it fixed, a lower price on the house or the right to walk away. Negotiating begins again. (Visit Chapter 11.)

Who Will Handle Your Closing?

As soon as you have a deal, you need to find someone to handle your closing. Closings can happen in a week in some areas or situations, if a buyer has all of his or her ducks in a row. But traditionally, closings are set up for 30, 45 or 60 days after the deal is signed. It takes time to set up financing, inspections and appraisals; move; and pack, in addition to everything else going on in your life. (The reason closings don't usually exceed 60 days is because it would be hard to lock in loan rates. If the rate goes up, the buyer may come across a situation where they are no longer able to pay for the home.)

As soon as you get a contract (or before), find a professional to handle your closing. Commonly, sellers turn to title companies, an attorney (try get an attorney that specializes in real estate) or an escrow firm to handle the closing (also called a settlement). In your area, evaluate who offers the best services, so that your needs are met. The house is your responsibility until it is in the buyer's hands. Meanwhile, evaluate the services and costs and determine what is best for you.

We have a comparison chart of using an attorney versus a title company. While every company and area is different, here is a jump start on their usual services.

Attorney	Title Company
There are several perks to having a real estate attorney handle your transaction. A real estate attorney that is in your area will have vast knowledge and experience with local laws, regulations, customs and ordinances. He can review the paperwork or contract before you close the deal. If you get an attorney early on in the process, he can help answer legal questions or situations that may come up while you are selling your home. He can also help you with disclosures so you don't have worries about lawsuits. Plus, he can help handle your closing. **The search:** The best way to find an attorney is through friends and family that had a positive experience. You can also turn to the Yellow Pages. To see a listing of all the real estate attorneys in your area Visit *www.FindLaw.com*.	Many title companies will provide you with the paperwork needed to sell your home and they will handle the closing for you. When you write a contract, the buyer expects the transfer of a "marketable title"—a title without liens against the property. "If you let the title company know that you are concerned about keeping your closing costs to a minimum, many companies will lower or waive certain discretionary fees to win your business," says TitleVest Agency, Inc. president Bill Baron. "Also, if you have the time and the inclination, calling on several title companies and getting competitive quotes can give you the knowledge you need to ask for or negotiate a reduction of certain fees."

What's Better Than a Discount?

Did you know that if you turn in your existing title insurance policy when you order a new one many title companies will give you a credit, discount or rebate? Ask if you are entitled to a discounted premium. TitleVest Agency, Inc. president Bill Baron says, "Discounts or no discounts, it is always a good idea to get a written, itemized breakdown of all the closing costs prior to placing your order with a title company."

Contract Terms You Should Know

Once you accept a written offer, the offer becomes a contract. Most real estate contracts include the following terms (depending on where you live):

Full names of buyers and sellers.

Address and legal description of the property: The legal description is on the tax records. For example, a legal description could look like: Starlight BL B LT 7 60 B2 19. The address is like any other, 8257 Starlight Court. (You can also get the legal description from the title work or your Register of Deeds county office.)

Purchase price: If you are writing the contract, it is common to write out the purchase price (like writing a check). If you were selling your home for $172,000, here's how you would fill it out:

Purchase price: <u>One-hundred and seventy-two thousand dollars</u>
Dollars: <u>$172,000</u>

Mortgage contingency/financing terms: The sale depends on the buyer getting a mortgage, interest rate and terms. (Sometimes in the contract, it will say the buyer has to make a written application for the loan within a certain number of days.) It will also tell you how the buyer is paying for the home: mortgage, mortgage assumption, cash or seller financing.

Conveyances: The Contract Include personal property that will be left in the house (if any). The buyer may ask if you will leave the washer, dryer, shades, door knockers—extras that you and the seller agree upon.

Deposit: The amount of the earnest money deposit will be listed, as well as what escrow agent will be holding the deposit.

Closing date, location and possession: Here you usually have the date of the closing (For example, "on or before Aug. 30.") If you don't know your settlement agent /settlement office's address yet, you can write "TBD," for "to be determined." You can always extend the closing date later on if needed, but both parties have to agree to it.

How the buyer will pay at closing: Payment will be made by bank wire or certified check.

Closing costs and who will pay them.

Inspection: "Know when the inspection will take place and a plan for any potential issues," says the Freddie Mac corporation (*www.freddiemac.com*). Sometimes, the sale of the house is contingent on the home inspection. The buyer has the right to execute or waive their right to a home inspection. If they choose to do a home inspection, they will have a certain number of days to complete it and provide a list of needed repairs. A buyer can get a whole house inspection, in addition to other inspections, such as radon, mold, soil, etc. Make sure to include time frames for getting these inspections done. (Sometimes, buyers will waive the right to an inspection in a hot market, to get the house.)

Final walk-through inspection: The buyer usually does a walk-through before closing. Make sure the house is clean and in the same condition or better than when they saw it.

Warranties: A list of any warranties that come with the home.

Well and septic: It has to be tested, as well as pass inspection if the property has either.

Property disclosures: Notification of any issues/problems with the property.

Property disclaimers.

Lead paint: Visit *www.epa.gov* for pamphlets to give buyers regarding lead paint. It provides up to date information on lead paint rules and regulations.

Acceptance/delivery date: Dates to respond to offers, counteroffers, etc.

Acknowledgement of deposit: States who is holding the deposit. If your title company or attorney is holding it, get them to sign.

Arbitration: How the buyer and seller will deal with disagreements.

Insurance: Whose insurance covers the home until the closing date.

Condominium: Any terms that come with purchasing a condominium.

Signatures: All parties must sign.

Standard terms, provisions: Make sure you understand everything in the contract.

Addendums: This lets you add, change or extend anything in the contract, without having to rewrite the whole contract. You just attach the addendum, have all parties sign and date all agreements.

Any contingencies: Make sure you understand the contingencies and add anything to the contract that you need to that is specialized to your needs in the sales transaction.

Common Contingencies and What They Mean

The fewer contingencies a contract has, the better the offer; this is the wise advice of mortgage expert Gibran Nicholas of Nicholas & Co. Your attorney can help guide you through any conditions, contingencies or terms. Make sure you understand everything in the contract. Every transaction is different because the needs of sellers and buyers vary. The needs of both parties are addressed in the contract. Sometimes additional terms, conditions and contingencies are added to the contract by using an addendum. According to The Attorney's Title Insurance Fund, they share common contingencies in real estate contracts. The Fund has about 6,000 real estate attorneys across Florida and it the leading title insurance underwriter in the state and sixth largest in the country. The Fund says this is what these common contingencies mean:

Financing contingency: The deal depends on the buyer being approved for a loan. A buyer will usually specify cancellation rights and return of the deposit if they cannot get acceptable financing to purchase the home.

Inspections: The buyer has a right to a home inspection as well as other inspections specified in the contract. This clause can request the seller to make repairs, lower the price or the buyer can shake hands with you and walk away from the deal. For more on inspections, review Chapter 11.

Clear title: A clear and marketable title to the house.

Home sale contingency: The buyer has a specific timeframe to sell their current home. You can do a kick-out clause (as mentioned earlier). There is also a way to deal with this to your benefit: Your home would stay for sale on the market, your buyer has a "right of first refusal." For example, if another buyer makes an offer on your home, you would then give the first buyer two options: (1) drop the contingency and buy your home, or (2) void the contract. You may also be asked to take your home off the market for a certain amount of time. Read the contingencies carefully—if there is anything you don't understand, ask.

Survey.

The follwing sample Offer to Purchase and Contract form 2-T and sample Additional Provisions Addendum form 2A11-T (please note that an addendum is not always necessary) are the property of and are reprinted with permission of the North Carolina Bar Association and the North Carolina Association of REALTORS®, Inc.

OFFER TO PURCHASE AND CONTRACT

_____, as Buyer,
hereby offers to purchase and _____. as Seller.
upon acceptance of said offer. agrees to sell and convey, all of that plot. piece or parcel of land described below. together with all
improvements located thereon and such fixtures and personal property as are listed below (collectively referred to as the "Property").
upon the following terms and conditions:

1. REAL PROPERTY: Located in the City of _____ .
County of _____. State of North Carolina. being known as and more particularly described as:
Street Address_____ Zip_____
Legal Description:_____
(☐ All   ☐ A portion of the property in Deed Reference: Book_____, Page No._____, _____County.)
NOTE: Prior to signing this Offer to Purchase and Contract, Buyer is advised to review Restrictive Covenants, if any, which may
limit the use of the Property, and to read the Declaration of Restrictive Covenants. By-Laws, Articles of Incorporation. Rules and
Regulations, and other governing documents of the owners' association and/or the subdivision, if applicable.

2. FIXTURES: The following items, if any, are included in the purchase price free of liens: any built-in appliances, light fixtures.
ceiling fans, attached floor coverings, blinds, shades, drapery rods and curtain rods. brackets and all related hardware, window and
door screens, storm windows, combination doors, awnings, antennas, satellite dishes and receivers. burglar/fire/smoke alarms, pool
and spa equipment, solar energy systems, attached fireplace screens. gas logs, fireplace inserts. electric garage door openers with
controls. outdoor plants and trees (other than in movable containers), basketball goals, storage sheds, mailboxes, wall and/or door
mirrors, and any other items attached or affixed to the Property. EXCEPT the following items:

_____
_____.

3. PERSONAL PROPERTY: The following personal property is included in the purchase price:_____
_____.

4. PURCHASE PRICE: The purchase price is $_____ and shall be paid as follows:
(a) $_____, EARNEST MONEY DEPOSIT with this offer by ☐ cash ☐ personal check ☐ bank check
    ☐ certified check ☐ other: _____ to be deposited and held in
    escrow by _____ ("Escrow Agent") until the sale is closed, at
    which time it will be credited to Buyer, or until this contract is otherwise terminated. In the event: (1) this offer is not accepted:
    or (2) any of the conditions hereto are not satisfied, then all earnest monies shall be returned to Buyer. In the event of breach of
    this contract by Seller. upon Buyer's request, all earnest monies shall be returned to Buyer, but such return shall not affect any
    other remedies available to Buyer for such breach. In the event this offer is accepted and Buyer breaches this contract. then all
    earnest monies shall be forfeited upon Seller's request, but receipt of such forfeited earnest monies shall not affect any other
    remedies available to Seller for such breach.
    NOTE: In the event of a dispute between Seller and Buyer over the return or forfeiture of earnest money held in escrow by a
    broker, the broker is required by state law to retain said earnest money in the broker's trust or escrow account until a written
    release from the parties consenting to its disposition has been obtained or until disbursement is ordered by a court of competent
    jurisdiction.
(b) $_____, ADDITIONAL EARNEST MONEY DEPOSIT to be paid to Escrow Agent no later than
    _____, TIME BEING OF THE ESSENCE WITH REGARD TO SAID DATE.
(c) $_____, BY ASSUMPTION of the unpaid principal balance and all obligations of Seller on the
    existing loan(s) secured by a deed of trust on the Property in accordance with the attached Loan Assumption Addendum.
(d) $_____, BY SELLER FINANCING in accordance with the attached Seller Financing Addendum.
(e) $_____, BALANCE of the purchase price in cash at Closing.

5. CONDITIONS: (State N/A in each blank that is not a condition to this contract.)
(a) Buyer must be able to obtain a ☐ FHA ☐ VA (attach FHA/VA Financing Addendum) ☐ Conventional
    ☐ Other: _____ loan at a ☐ Fixed Rate ☐ Adjustable Rate in the principal amount of
    _____ (plus any financed VA Funding Fee or FHA MIP) for a term of _____ year(s).
    at an initial interest rate not to exceed _____ % per annum. with mortgage loan discount points not to exceed _____ %
    of the loan amount. Buyer shall apply for said loan within _____ days of the Effective Date of this contract. Buyer shall use

Page 1 of 5

This form jointly approved by:
North Carolina Bar Association
North Carolina Association of REALTORS*, Inc.

STANDARD FORM 2 - T
© 7/2004

Buyer Initials _____ _____   Seller Initials _____ _____

Buyer's best efforts to secure the lender's customary loan commitment letter on or before
_____ and to satisfy all terms and conditions of the loan commitment letter by Closing. After the above letter date, Seller may request in writing from Buyer a copy of the loan commitment letter. If Buyer fails to provide Seller a copy of the loan commitment letter or a written waiver of this loan condition within five days of receipt of Seller's request, Seller may terminate this contract by written notice to Buyer at any time thereafter, provided Seller has not then received a copy of the letter or the waiver.

(b) There must be no restriction, easement, zoning or other governmental regulation that would prevent the reasonable use of the Property for _____ purposes.

(c) The Property must be in substantially the same or better condition at Closing as on the date of this offer (or as of the Option Termination Date if Alternative 2 of paragraph 13 applies), reasonable wear and tear excepted.

(d) All deeds of trust, liens and other charges against the Property, not assumed by Buyer, must be paid and satisfied by Seller prior to or at Closing such that cancellation may be promptly obtained following Closing. Seller shall remain obligated to obtain any such cancellations following Closing.

(e) Title must be delivered at Closing by GENERAL WARRANTY DEED unless otherwise stated herein, and must be fee simple marketable and insurable title, free of all encumbrances except: ad valorem taxes for the current year (prorated through the date of Closing); utility easements and unviolated restrictive covenants that do not materially affect the value of the Property; and such other encumbrances as may be assumed or specifically approved by Buyer. The Property must have legal access to a public right of way.

6. SPECIAL ASSESSMENTS: Seller warrants that there are no pending or confirmed governmental special assessments for sidewalk, paving, water, sewer, or other improvements on or adjoining the Property, and no pending or confirmed owners' association special assessments, except as follows: _____

(Insert "None" or the identification of such assessments, if any.) Seller shall pay all owners' association assessments and all governmental assessments confirmed through the time of Closing, if any, and Buyer shall take title subject to all pending assessments, if any, unless otherwise agreed as follows: _____

7. PRORATIONS AND ADJUSTMENTS: Unless otherwise provided, the following items shall be prorated and either adjusted between the parties or paid at Closing: (a) Ad valorem taxes on real property shall be prorated on a calendar year basis through the date of Closing; (b) Ad valorem taxes on personal property for the entire year shall be paid by the Seller unless the personal property is conveyed to the Buyer, in which case, the personal property taxes shall be prorated on a calendar year basis through the date of Closing; (c) All late listing penalties, if any, shall be paid by Seller; (d) Rents, if any, for the Property shall be prorated through the date of Closing; (e) Owners' association dues and other like charges shall be prorated through the date of Closing. Seller represents that the regular owners' association dues, if any, are $_____ per _____.

8. CLOSING EXPENSES: Buyer shall be responsible for all costs with respect to any loan obtained by Buyer. Buyer shall pay for recording the deed and for preparation and recording of all instruments required to secure the balance of the purchase price unpaid at Closing. Seller shall pay for preparation of a deed and all other documents necessary to perform Seller's obligations under this agreement, and for excise tax (revenue stamps) required by law. If Seller is to pay any of Buyer's expenses associated with the purchase of the Property, the amount thereof shall be $_____, including any FHA/VA lender and inspection costs that Buyer is not permitted to pay, but excluding any portion disapproved by Buyer's lender.

9. FUEL: Buyer agrees to purchase from Seller the fuel, if any, situated in any tank on the Property at the prevailing rate with the cost of measurement thereof, if any, being paid by Seller.

10. EVIDENCE OF TITLE: Seller agrees to use his best efforts to deliver to Buyer as soon as reasonably possible after the Effective Date of this contract, copies of all title information in possession of or available to Seller, including but not limited to: title insurance policies, attorney's opinions on title, surveys, covenants, deeds, notes and deeds of trust and easements relating to the Property. Seller authorizes (1) any attorney presently or previously representing Seller to release and disclose any title insurance policy in such attorney's file to Buyer and both Buyer's and Seller's agents and attorneys; and (2) the Property's title insurer or its agent to release and disclose all materials in the Property's title insurer's (or title insurer's agent's) file to Buyer and both Buyer's and Seller's agents and attorneys.

11. LABOR AND MATERIAL: Seller shall furnish at Closing an affidavit and indemnification agreement in form satisfactory to Buyer showing that all labor and materials, if any, furnished to the Property within 120 days prior to the date of Closing have been paid for and agreeing to indemnify Buyer against all loss from any cause or claim arising therefrom.

Buyer Initials _____ _____   Seller Initials _____ _____

STANDARD FORM 2 – T
© 7/2004

12. PROPERTY DISCLOSURE:
- ❑ Buyer has received a signed copy of the N.C. Residential Property Disclosure Statement prior to the signing of this Offer to Purchase and Contract.
- ❑ Buyer has NOT received a signed copy of the N.C. Residential Property Disclosure Statement prior to the signing of this Offer to Purchase and Contract and shall have the right to terminate or withdraw this contract without penalty prior to WHICHEVER OF THE FOLLOWING EVENTS OCCURS FIRST: (1) the end of the third calendar day following receipt of the Disclosure Statement; (2) the end of the third calendar day following the date the contract was made; or (3) Closing or occupancy by the Buyer in the case of a sale or exchange.
- ❑ Exempt from N.C. Residential Property Disclosure Statement because (SEE GUIDELINES)
- ❑ The Property is residential and was built prior to 1978 (Attach Lead-Based Paint or Lead-Based Paint Hazards Disclosure Addendum.)

13. PROPERTY INSPECTION, APPRAISAL, INVESTIGATION (Choose ONLY ONE of the following Alternatives):

❑ ALTERNATIVE 1:
(a) Property Inspection: Unless otherwise stated herein, Buyer shall have the option of inspecting, or obtaining at Buyer's expense inspections, to determine the condition of the Property. Unless otherwise stated herein, it is a condition of this contract that: (i) the built-in appliances, electrical system, plumbing system, heating and cooling systems, roof coverings (including flashing and gutters), doors and windows, exterior surfaces, structural components (including foundations, columns, chimneys, floors, walls, ceilings and roofs), porches and decks, fireplaces and flues, crawl space and attic ventilation systems (if any), water and sewer systems (public and private), shall be performing the function for which intended and shall not be in need of immediate repair; (ii) there shall be no unusual drainage conditions or evidence of excessive moisture adversely affecting the structure(s); and (iii) there shall be no friable asbestos or existing environmental contamination. Any inspections shall be completed and written notice of necessary repairs shall be given to Seller on or before _____. Seller shall provide written notice to Buyer of Seller's response within _____ days of Buyer's notice. Buyer is advised to have any inspections made prior to incurring expenses for Closing and in sufficient time to permit any required repairs to be completed by Closing.
(b) Wood-Destroying Insects: Unless otherwise stated herein, Buyer shall have the option of obtaining, at Buyer's expense, a report from a licensed pest control operator on a standard form in accordance with the regulations of the North Carolina Structural Pest Control Committee, stating that as to all structures, except _____, there was no visible evidence of wood-destroying insects and containing no indication of visible damage therefrom. The report must be obtained in sufficient time so as to permit treatment, if any, and repairs, if any, to be completed prior to Closing. All treatment required shall be paid for by Seller and completed prior to Closing, unless otherwise agreed upon in writing by the parties. The Buyer is advised that the inspection report described in this paragraph may not always reveal either structural damage or damage caused by agents or organisms other than wood-destroying insects. If new construction, Seller shall provide a standard warranty of termite soil treatment.
(c) Repairs: Pursuant to any inspections in (a) and/or (b) above, if any repairs are necessary, Seller shall have the option of completing them or refusing to complete them. If Seller elects not to complete the repairs, then Buyer shall have the option of accepting the Property in its present condition or terminating this contract, in which case all earnest monies shall be refunded. Unless otherwise stated herein, any items not covered by (a)(i), (a)(ii), (a)(iii) and (b) above are excluded from repair negotiations under this contract.
(d) Radon Inspection: Buyer shall have the option, at Buyer's expense, to have the Property tested for radon on or before the date for completion of inspections as set forth in paragraph 13 (a) above. The test result shall be deemed satisfactory to Buyer if it indicates a radon level of less than _____ pico curies per liter of air (as of January 1, 1997, EPA guidelines reflect an "acceptable" level as anything less than 4.0 pico curies per liter of air). If the test result exceeds the above-mentioned level, Seller shall have the option of: a) completing necessary corrective measures to bring the radon level within the satisfactory range; or b) refusing to complete any corrective measures. Upon the completion of corrective measures, Buyer may have a radon test performed at Seller's expense, and if the test result indicates a radon level at or below the level listed above, it shall be deemed satisfactory to the Buyer. If Seller elects not to complete necessary corrective measures, or if corrective measures are attempted but fail to bring the radon level within the satisfactory range, Buyer shall have the option of: a) accepting the Property with its then current radon level; or b) terminating the contract, in which case all earnest monies shall be refunded.
(e) Cost Of Repair Contingency: Notwithstanding the above and as an additional remedy of Buyer, if a reasonable estimate of the total cost of repairs and/or corrective measures required by (a), (b) and (d) above equals or exceeds $_____, then Buyer shall have the option to terminate this contract and all earnest monies shall be returned to Buyer.
(f) Appraisal Contingency: The Property must appraise at a value equal to or exceeding the purchase price or, at the option of Buyer, this contract may be terminated and all earnest monies shall be refunded to Buyer. If this contract is not subject to a financing contingency requiring an appraisal, Buyer shall arrange to have the appraisal completed on or before _____. The cost of the appraisal shall be borne by Buyer.
(g) CLOSING SHALL CONSTITUTE ACCEPTANCE OF THE PROPERTY IN ITS THEN EXISTING CONDITION UNLESS PROVISION IS OTHERWISE MADE IN WRITING.

Buyer Initials _____ _____ Seller Initials _____ _____

STANDARD FORM 2 – T
© 7/2004

❑ **ALTERNATIVE 2:** *(This Alternative applies ONLY if Alternative 2 is checked AND Buyer has paid the Option Fee.)*
(a) Property Investigation with Option to Terminate: In consideration of the sum of $_____ (do *not* insert $0, N/A, or leave blank) paid by Buyer to Seller (not Escrow Agent) and other valuable consideration, the receipt and sufficiency of which is hereby acknowledged (the "Option Fee"), Buyer shall have the right to terminate this contract **for any reason or no reason, whether related to the physical condition of the Property or otherwise,** by delivering to Seller written notice of termination (the "Termination Notice") by 5:00 p.m. on _____, 20____, *time being of the essence* (the "Option Termination Date"). At any time prior to Closing, Buyer shall have the right to inspect the Property at Buyer's expense (Buyer is advised to have all inspections and appraisals of the Property, including but not limited to those matters set forth in Alternative 1, performed prior to the Option Termination Date).
(b) Exercise of Option: If Buyer delivers the Termination Notice prior to the Option Termination Date, *time being of the essence,* this contract shall become null and void and all earnest monies received in connection herewith shall be refunded to Buyer; however, the Option Fee will not be refunded and shall be retained by Seller. If Buyer fails to deliver the Termination Notice to Seller prior to the Option Termination Date, then Buyer will be deemed to have accepted the Property in its physical condition existing as of the Option Termination Date, excluding matters of survey. The Option Fee is not refundable, is not a part of any earnest monies, and will be credited to the purchase price at Closing.
(c) **CLOSING SHALL CONSTITUTE ACCEPTANCE OF THE PROPERTY IN ITS THEN EXISTING CONDITION UNLESS PROVISION IS OTHERWISE MADE IN WRITING.**

14. REASONABLE ACCESS: Seller will provide reasonable access to the Property (including working, existing utilities) through the earlier of Closing or possession by Buyer, to Buyer or Buyer's representatives for the purposes of appraisal, inspection, and/or evaluation. Buyer may conduct a walk-through inspection of the Property prior to Closing.

15. CLOSING: Closing shall be defined as the date and time of recording of the deed. All parties agree to execute any and all documents and papers necessary in connection with Closing and transfer of title on or before _____, at a place designated by Buyer. The deed is to be made to _____.

16. POSSESSION: Unless otherwise provided herein, possession shall be delivered at Closing. In the event possession is NOT to be delivered at Closing: ❑ a Buyer Possession Before Closing Agreement is attached. OR ❑ a Seller Possession After Closing Agreement is attached.

17. OTHER PROVISIONS AND CONDITIONS: (ITEMIZE ALL ADDENDA TO THIS CONTRACT AND ATTACH HERETO.)

18. RISK OF LOSS: The risk of loss or damage by fire or other casualty prior to Closing shall be upon Seller. If the improvements on the Property are destroyed or materially damaged prior to Closing, Buyer may terminate this contract by written notice delivered to Seller or Seller's agent and all deposits shall be returned to Buyer. In the event Buyer does NOT elect to terminate this contract, Buyer shall be entitled to receive, in addition to the Property, any of the Seller's insurance proceeds payable on account of the damage or destruction applicable to the Property being purchased.

19. ASSIGNMENTS: This contract may not be assigned without the written consent of all parties, but if assigned by agreement, then this contract shall be binding on the assignee and his heirs and successors.

20. PARTIES: This contract shall be binding upon and shall inure to the benefit of the parties, i.e., Buyer and Seller and their heirs, successors and assigns. As used herein, words in the singular include the plural and the masculine includes the feminine and neuter genders, as appropriate.

21. SURVIVAL: If any provision herein contained which by its nature and effect is required to be observed, kept or performed after the Closing, it shall survive the Closing and remain binding upon and for the benefit of the parties hereto until fully observed, kept or performed.

22. ENTIRE AGREEMENT: This contract contains the entire agreement of the parties and there are no representations, inducements or other provisions other than those expressed herein. All changes, additions or deletions hereto must be in writing and signed by all parties. Nothing contained herein shall alter any agreement between a REALTOR® or broker and Seller or Buyer as contained in any listing agreement, buyer agency agreement, or any other agency agreement between them.

Page 4 of 5

STANDARD FORM 2 – T
© 7/2004

Buyer Initials _____ _____   Seller Initials _____ _____

23. NOTICE AND EXECUTION: Any notice or communication to be given to a party herein may he given to the party or to such party's agent. This offer shall become a binding contract (the "Effective Date") when signed by both Buyer and Seller and such signing is communicated to the offering party. This contract is executed under seal in signed multiple originals, all of which together constitute one and the same instrument, with a signed original being retained by each party and each REALTOR[b] or broker hereto, and the parties adopt the word "SEAL" beside their signatures below.

Buyer acknowledges having made an on-site personal examination of the Property prior to the making of this offer.

THE NORTH CAROLINA ASSOCIATION OF REALTORS®, INC. AND THE NORTH CAROLINA BAR ASSOCIATION MAKE NO REPRESENTATION AS TO THE LEGAL VALIDITY OR ADEQUACY OF ANY PROVISION OF THIS FORM IN ANY SPECIFIC TRANSACTION. IF YOU DO NOT UNDERSTAND THIS FORM OR FEEL THAT IT DOES NOT PROVIDE FOR YOUR LEGAL NEEDS, YOU SHOULD CONSULT A NORTH CAROLINA REAL ESTATE ATTORNEY BEFORE YOU SIGN IT.

Date: _____   Date: _____

Buyer _____ (SEAL)   Seller _____ (SEAL)

Date: _____   Date: _____

Buyer _____ (SEAL)   Seller _____ (SEAL)

Escrow Agent acknowledges receipt of the earnest money and agrees to hold and disburse the same in accordance with the terms hereof.

Date_____   Firm:_____

                                 By:_____
                                      (Signature)

Selling Agent/Firm/Phone_____
        Acting as ☐ Buyer's Agent   ☐ Seller's (sub)Agent   ☐ Dual Agent

Listing Agent/Firm/Phone_____
        Acting as ☐ Seller's (sub)Agent   ☐ Dual Agent

STANDARD FORM 2 – T
© 7/2004

ADDITIONAL PROVISIONS ADDENDUM

Property Address: _____

NOTE: All of the following provisions which are marked with an "X" shall apply to the attached Offer to Purchase and Contract or Vacant Lot Offer to Purchase and Contract ("Contract"). Those provisions marked "N/A" shall not apply.

1. _____   **EXPIRATION OF OFFER:** This offer shall expire unless acceptance is delivered to Buyer or to _____
_____, on or before _____ ❑ AM ❑ PM, on
_____, or until withdrawn by Buyer, whichever occurs first.

2. _____   **INTEREST BEARING TRUST ACCOUNT:** Any earnest monies deposited by Buyer may be placed in the interest bearing trust account of the Escrow Agent named in the Contract. Any interest earned thereon shall belong to the Escrow Agent in consideration of the expenses incurred by maintaining such account and records associated therewith.

3. _____   **SEWER SYSTEM:** This Contract is contingent upon Buyer obtaining ~~~~~~~ment Permit or written evaluation from the County Health Department ("County") for a (check on ~~~~) ❑ conventional or ❑ other _____ ground absorption sewe~ ~~stem ~ a _____ bedroom home. All costs and expenses of obtaining such Permit or wri~ ~luation sha~ ~~~uyer, except Seller, by no later than _____, shall be ~~spons~ ~ clearing tha~ ~ the Property required by the County to perform its tests and/or inspectio~ ~~ha~ ~ Buyer's best ~ s to obtain such Permit or written evaluation. If the ground absorption s~ ~~ ~or ~d, Buyer m~ ~ina~ ~ Contract and the Earnest Money Deposit shall be re~ ~d to~ B~ ~iv~ ~condition u~ ~ides written notice to Seller by _____ ~is c~ ~n c~ ~e satisfied, ~ ~f the essence.

4. _____   **FLOOD HAZARD ZON~** ~ha~ ~ise~ ~perty i~ ~rea which the Secretary of HUD has found to have spe~ ~ha~ ~than ~ ~be necessar~ ~e flood insurance in order to obtain any loa~ ~d by th~ ~fi~ ~der~ ~ulated institu~ ~or a loan insured or guaranteed by an agency of th~ ~overnm~

5. _____   **~G OF ~ CON~ ~ ~TI~ ~NC~** ~ This Contract is contingent upon closing of an ~ ~tract o~ ~er~ ~ prop~ ~loc~ _____
_____
~ ~fo~ ~ ~f this contingency is not removed on or before midnight of
~ ~Seller may terminate this Contract and all earnest monies shall be
re~

6. _____   **RENT~ ~INC~ ~VI~ ~TMENT PROPERTY:** The Property is subject to existing leases and/or rights of tenant~ ~n ~der month-to-month tenancies. Seller agrees to deliver to Buyer on or before _____, true and complete copies of all existing leases, rental agreements, outstanding tenant notic~ ~ritten statements of all oral tenant agreements, statement of all tenant's deposits, uncured defaults by Seller or tenants, and claims made by or to tenants, if any. This Contract is contingent upon Buyer's approval of said documents. Buyer shall be deemed to have approved said documents unless written notice to the contrary is delivered to Seller or Seller's agent within seven (7) days of receipt of same. If Buyer does not approve said documents and delivers written notice of rejection within the seven day period, this Contract shall be terminated and all earnest monies shall be returned to Buyer. **NOTE:** DO NOT USE THIS PROVISION FOR PROPERTY SUBJECT TO THE NORTH CAROLINA VACATION RENTAL ACT. A VACATION RENTAL ADDENDUM SHOULD BE USED IN SUCH CASES.

Page 1 of 2

REALTOR®

This form jointly approved by:
North Carolina Bar Association
North Carolina Association of REALTORS®, Inc.

STANDARD FORM 2A11 - T
© 7/2004

Buyer Initials _____ _____   Seller Initials _____ _____

This sample form is the property of and may not be reproduced without permission from
the North Carolina Bar Association and the North Carolina Association of REALTORS®, Inc.

IN THE EVENT OF A CONFLICT BETWEEN THIS ADDENDUM AND THE OFFER TO PURCHASE AND CONTRACT OR
THE VACANT LOT OFFER TO PURCHASE AND CONTRACT, THIS ADDENDUM SHALL

THE NORTH CAROLINA ASSOCIATION OF REALTORS®, INC. AND THE NORTH CAROLINA BAR ASSOCIATION
MAKE NO REPRESENTATION AS TO THE LEGAL VALIDITY OR ADEQUACY OF ANY PROVISION OF THIS FORM IN
ANY SPECIFIC TRANSACTION. IF YOU DO NOT UNDERSTAND THIS FORM OR FEEL THAT IT DOES NOT PROVIDE
FOR YOUR LEGAL NEEDS, YOU SHOULD CONSULT A NORTH CAROLINA REAL ESTATE ATTORNEY BEFORE YOU
SIGN IT.

Buyer: _____ Date: _____

Buyer: _____ Date: _____

Seller: _____ Date: _____

Seller: _____ Date: _____

Page 2 of 2

STANDARD FORM 2A11 - T
© 7/2004

Chapter 10

Steps to a Hassle-Free Closing

"A seller doesn't have to do anything unless a buyer makes an issue of the survey or title commitment. A smart seller will fix problems before putting their home up for sale."
—Richard Barrett-Cuetara, real estate attorney
Cowles & Thompson

Here is a bird's-eye view between signing the contract to closing. After your contract is signed and dated and earnest money is deposited, the buyer takes care of the loan application. Meanwhile, select an attorney, title insurance company or escrow company to handle closing for you. Experts say the best way to go is by recommendation. Your closing agent will provide proof of a marketable title and deed. Experts say the seller doesn't have much to worry about unless problems arise with the title or survey. What's next? Following is a brief checklist of what will happen between now and closing and who will handle it.

Now to Closing	Who Sets It up
Home inspection.	Buyer.
Appraisal.	Loan officer.
Repairs: Lender-required repairs from appraisal (if any) and buyer requests, after home inspection.	Seller.
Lender approves buyer for a loan.	Buyer and loan officer.
Termite inspection/well and septic inspection—you should not set up either one more than 30 days before closings. (If, in the last five years, your septic has not been pumped, get it taken care of.)	Buyer or seller arranges. (If a VA [Veterans Administration] loan, seller is usually required to set it up.)
Any other inspections (roof, radon, etc.).	Buyer.
Utilities.	Buyer and seller.
Survey.	Title company.
Title search.	Title company.
Repairs approved by lender and buyer.	Lender, buyer and seller.
Home insurance.	Buyer.
Go over closing costs and paperwork.	Buyer and seller.
Final walk-through.	Buyer and seller.
Bring cashier's check or certifies funds to closing. (The closing officer will let you know what you need to pay at settlement.)	Buyer and seller. (Seller also needs to bring keys and garage door opener.)
Closing.	Buyer and seller.

As a seller, the most action you will have between now and closing is dealing with inspections. What happens during a home inspection, your option for repairs and how you will be affected is next.

Three Key Points

After the contract is signed, there are three areas that are important in getting your deal to the closing table, as outlined in the following checklist. It is important to keep in touch with the buyer to make sure he or she is getting the other side of the transaction taken care of too. The sale of your home usually depends on these areas (usually also specified in your contract):

✦ **Buyer needs to obtain financing.** The sale depends on the buyer being approved for a loan to be able to afford your home. This is the reason sellers prefer it if a buyer has a preapproval letter for a loan. Check in with the buyer's lender to see how the loan process is going.

+ **Lender's conditions.** You and the buyer aren't the only ones in this transaction. The lender has requirements before granting the loan. The lender will want a survey, appraisal (to assure the home's value), termite inspections (usually you have to set this up, make repairs or have damage treated, and show proof that it has been taken care of), title insurance (this protects against errors with the title) and title exam.

+ **Inspections.** Buyers want to inspect what they are buying. Many buyers set up whole house inspections to get a physical examination of the property. (Even though the buyer will be setting up and paying for the inspection, you will also want to make sure the inspector is certified.) For more on inspections, check out Chapter 11.

Calendar
Keep track of important deadlines.

Sunday	Monday	Tuesday	Wednesday	Thursday	Friday	Saturday
—	—	—	—	—	—	—
—	—	—	—	—	—	—
—	—	—	—	—	—	—
—	—	—	—	—	—	—
—	—	—	—	—	—	—

Contact Info
Handy numbers while selling your home.

Name _____   Name _____

Phone _____   Phone _____

E-mail _____   E-mail _____

Fax _____   Fax _____

Address _____   Address _____

_____   _____

Name _____   Name _____

Phone _____   Phone _____

E-mail _____   E-mail _____

Fax _____   Fax _____

Address _____   Address _____

_____   _____

Name _____   Name _____

Phone _____   Phone _____

E-mail _____   E-mail _____

Fax _____   Fax _____

Address _____   Address _____

_____   _____

Name _____   Name _____

Phone _____   Phone _____

E-mail _____   E-mail _____

Fax _____   Fax _____

Address _____   Address _____

_____   _____

Chapter 11

Quality Home Inspections: What Happens During a Home Inspection and How It Affects the Transaction

"A house is like a patient in a doctor's office, each one is uniquely challenged, depending on age, general health and nature."

—Rich Matzen
American Society of Home Inspectors

Steve sat down on the soft bed in the spacious master bedroom and looked around. The morning light streamed in through the double windows, and with a content face, he said, "I can imagine growing old in this home." Meanwhile, the home inspector was pensive and thoughtful, looking around the two-story colonial. His eyes saw what Steve and his Realtor did not. While it was a fairly new home, it had problems.

Some of the siding was warped from rain, the hot water heater needed to be replaced and the washer was leaking—among other issues.

For more than two hours, the home inspector visually examined the home closely. He looked at the roof, basement, foundation, crawlspace, heating, cooling, plumbing, electrical, fireplace, attic, ventilation, insulation, doors, windows, interior and exterior.

As a seller, keep in mind:

◆ The buyer will set up the home inspection and pay for it.

◆ The home inspector will tell you and the buyer what is wrong with the home (and may estimate costs).

◆ The buyer will come back with a list of repair requests.

◆ You and the buyer will negotiate.

◆ If you're selling your home "as is," there is nothing to negotiate or fix. But tell the buyer upfront you are selling your home "as is." "State laws vary and, in some cases, an 'as is' clause may not limit your responsibilities," says American Society of Home Inspector member Rich Matzen.

If a buyer does a whole-house inspection (or additional inspections), it doesn't obligate you to make repairs as a result of those inspections. But in most cases, buyers use the inspection to negotiate repairs, correct environmental hazards and may remedy safety issues or other problems.

Most contracts will have a home-inspection contingency that gives the buyer the right to inspections, in addition to terms and conditions in dealing with what is found in the inspection. The buyer sets up the inspection for the time frame specified in the contract. Say the inspection identifies $3,000 in repairs. Many times, a buyer will ask the seller to make the repairs. If you don't want to make repairs, a buyer will request a reduction in the price to equal the price of the repairs. Otherwise, the buyer has the option to pass on the house and have their earnest money deposit refunded, says real estate attorney Richard Barrett-Cuetara, of Cowles & Thompson in Dallas, Texas.

He says contracts will have a dollar amount associated with inspections. For example, a contract would say:

> If the inspection shows more than $2,000 in expenses, the buyer has the
> following options:
> 1. Seller is responsible for repairs.
> 2. Seller has to reduce the price by $2,000.
> 3. Buyer can pass on the house and have earnest money refunded.

Sometimes another option is for sellers to give money to the buyers for the repairs at closing ("credit" repair costs) or the buyer and seller can negotiate what gets repaired. It all depends on the situation.

Be aware, however, "If the buyer defaults, it is impossible, in court, to force the buyer to buy," says Barrett-Cuetara. "If the seller defaults, a buyer can force the sale of a house."

For Steve, this was house number two. Since the divorce, his wife lived in their old home with their son, and Steve had been living in a town house. He was excited about his new home and had already picked which room he would give his son.

After signing the contract, he set up the home inspection. He wanted to know what was wrong with the house, and he, like all buyers, trusted the inspector to tell him. The inspector would let him know what was in good working order, today. (An inspector can't guarantee what will work tomorrow or for how long.) After Steve got his home inspection report, he created a list of requested repairs to negotiate with the seller.

Buyer Waits Too Long to Do a Home Inspection

Hot Tip

According to Richard Barrett-Cuetara of Cowles & Thompson, in the contract, it usually states how many days a buyer has to do an inspection and request repairs from the seller. If the buyer waits too long to do this, they waive their right to an inspection.

Home Inspection Scenarios

When you have a home inspection, you can come across several scenarios. Following are true stories. This is just a sampling.

Scenario #1: John was purchasing his first home for his family of five. His oldest son was in college, and his youngest son was entering middle school. They longed to move out of their three-bedroom town house. They found a two-story home with four bedrooms on more than two acres. The contract was written, but it was contingent upon them having a whole house inspection.

The inspector arrived. For several hours he explored the home and found a series of problems: the banister needed to be repaired, the fan in the attic was broken and there was an electrical problem with the downstairs bathroom. The buyers made a list of repairs they needed the seller to fix. The For Sale By Owner agreed and made the needed repairs.

Before closing, the buyers had a final walk-through, and they were relieve to see that all the repairs had been made.

Scenario #2: Remember Steve? The inspector spent several hours and gave him a list of problems with the two-story colonial. The complete list had the following problems:

- ✦ Exterior: Replace damaged siding at the garage door, patio door and on the side of the house. Rotted wood at the garage door, porch rails and posts. Estimated repair cost: $2,500.
- ✦ Heat and A/C repair: Damaged duct. Estimated repair cost: $300.
- ✦ Replace hot water heater. Estimated repair cost: $400.
- ✦ Replace storm door. Estimated repair cost: $200.
- ✦ Plumbing: Replace leaking pipes and reseat/reseal toilet. Estimated repair cost: $250.

   Estimate Total: $3,650

The seller was shocked at the cost of repairs. Steve asked the FSBO to make the repairs or credit the cost at closing. But, the seller did not want to make the repairs or credit the cost, because he was offering his home at below market value.

The buyer wanted the repairs fixed or money to fix it at closing or no deal. The seller wanted to sell the home "as is" and had that right. Over the inspection, because the buyer and seller couldn't come to an agreement that was suitable for both parties, the sale of the house did not go through.

Scenario #3: Bob also came across a home he was interested in. But the inspection revealed thousands of dollars worth of termite damage to the structure of the home. He walked away from the deal completely.

Whole-House Inspections: Steps 1–5

Rich Matzen has been in the home inspection business since 1976. This Seattle professional has seen it all inspecting homes. He has seen where a builder forgot to connect a shower to the sewer (the crawlspace was a pond) and an unusually cold home that didn't have insulation because it was still in bundles in the attic.

Rich has seen a lot and he knows how it all works. He took us through the basic steps in the home inspection process:

✦ **Step 1:** A family enters into a purchase sales agreement to buy the house. Typically there is a clause in the contract that allows the buyer the right to get a home inspection within five to 10 days of signing the contract. (Sometimes sales are contingent on the home inspection.)

✦ **Step 2:** The homebuyer quickly contacts a home inspector to make the appointment. The homebuyer makes sure the time for the inspection works for the seller because the seller will need to provide access for the inspector to do the inspection.

✦ **Step 3:** At the appointment, the inspector conducts the actual whole-house inspection for two to three hours. Who will attend? The buyer, the buyer's Realtor (if the buyer has one) and possibly the seller (if you want to attend).

✦ **Step 4:** The inspector gives you a home inspection report. The report can range from an on-site checklist, to an on-site narrative report, to a computer-generated report. Eeventually the buyer will receive a report expressing what repairs need to be made. It may include estimated costs and discussion of the overall integrity of the items inspected. (Every inspection report is different, but it does have to be in writing.)

✦ **Step 5:** Buyers and sellers negotiate repairs. Usually written in the contract, the buyer may request that the seller makes the repairs. If the seller doesn't want to make repairs, the buyer may request a lower sale price. Or the buyer can walk away from the deal and get their earnest money deposit back. (Sometimes sellers can credit money toward repairs at closing.)

Hot Tip

Revealing the Inspection

Richard Barrett-Cuetara explains that if a buyer had a home inspection and walked away from the deal, you have to sell again. According to most laws, you have to show your inspection report (disclosing problems in your home) to potential buyers. If you get another buyer, they get another inspection and walk away from the deal too, then you have to show *both* inspection reports to potential buyers. The worst-case scenario is having multiple home inspection reports to reveal, from buyers that walked away from your home.

Disclosures

Most states require sellers to let buyers know all known problems with the house (structural, mechanical and legal), plus disclosures for lead paint (if your home is built before 1978, you need a lead disclosure form that can be found on *www.hud.gov or www.epa.gov*) and other hazards.

Do's and Don'ts During a Home Inspection

✦ Don't argue negative comments about your home during the inspection. For example, a FSBO was following the inspector during the house inspection. The inspector pointed out the visible water damage around the sliding glass door. "Oh, that's not a problem. Why is that a problem?" said the FSBO. Don't take problems with your home personally.

✦ Don't purposely hide problems from the inspector or block areas that need to be inspected. "A seller should prepare and clean a home," says Rich. But don't attempt to "trick or obscure" problems. For example, "preventing access to the furnace is not acceptable."

✦ Don't make statements about your home that can't be verified. If you don't know when the roof was added or when the appliance was installed, check documents before you answer. And if you don't know, you don't know.

✦ If the buyer makes reasonable requests for repairs and you agree, address repairs promptly; don't linger. Usually a contract says how many days you have to make repairs. The buyer can have an inspector check out the property again to ensure repairs were made properly. If you wait a long time to make repairs, it can sometimes delay closing.

Pre-inspection?

Get a pre-inspection to tell buyers up front what is wrong with the home, to avoid problems later in the transaction. It may prevent them from choosing to do another inspection (speeding up the process), and they can never come back and sue you for undisclosed problems with the house, because you showed them the inspection report from the very beginning of the transaction. All parties know what cards are on the table in this transaction. For more on how to get a pre-inspection, review Chapter 5.

10 Top Defects

The National Association of Certified Home Inspectors (NACHI) has a top-10 list of defects found in homes. Following is a list of these problems, along with suggestions for repairs:.

1. **The house has poor drainage.** This is the most common problem found by home inspectors. To improve drainage, you may have to install a new system of roof gutters and downspouts or have the lot regraded to better channel water away from the house.

2. **The house has faulty wiring.** An insufficient or out-of-date electrical system is a common problem, especially in older homes. This is a potentially hazardous defect and not to be taken lightly. You may have to replace the entire electrical system, or at least part of it, to bring this home up to code or make it safe.

3. **The roof leaks.** If the roof has water damage. It may be caused by old or damaged shingles or improper flashing. It's cheap and relatively easy to repair shingles and small amounts of flashing, but if the roof is old, you face a much larger expense to replace the whole thing.

4. **The house has an unsafe heating system.** An older heating system or one that has been poorly maintained can be a serious health and safety hazard. You may have to repair or replace the old furnace. This is a major expense, but new furnaces are more energy-efficient, which will probably save you money down the line. If your heating system is anything but electrical, install carbon monoxide detectors in a couple of locations in the house.

5. **The whole house has been poorly maintained.** Examples of poor maintenance include cracked or peeling paint, crumbling masonry, broken fixtures or shoddy wiring or plumbing. You can easily repaint a wall, replace a fixture or repair a brick wall, but makeshift electrical or plumbing situations are serious and potentially dangerous problems. Replace any such wires or pipes.

6. **The house has minor structural damage.** Minor structural damage means the house is not likely to fall down, but you should deal with the problem before it becomes more serious. Such damage is usually caused by water seeping into the foundation, floor joists, rafters or window and door headers. First you need to fix the cause of the problem (a leaky roof, for example), then repair or replace any damaged pieces. The more extensive the damage, the more expensive it will be to repair.

7. **The house has plumbing problems.** The most common plumbing defects include old or incompatible piping materials and faulty fixtures or waste lines. These may require simple repairs, such as replacing a fixture, or more expensive measures, such as replacing the plumbing itself.

8. **The house's exterior lets in water and air around windows and doors.** This usually does not indicate a structural problem, but is commonly due to poor caulking, requiring relatively simple and inexpensive repairs around windows and doors.

9. **The house is inadequately ventilated.** Poor ventilation can result in too much moisture that wreaks havoc on interior walls and structural elements. It can also exacerbate allergic reactions. Install ventilation fans in every bathroom if there are no windows, and regularly open all the windows in your home. To repair damage caused by poor ventilation, you may only

have to replace drywall and other inexpensive pieces. If you have to replace a structural element, it will be more expensive.

10. **The house has an environmental hazard.** Environmental problems are a new and growing area of home defects. They include lead-based paint (common in homes built before 1978), asbestos, formaldehyde, contaminated drinking water, radon and leaking underground oil tanks. You usually need to arrange a special inspection to determine environmental problems, and they're usually expensive to fix. For example, it costs $1,000 to install a radon-ventilation system, and about $6,000 to remove a leaking oil tank.

What You Need to Know About Defects

There are also legal defects that can come up when selling your home. Richard Barrett-Cuetara says a real estate attorney will spot liens or other issues associated with the title. As a seller, you can take care of liens before you sell the home, so this issue doesn't present itself on the way to closing.

Items that aren't really defects are sticking doors and windows and old paint jobs. But buyers may use it as a negotiating point to get a few dollars off the price or other requests.

Repair/Replacement Costs

US Inspect shares the following typical maintenance and repair costs for single-family residential housing. According to US Inspect, "These cost projections are only meant to help you gauge how much to budget in order to repair or replace common household systems and components."

Repair/Replacement Items	Cost Projections
Replace metal chimney flashings and roof valleys. Each side.	$275–350 per item
Regrade ground surface to divert surface water. Average home, 30'–40'.	$600–1,200 ($20–30/LF)
Upgrade **electric service** to 200 amps; includes new service cable and main distribution panel (no additional wiring or circuits).	$1,100–1,500 LS
Remove **ceramic tile and damaged substrate**. Install waterproof substrate and new tile in damaged area only.	$300–400
Install **20-year, standard fiberglass reinforced asphalt composition shingles**. Average home, 1,500 SF roof. Removal of existing shingles not included.	$2,500–3,500
Replace standard gas-fired, forced-air heating **unit**. Average home, approximately 100,000 BTU input.	$1,800–2,600
Repair concrete block **foundation wall**. Average conditions, 30 LF wall.	$4,500–6,000 ($150–200/LF)
Remove and replace concrete **foundation wall**. Average conditions, 30 LF wall.	$9,000–10,500 ($300–350/LF)
Replace failed **chimney lining**. Average two-story home. Average difficulty; stainless steel.	$1,500–2,000
Treatment of **soil** for termites. Average home. Average difficulty.	$700–900
Replace **pipe from septic tank** to distribution box.	$250–350
Replace **septic tank**.	$1,500–2,000
Replace **drainage/leaching fields**.	$6,000–20,000

(LF = linear feet, LS = lump sum, SF = square feet)

What Will an Inspector Look at in Your Home?

If you wonder why the home inspection will take so long, take a look at what the inspector will be taking a look at during the inspection. Courtesy of NACHI, here are areas a home inspector will typically look at in your home, so you know what to expect:

✦ **Roof:** Gutters, downspouts, vents, flashings, skylights, chimney, other roof penetrations, roof covering, general structure of the roof from accessible panels, doors or stairs.

✦ **Exterior:** Doors, decks, stoops, steps, porches, railings, eaves, fascias, grading, walkways, balusters, spindles, balconies, surface drainage and retaining walls likely to adversely affect the building.

+ **Basement, foundation and crawl space:** Basement, foundation, crawlspace, visible structural components. Inspect for conditions of water penetration where deterioration is present. Report general indications of foundation movement, such as: cracks, brick cracks, out-of-square doorframes, sheetrock or floor slopes.

+ **Heating:** Inspect the heating system; describe the energy source and heating method using normal operating controls. Report as in need of repair, electric furnaces that do not operate. Report if the furnace is inaccessible.

+ **Cooling:** Central cooling equipment using normal operating controls.

+ **Plumbing:** Inspect the main water shut off valve and inspect water-heating system. Flush toilets. Run water in sinks, tubs and showers. Inspect fixtures, faucets, drain, waste and vent systems. Describe any visible fuel storage. Inspect drainage sump pumps (testing sumps with accessible floats). Inspect/describe water supply, drain, waste, main fuel shut-off.

+ **Attic, ventilation and insulation:** Insulation in unfinished spaces, ventilation in the attic, mechanical ventilation systems, and report any general lack of insulation.

+ **Doors, windows and interior:** Open and close windows and doors. Inspect walls, ceilings, steps, stairways, railings, garage-doors and door openers, electronic sensors and door locks. Check for windows in need of repair that are fogged or display other evidence of broken seals.

+ **Electrical:** Service line, meter box, main disconnect, service amperage, panels, breakers, fuses, grounding, bonding, switches, receptacles, light fixtures, ground circuit interrupters, service entrance conductors (condition of their sheathing), ground fault circuit interrupters with GFCI tester, and service entrance cables. Report: Absence of smoke detectors, presence of solid conductor aluminum branch circuit wiring if readily visible, GFCI-tested receptacles where power isn't present, polarity is incorrect, not grounded, evidence of arcing or excessive heat, is not secured to the wall, cover is not in place or the ground fault circuit interrupter devices are not properly installed or do not operate properly.

+ **Fireplace:** Open/close the damper door if readily accessible and operable. Hearth extensions and other permanently installed components. Also, report those things in need of repair, such as deficiencies in the lintel, hearth and material surrounding the fireplace, including clearance from combustible materials.

Did You Know? Other Types of Inspections

It is also important to note that buyers may want to run a variety of different specialized inspections. Following are a few additional inspections available to buyers. (The buyer would pay for any inspections they select to do.) There are hidden defects that sometimes an inspector might not spot, such as problems with the roof, chimney, termite damage, poor electrical wiring or mold. Specialized inspectors with fine-tuned eyes will be able to investigate some areas further.

Other Inspections

- ✦ Roof.
- ✦ Chimney.
- ✦ Water, sewer.
- ✦ Radon.
- ✦ Mold.
- ✦ Structural inspection.
- ✦ Electrical.
- ✦ Soil.
- ✦ Lead paint.
- ✦ Termite.
- ✦ Plumbing.
- ✦ Heating, air conditioning, ventilation.
- ✦ Septic dye.
- ✦ Seawall.
- ✦ Asbestos.
- ✦ Well.
- ✦ Underground storage tank.

Termite Inspections

After you get a contract on your home, you or the buyer will usually set up a termite inspection. An exterminator checks for termites, powder post beetles, old house bores, carpenter ants, carpenter bees and wood destroying fungus. The termite inspection will let you know what they found and your options for treating it. There are different treatments for termites: repellent liquid treatments, non-repellant liquids and baits. You can be proactive and opt to do a termite inspection before you sell your home so you don't come across surprises later, says Nick Lupini, vice-president of Loyal Termite and Pest Control in Richmond, Virginia.

Lupini says the best way to avoid termite problems is to get a "termite inspection once a year." To help prevent termites, he recommends opening the foundation vents on a regular basis, removing wood debris on the crawl space floor, keeping the area free of moisture and putting down a vapor barrier, such as plastic.

Different Termite Treatment Options

Liquid Treatment: Liquid is injected in the soil around and under the foundation. Crawl spaces and trenches tunneled around the foundation are filled with the treatment to repel termites from the structure.

Non-repellent Liquids: The structure is drilled, trenched and injected with treatment, but the termites cannot detect the liquid in the soil, so they tunnel into the treated soil and die.

Bait Systems: "Wood monitoring stakes" are placed in the ground around the home. If termites are found eating them, a bait is put there instead. Termites eat the bait and it gets rid of them.

Toxic Hazards

Buyers are becoming increasingly concerned about potential toxic hazards in homes that pose health risks. A growing concern among homebuyers is common toxic hazards such as: lead paint, asbestos, carbon monoxide, radon and formaldehyde. Sometimes buyers will request testing for these substances. For example, lead that can be found in chipping paint in homes built before 1978 can cause damage to the nervous system, joints, hearing, circulation or kidneys. Asbestos found in insulation in homes built from the 1930s to 1950s can cause lung damage. Radon is getting an increasing amount of attention because it can cause lung cancer. Mold is also getting a lot of attention.

If you know of any hazards that exist in your home or if you have had problems with certain hazards in the past, it's always a good idea to get your home tested for it. Disclose everything to the buyer.

Where Would These Toxic Materials Be?

Asbestos: Found in wall insulation. (This would appear mostly in homes built from 1930 to 1950). It could also appear in older homes pipe insulation, vinyl floor tiles, siding, textured paint, wall patching, and shingles.

Carbon monoxide: This odorless, invisible gas can be a hazard found in stoves, wood-burning or gas fireplaces, automobiles, furnaces or space heaters.

Formaldehyde: A colorless, acrid gas found in building materials (plywood, hardwood, paneling, particleboard, etc.), paints, glues, foam insulation (homes built in 1970s), preservatives, some gas stoves and kerosene space heaters.

Lead: Federal law requires disclosure of lead-based paint in your home and a federal form about lead-based paint in your purchase contract, if your home was built before 1978. (Visit *www.hud.gov*.) Lead is found in chipped, cracked or peeling paint (in homes built before 1978); pipes in older homes; and soldered copper pipes in newer homes. Give out an EPA-approved lead-based paint hazard pamphlet called *Protect Your Family From Lead in Your Home* (visit *www.epa.gov*).

Radon: Invisible, odorless gas (caused by the breakdown of uranium in soil) found in wells, sump pumps, foundation cracks, basements, gaps in plumbing, wiring, ducts or joints. Be aware of environmental hazards not only when selling your home, but when you go to purchase your next home as well.

Checklists

Here are some checklists you can use to do a personal inspection of your home to scope it out for potential problems and a checklist to prepare before the whole house inspection.

Personal Inspection

You can take a look at a few key areas in your home to get a basic idea of its condition. Following are a few common areas to look at personally, but nothing beats the fine-tuned eye of a home inspector who has seen numerous homes.

❏ Do you see any shifts or cracks in the home's foundation?

❏ Are there any leaks inside or outside the home?

❏ Is there dampness in the crawlspace or basement? Is there insulation?

❑ How is the attic's interior structure?

❑ What is the overall condition of your roof? How old is it?

❑ How are the heating and AC units working?

❑ Do you see any obvious electrical problems?

❑ What is the condition and age of your appliances?

❑ Are there outside repairs or paint needed? Other exterior problems?

Prepare for the Inspection

The buyer will usually set up the home inspection, but before the inspector drops by, tackle these small tasks:

❑ Make sure the utilities are on.

❑ Turn on lights.

❑ Make sure the inspector will have easy access to the entire property. Don't try to hide any problems.

❑ Have your pet spend time with a friend or family during the inspection.

❑ If there is any information you think would be helpful to the inspector, discuss it. They are amazing resources of information too.

(See a sample whole-house inspection report in Chapter 13.)

Chapter 12

Hassle-Free Closing: The Day You've Been Waiting For

Closing is when you get paid and the buyer gets the keys to the home. Closing goes by many names, including *settlement* and *escrow*. But it all means the same thing—it's transferring of ownership (or title) of the home. All the details are finalized, all the paperwork is signed and the agreements between you and the buyer are finalized.

Here are the bare bones of what happens: You arrive at the office of whoever is handling your closing. You sign all the paperwork, and you receive the funds from the sale of your home (either by check or wired to your account). It's the easiest part of the transaction. You're in and out in about an hour.

Ok, now for the specific details.

What Happens?

Your closing agent will pull all the paperwork together for you. You have nothing to worry about. All you need to do is review the paperwork before the closing so you are familiar with the costs and profit of selling your home. Take a look at the HUD-1 settlement statement before closing; it lets you know what costs you and the buyer will be paying. When you show up for closing, you will "sign the dotted line." All the paperwork will be prepared for you. You will receive your funds, and the buyer will get the keys.

A good closing agent:

✦ Reviews the sales contract.
✦ Figures out what payments are for whom.
✦ Prepares documents for the closing.
✦ Ensures taxes, title, real estate commissions (if any) and other closing costs are paid.

+ Makes sure the title is real.
+ Ensures that you are paid.

All you have to do is show up for closing. Your closing agent will let you know what money the buyer owes you (the remainder of the down payment, etc.). You will also find out what money you owe (such as for unpaid taxes, etc.). You will provide proof of inspections and repairs. You'll pass the buyer the title to the property as a signed deed.

Good to Know

While you have been busy packing up boxes and searching for a new home, your escrow agent has been busy preparing and ordering documents for closing. They usually gather the following: warranty deed, note, payoff figures from existing loans, release of liens, deed of trust, termite reports, proof of insurance and the survey.

Closing Costs

At the heart of it, you want to know what you will pay at closing. Meet with your closing officer before the settlement to know your costs. Here's an up-close look at the closing costs you may encounter.

Seller's Closing Costs	Buyer's Closing Costs
+ Paying off your mortgage. + Real estate taxes. + Recording fees. + Your attorney and escrow fees. + Inspections/repairs. + Title insurance (depending on area). + Transfer tax, if applicable. + Other local fees set by area customs.	+ Fees for obtaining a mortgage. + Inspection fees. + Homeowners insurance. + Title insurance. + Escrow fees, if applicable. + Transfer taxes, if there are any. + Attorney's fees, if you used one.

Closer Look at Seller's Costs

Following is an overview of some closing costs sellers often encounter during settlement. This is an overview and brief explanation of the costs, but not all of the fees will apply to your sale.

Common Seller's Costs

Attorney's fee or escrow fees: For example, if you use an attorney to help with your transaction.

Title insurance: The cost of the title insurance varies, depending on the price of your house.

Transfer tax: State and county transfer tax and state capital gains tax (charges for selling your home), if applicable.

Survey: The boundary lines of the property are measured. Not all states require surveys.

Claims against the property, such as unpaid property taxes: For the prior or current year, unpaid taxes need to be credited to the buyer.

Real estate tax: The seller has to pay the current year's taxes up to the date of closing.

Mortgage payoff and recorded release of mortgage: Proceeds from the sale of your home are paid to your lender. The record lease of mortgage is proof your mortgage has been entirely paid off by the sale of your house. You may also pay prepayment penalties, if that applies.

Recording fee: Local government charges you a fee to process paperwork to record the real estate purchase.

Taxes or document stamps: Associated with the deed.

FHA fees: These costs are negotiable between you and the buyer.

Utility bills: Some localities require proof that you are current on your utility bills.

Association transfer fees: Usually for town house or condo buyers, but sometimes sellers have picked up the tab on this, too.

Condo/co-op move-out fee: This is a building charge.

Association reserves: Reserves held by homeowners and condo associations are usually credited to sellers on basis of your percentage of ownership in the association.

Inspections: Some areas dictate that a seller pays for inspections such as pest, radon, etc.

Repairs: If a buyer has a home inspection done and problems are found, you will be asked to fix or credit some or all of these costs. Whether you agree or not is up to you. For termite damage, you will need proof it has been repaired and treated.

Real estate broker's commission: If your buyer has a Realtor or if you used a discount broker to sell your home, for instance.

Unpaid special assessments: This would apply to situations such as local government charges for new sidewalks.

Seller's Homeowner's Insurance

Experts recommend not canceling your homeowner's insurance until the home sale has been recorded. Meanwhile, the buyer should start his homeowner's insurance quickly.

Hot Tip

What Documents Will You Sign?

There are common documents you and the buyer will be asked to sign at closing. Really take the time to read the documents and, if you have any questions at all during the transaction, always feel free to ask your closing agent.

◆ **The seller typically signs:** HUD-1 settlement statement, grant or warranty deed, escrow instruction, the bill of sale and any additional documents associated with the individual transaction.

◆ **The buyer typically signs:** According to Ginnie Mae, buyers sign the HUD-1 settlement statement, warranty deed, Truth in Lending disclosure statement, Real Estate Settlement Procedures Act (RESPA), mortgage note, "deed of trust" or mortgage, loan application, tax authorization, escrow analysis and any other forms, depending on local laws and customs. Other forms: Title insurance and homeowners insurance. (See Chapter 19 for when you go to buy your next home.)

What happens if you or the buyer can't be there for closing? Not a problem. A power of attorney can be used to allow another individual to sign for you. The other solution is having the documents sent beforehand and pre-signing.

Common Closing Issue

Sometimes a problem arises when loan documents arrive at closing and the terms and conditions are different than the buyer was expecting. The solution for this situation is having the buyer look at the documents well in advance and keep in touch with the closing officer, attorney or title company.

What Should You Bring With You to Closing?

You will be traveling light for closing day; you will only need to remember to bring a few key items. Your closing agent will tell you exactly what you need to bring, but here are some common items needed for closing:

❑ Forms of ID (For example, picture ID, driver's license, social security card, etc.)

❑ House keys.

❑ Deed, if necessary.

❑ Garage door opener, if this applies to you

❑ Proof of any inspections and repairs that were taken care of in the transaction.

❑ Proof you have paid your water bill.

❑ Receipts to show proof you paid your tax bill (this avoids any problems that may arise with prorations).

❑ Any information you want to pass to the buyer, such as instructions or paperwork for some of the appliances.

Bring the following items your closing agent asked you to bring:

❏ _____

❏ _____

❏ _____

❏ _____

❏ _____

❏ _____

❏ _____

Where Will Closing Be Held?

Closing customs vary across the country. Commonly, the closing will happen at the office of your attorney, title company or escrow company. Your closing agent will let you know when and where you will need to be for the big day, so don't worry. (Now, if you don't hear such information from your closing agent, call and ask. It's always a good idea to keep in contact with your closing agent until closing day to ensure everything is going smoothly and as planned. It always boils down to preparation.) Here are various examples of how closing meetings are held:

✦ **All attend:** Buyers, sellers and any real estate agents who may be involved attend the closing.

✦ **One-on-one:** In other areas, a buyer will go to his closing at one location. Then, the seller will go to his closing meeting at another location. Usually in this case, the buyer will have the closing scheduled first and the seller will have the closing second.

✦ **No meeting:** In some locations, there aren't closing meetings. For that situation, a closing agent will process the paperwork, as well as get everything signed and collected.

The Big Day

The closing usually lasts about an hour. It is held at the office of your closing agent. You will sign the deed, giving the buyer the title to the house. The transfer is not official until it is recorded at the county Recorder's Office. The funds are distributed.

If you want to buy another home soon, it's good advice to close on the sale of your home before closing on a new home. Then, if something comes up that prevents the sale from happening, you won't be tied to two mortgages. (If you end up in a situation where you are responsible for two homes for a brief time—one you're selling and one you purchased—you can talk to your mortgage officer about bridge loans and other options to help in this scenario.)

On an additional note, sometimes it takes several days following closing before funding happens. The lender may have to review, as well as approve, the paperwork. In other instances, there is an immediate distribution of funds (also called *table funding*); you can ask in advance to have this arranged.

PART THREE

FOR SALE
BY OWNER

What You Should Know

Chapter 13

Contracts You Can Use to Sell Your Home

This chapter features a sample filled out contract, inspection report, disclosure/disclaimer statement and paperwork often associated with selling your home. Every contract looks different, these simply serve as examples to give you a feel for the process. You can find the following in this chapter:

✦ Contract for the sale and purchase of real estate (without a broker).

✦ Residential property disclosure and disclaimer statement.

✦ Lead-based paint disclosure.

✦ Sample contract addendum.

✦ Whole house inspection report.

CONTRACT FOR THE SALE AND PURCHASE OF REAL ESTATE
(NO BROKER)

WARNING: THIS CONTRACT HAS SUBSTANTIAL LEGAL CONSEQUENCES AND THE PARTIES ARE ADVISED TO CONSULT LEGAL AND TAX COUNSEL.

FOR VALUABLE CONSIDERATION OF TEN DOLLARS and other good and valuable consideration, the receipt and sufficiency of which is hereby acknowledged, ___John Smith and Jane Smith___ (Seller), whether one or more, and ___Tom Brown___ (Buyer), whether one or more, do hereby covenant, contract and agree as follows:

1.   AGREEMENT TO SALE AND PURCHASE: Seller agrees to sell, and Buyer agrees to buy from Seller the property described as follows: *(complete adequately to identify property)*

Jasper County, Alabama.
Address: 123 Any Street, Anytown, Alabama .

Legal Description:
Lot 12, Block 5, Subdivision 32, Jasper County, Alabama .

☐ As described in attached Exhibit.

Together with the following items, if any: *(Strike items to be retained by Seller)* curtains and rods, draperies and rods, valances, blinds, window shades, screens, shutters, awnings, wall-to-wall carpeting, mirrors fixed in place, ceiling fans, attic fans, mail boxes, ~~television antennas and satellite dish system with controls and equipment~~, permanently installed heating and air-conditioning units, window air-conditioning units, built-in security and fire detection equipment, plumbing and lighting fixtures including chandeliers, water softener, stove, built-in kitchen equipment, garage door openers with controls, built-in cleaning equipment, all swimming pool equipment and maintenance accessories, shrubbery, landscaping, permanently installed outdoor cooking equipment, built-in fireplace screens, artificial fireplace logs and all other property owned by Seller and attached to the above described real property except the following property which is not included *(list items not included)*:
Bird house

All property sold by this contract is called the "Property."

2.   SALES PRICE: The parties agree to the following sales price:

	Amount	Amount
Purchase Price	$250,000	
Earnest Money		$2,500
New Loan		$247,500
Assumption of Loan		$
Seller Financing		$
Cash at Closing		$
Total (both columns should be equal)	$250,000	$250,000

Both columns should be an equal amount.

If the unpaid principal balance(s) of any assumed loan(s), if any, as of the Closing Date varies from the loan balance(s) stated above, the cash payable at closing will be adjusted by the amount of any variance.

Buyer Initials __TB____   - 1 -   Seller Initials __JS__ __JS__

3. FINANCING: The following provisions apply with respect to financing:

☐   CASH SALE: This contract is not contingent on financing.

☐   OWNER FINANCING: Seller agrees to finance _____ dollars of the purchase price pursuant to a promissory note from Buyer to Seller of $_____, bearing _____% interest per annum, payable over a term of _____ years with even monthly payments, secured by a deed of trust or mortgage lien with the first payment to begin on the _____ day of _____, 20_____.

Credit Information. If Buyer is to pay all or part of the purchase price by executing a promissory note in favor of Seller or if an existing loan is not to be released at closing, this contract is conditional upon Seller's approval of Buyer's financial ability and creditworthiness, which approval shall be at Seller's sole and absolute discretion. In such case: (1) Buyer shall supply to Seller on or before _____, _____ , at, Buyer's expense, information and documents concerning Buyer's financial, employment and credit condition; (2) Buyer consents that Seller may verify Buyer's financial ability and creditworthiness; (3) any such information and documents received by Seller shall be held by Seller in confidence, and not released to others except to protect Seller's interest in this transaction; (4) if Seller does not provide written notice of Seller's disapproval to Buyer on or before _____, _____ , then Seller waives this condition.

☒   NEW LOAN OR ASSUMPTION: This contract is contingent on Buyer obtaining financing. Within 30 days after the effective date of this contract Buyer shall apply for all financing or noteholder's approval of any assumption and make every reasonable effort to obtain financing or assumption approval. Financing or assumption approval will be deemed to have been obtained when the lender determines that Buyer has satisfied all of lender's financial requirements (those items relating to Buyer's net worth, income and creditworthiness). If financing or assumption approval is not obtained within 30 days after the effective date hereof, this contract will terminate and the earnest money will be refunded to Buyer. If Buyer intends to obtain a new loan, the loan will be of the following type:

☒ Conventional ☐ VA ☐ FHA ☐ Other: _____

Existing Loan Review. If an existing loan is not to be released at closing, Seller shall provide copies of the loan documents (including note, deed of trust or mortgage, modifications) to Buyer within _____ calendar days from acceptance of this contract. This contract is conditional upon Buyer's review and approval of the provisions of such loan documents. Buyer consents to the provisions of such loan documents if no written objection is received by Seller from Buyer within _____ calendar days from Buyer's receipt of such documents. If the lender's approval of a transfer of the Property is required, this contract is conditional upon Buyer's obtaining such approval without change in the terms of such loan, except as may be agreed by Buyer. If lender's approval is not obtained on or before _____, _____, this contract shall be terminated on such date. The Seller ☐ shall ☐ shall not, be released from liability under such existing loan. If Seller is to be released and release approval is not obtained, Seller may nevertheless elect to proceed to closing, or terminate this agreement in the sole discretion of Seller.

The following provisions apply if a VA or FHA loan is to be obtained:

FHA. It is expressly agreed that notwithstanding any other provisions of this contract, the Purchaser (Buyer) shall not be obligated to complete the purchase of the Property described herein or to incur any penalty by forfeiture of earnest money deposits or otherwise unless the Purchaser (Buyer) has been given in accordance with HUD/FHA or VA requirements a written statement by the Federal Housing Commissioner, Veterans Administration, or a Direct Endorsement lender setting forth the appraised value of the Property of not less than $ _____ . The Purchaser (Buyer) shall have the privilege and option of proceeding with consummation of the contract without regard to the amount of the appraised valuation. The appraised valuation is arrived at to determine the maximum mortgage the Department of

Buyer Initials   TB   _____   - 2 -   Seller Initials   JS   JS

Housing and Urban Development will insure. HUD does not warrant the value nor the condition of the Property. The Purchaser (Buyer) should satisfy himself/herself that the price and condition of the Property are acceptable.

VA. If Buyer is to pay the purchase price by obtaining a new VA-guaranteed loan: It is agreed that, notwithstanding any other provisions of this contract, Buyer shall not incur any penalty by forfeiture of earnest money or otherwise be obligated to complete the purchase of the Property described herein, if the contract purchase price or cost exceeds the reasonable value of the Property established by the Veterans Administration. Buyer shall, however, have the privilege and option of proceeding with the consummation of this contract without regard to the amount of the reasonable value established by the Veterans Administration.

4.   EARNEST MONEY: Buyer shall deposit $ __2,500_____ as earnest money with __Seller_____ upon execution of this contract by both parties.

5.   PROPERTY CONDITION:

SELLER'S DISCLOSURE OF LEAD-BASED PAINT AND LEAD-BASED PAINT HAZARDS is required by Federal law for a residential dwelling constructed prior to 1978. An addendum providing such disclosure ☐ is attached ☒ is not applicable.

Buyer hereby represents that he has personally inspected and examined the above-mentioned premises and all improvements thereon. Buyer hereby acknowledges that unless otherwise set forth in writing elsewhere in this contract neither Seller nor Seller's representatives, if any, have made any representations concerning the present or past structural condition of the improvements. Buyer and Seller agree to the following concerning the condition of the property:

☐   Buyer accepts the property in its "as-is" and present condition.

☒   Buyer may have the property inspected by persons of Buyer's choosing and at Buyer's expense. If the inspection report reveals defects in the property, Buyer shall notify Seller within 5 days of receipt of the report and may cancel this contract and receive a refund of earnest money, or close this agreement notwithstanding the defects, or Buyer and Seller may renegotiate this contract, in the discretion of Seller. All inspections and notices to Seller shall be complete within 14 days after execution of this agreement.

☐   Buyer accepts the Property in its present condition; provided Seller, at Seller's expense, shall complete the following repairs and treatment: _____

_____

_____

Buyer agrees that he will not hold Seller or its representatives responsible or liable for any present or future structural problems or damage to the foundation or slab of said property. **If the subject residential dwelling was constructed prior to 1978, Buyer may conduct a risk assessment or inspection for the presence of lead-based paint and/or lead-based paint hazards, to be completed within 14 days after execution of this agreement. In the alternative, Buyer may waive the opportunity to conduct an assessment/inspection by indicating said waiver on the attached Lead-Based Paint Disclosure form.**

MECHANICAL EQUIPMENT AND BUILT IN APPLIANCES: All such equipment is sold ☐ "as-is" without warranty, or ☒ shall be in good working order on the date of closing. Any repairs needed to mechanical equipment or appliances, if any, shall be the responsibility of ☐ Seller ☒ Buyer.

UTILITIES: Water is provided to the property by ___Water Co., Inc._____, Sewer is provided

Buyer Initials __TB_____   - 3 -   Seller Initials __JS___ __JS__

by _____City of Anytown_____. Gas is provided by _Anytown Gas Providers, Inc._. Electricity
is provided by _____Anytown Electric, Inc._____. Other: _____
_____
_____
_____

The present condition of all utilities is accepted by Buyer.

6.   CLOSING: The closing of the sale will be on or before _____December 21_____, 2005, unless extended pursuant to
       the terms hereof.

       Closing may be extended to within 7 days after objections to matters disclosed in the title abstract, certificate or
       commitment or by the survey have been cured.

       If financing or assumption approval has been obtained, the Closing Date will be extended up to 15 days if necessary
       to comply with lender's closing requirements (for example, appraisal, survey, insurance policies, lender-required
       repairs, closing documents). If either party fails to close this sale by the Closing Date, the non-defaulting party will be
       entitled to exercise the remedies contained herein. The closing date may also be extended by written agreement of the
       parties.

7.   TITLE AND CONVEYANCE: Seller is to convey title to Buyer by Warranty Deed or _____(as
       appropriate) and provide Buyer with a Certificate of Title prepared by an attorney, title or abstract company upon
       whose Certificate or report title insurance may be obtained from a title insurance company qualified to do and doing
       business in the State of Alabama. Seller will also execute a Bill of Sale, if necessary, for the transfer of any personal
       property. Seller shall, prior to or at closing, satisfy all outstanding mortgages, deeds of trust and special liens
       affecting the subject property which are not specifically assumed by Buyer herein. Title shall be good and
       marketable, subject only to (a) covenants, conditions and restrictions of record, (b) public, private utility easements
       and roads and rights-of-way, (c) applicable zoning ordinances, protective covenants and prior mineral reservations,
       d) special and other assessments on the property, if any, (e) general taxes for the year ____2005____and subsequent
       years and (e) other_____.

       A title report shall be provided to Buyer at least 5 days prior to closing. If there are title defects, Seller shall notify
       Buyer within 5 days of closing and Buyer, at Buyer's option, may either (a) if defects cannot be cured by designated
       closing date, cancel this contract, in which case all earnest money deposited shall be returned, (b) accept title as is, or
       (c) if the defects are of such character that they can be remedied by legal action within a reasonable time, permit Seller
       such reasonable time to perform curative work at Seller's expense. A deadline should be agreed to in a separate
       written agreement. In the event that the curative work is performed by Seller, the time specified herein for closing of
       this sale shall be extended for a reasonable period necessary for such action. Seller represents that the property may
       be legally used as zoned and that no government agency has served any notice to Seller requiring repairs, alterations
       or corrections of any existing condition except as stated herein.

8.   APPRAISAL, SURVEY AND TERMITE INSPECTION: Any appraisal of the property shall be the responsibility of
       ☒ Buyer ☐ Seller. A survey is: ☒ not required ☐ required, the cost of which shall be paid by ☐ Seller   ☐
       Buyer. A termite inspection is ☐ not required ☒ required, the cost of which shall be paid by ☒ Seller ☐ Buyer. If
       a survey is required it shall be obtained within 5 days of closing.

9.   POSSESSION AND TITLE: Seller shall deliver possession of the Property to Buyer at closing. Title shall be conveyed
       to Buyer, if more than one as ☐ Joint tenants with rights of survivorship ☐ tenants in common,
       ☒ Other:____single purchaser_____. Prior to closing the property shall remain in
       the possession of Seller and Seller shall deliver the property to Buyer in substantially the same condition at closing,
       as on the date of this contract, reasonable wear and tear excepted.

Buyer Initials __TB__ _____   - 4 -   Seller Initials _JS_   _JS_

10. CLOSING COSTS AND EXPENSES: The following closing costs shall be paid as provided. *(Leave blank if the closing cost does not apply.)*

Closing Costs	Buyer	Seller	Both*
Attorney Fees	☐	☐	☒
Title Insurance	☐	☐	☒
Title Abstract or Certificate	☐	☐	☒
Property Insurance	☐	☐	☒
Recording Fees	☐	☐	☒
Appraisal	☒	☐	☐
Survey	☐	☐	☒
Termite Inspection	☐	☒	☐
Origination fees	☒	☐	☐
Discount Points	☒	☐	☐
If contingent on rezoning, cost and expenses of rezoning	☒	☐	☐
Other:			
	☐	☐	☐
	☐	☐	☐
	☐	☐	☐
	☐	☐	☐
	☐	☐	☐
All other closing costs	☐	☐	☒

* 50/50 between buyer and seller.

11. PRORATIONS: Taxes for the current year, interest, maintenance fees, assessments, dues and rents, if any, will be prorated through the Closing Date. If taxes for the current year vary from the amount prorated at closing, the parties shall adjust the prorations when tax statements for the current year are available. If a loan is assumed and the lender maintains an escrow account, the escrow account must be transferred to Buyer without any deficiency. Buyer shall reimburse Seller for the amount in the transferred account. Buyer shall pay the premium for a new insurance policy. If taxes are not paid at or prior to closing, Buyer will be obligated to pay taxes for the current year.

12. CASUALTY LOSS: If any part of the Property is damaged or destroyed by fire or other casualty loss after the effective date of the contract, Seller shall restore the Property to its previous condition as soon as reasonably possible. If Seller fails to do so due to factors beyond Seller's control, Buyer may either (a) terminate this contract and the earnest money will be refunded to Buyer, (b) extend the time for performance and the Closing Date will be extended as necessary, or (c) accept the Property in its damaged condition and accept an assignment of insurance proceeds.

13. DEFAULT: If Buyer fails to comply with this contract, Buyer will be in default, and Seller may either (a) enforce specific performance, seek such other relief as may be provided by law, or both, or (b) terminate this contract and receive the earnest money as liquidated damages, thereby releasing both parties from this contract. If, due to factors beyond Seller's control, Seller fails within the time allowed to make any non-casualty repairs or deliver evidence of clean title, Buyer may either (a) extend the time for performance up to an agreed deadline, and the Closing Date will be extended as necessary or (b) terminate this contract as the sole remedy and receive a refund of the earnest money. If Seller fails to comply with this contract for any other reason, Seller will be in default and Buyer may either (a) enforce specific performance, seek such other relief as may be provided by law, or both, or (b) terminate this contract and receive the earnest money, thereby releasing both parties from this contract.

14. ATTORNEY'S FEES: The prevailing party in any legal proceeding brought under or with respect to the transaction described in this contract is entitled to recover from the non-prevailing party all costs of such proceeding and reasonable attorney's fees.

Buyer Initials **TB**   - 5 -   Seller Initials **JS** **JS**

15.   REPRESENTATIONS: Seller represents that as of the Closing Date (a) there will be no liens, assessments, or security interests against the Property which will not be satisfied out of the sales proceeds unless securing payment of any loans assumed by Buyer and (b) assumed loans will not be in default. If any representation in this contract is untrue on the Closing Date, this contract may be terminated by Buyer and the earnest money will be refunded to Buyer. All representations contained in this contract will survive closing.

16.   FEDERAL TAX REQUIREMENT: If Seller is a "foreign person", as defined by applicable law, or if Seller fails to deliver an affidavit that Seller is not a "foreign person", then Buyer shall withhold from the sales proceeds an amount sufficient to comply with applicable tax law and deliver the same to the Internal Revenue Service together with appropriate tax forms. IRS regulations require filing written reports if cash in excess of specified amounts is received in the transaction.

17.   AGREEMENT OF PARTIES: This contract contains the entire agreement of the parties and cannot be changed except by their written agreement.

18.   NOTICES: All notices from one party to the other must be in writing and are effective when mailed to, hand-delivered at, or transmitted by facsimile machine as follows:

To Buyer at: To Seller at:

Tom Brown   John and Jane Smith

456 Buyer Blvd.   123 Any Street

Anytown, AL 83838   Anytown, AL 83838

Telephone (555)555-5555   Telephone (555)555-1223

Facsimile (555)555-3434   Facsimile (555)555-1224

19.   ASSIGNMENT: This agreement may not be assigned by Buyer without the consent of Seller. This agreement may be assigned by Seller and shall be binding on the heirs and assigns of the parties hereto.

20.   PRIOR AGREEMENTS: This contract incorporates all prior agreements between the parties, contains the entire and final agreement of the parties, and cannot be changed except by their written consent. Neither party has relied upon any statement or representation made by the other party or any sales representative bringing the parties together. Neither party shall be bound by any terms, conditions, oral statements, warranties, or representations not herein contained. Each party acknowledges that he has read and understands this contract. The provisions of this contract shall apply to and bind the heirs, executors, administrators, successors and assigns of the respective parties hereto. When herein used, the singular includes the plural and the masculine includes the feminine as the context may require.

21.   NO BROKER OR AGENTS: The parties represent that neither party has employed the services of a real estate broker or agent in connection with the property, or that if such agents have been employed, that the party employing said agent shall pay any and all expenses outside the closing of this agreement.

22.   EMINENT DOMAIN: If the property is condemned by eminent domain after the effective date hereof, the Seller and Buyer shall agree to continue the closing, or a portion thereof, or cancel this contract. If the parties cannot agree, this contract shall ☐ remain valid with Buyer being entitled to any condemnation proceeds at or after closing, or ☒ be cancelled and the earnest money returned to Buyer.

Buyer Initials ___TB___ _____   - 6 -   Seller Initials ___JS___ ___JS___

23.   OTHER PROVISIONS

_____
_____
_____
_____
_____
_____
_____
_____
_____

24.   TIME IS OF THE ESSENCE IN THE PERFORMANCE OF THIS AGREEMENT.

25.   GOVERNING LAW: This contract shall be governed by the laws of the State of Alabama.

26.   DEADLINE LIST *(Optional) (complete all that apply)*. Based on other provisions of this contract.

Deadline	Date
Loan Application Deadline, if contingent on loan	12-01-05
Loan Commitment Deadline	12-04-05
Buyer(s) Credit Information to Seller	12-05-05
Disapproval of Buyers Credit Deadline	12-06-05
Survey Deadline	12-07-05
Title Objection Deadline	12-08-05
Survey Deadline	12-10-05
Appraisal Deadline	12-15-05
Property Inspection Deadline	12-18-05

Whether or not listed above, deadlines contained in this contract may be extended informally by a writing signed by the person granting the extension except for the closing date which must be extended by a writing signed by both Seller and Buyer.

EXECUTED the 13 day of November_____, 2005 (THE EFFECTIVE DATE).

___John Smith_____   ___Tom Brown_____
Seller   Buyer

___Jane Smith_____   _____
Seller   Buyer

Buyer Initials **TB** _____   - 7 -   Seller Initials **JS**   **JS**

These forms are samples only and
are illegal to reproduce without
permission from USLeagalForms.com.

EXHIBIT FOR DESCRIPTION OR ATTACH SEPARATE DESCRIPTION

(There are no attachments)

Buyer Initials __TB__ _____   - 8 -   Seller Initials __JS__ __JS__

RECEIPT

Receipt of Earnest Money in the amount of $2,500.00   is acknowledged.

Signature: John Smith   Date: November 13, 2005

By: John Smith

123 Any Street   Telephone: (555)555-1223
Address
Anytown   AL   38383   Facsimile: (555)555-1224
City   State   Zip Code

Buyer Initials **TB**   - 9 -   Seller Initials **JS** **JS**

RESIDENTIAL PROPERTY DISCLOSURE AND DISCLAIMER STATEMENT

INSTRUCTIONS TO THE SELLER

Please complete the following form. Do not leave any spaces blank. If the question clearly does not apply to the property write "NA". If the answer to any items requires explanation, explain on attached sheets, if necessary.

NOTICE TO THE BUYER

THE FOLLOWING DISCLOSURES ARE MADE BY THE SELLER(S), CONCERNING THE CONDITION OF THE PROPERTY LOCATED AT ___123 Any Street, Anytown, Alabama, 38383___. ("THE PROPERTY"), OR AS LEGALLY DESCRIBED ON ATTACHED EXHIBIT A.

DISCLOSURES CONTAINED IN THIS FORM ARE PROVIDED BY THE SELLER ON THE BASIS OF SELLER'S ACTUAL KNOWLEDGE OF THE PROPERTY AT THE TIME THIS DISCLOSURE FORM IS COMPLETED BY THE SELLER. THE FOLLOWING ARE DISCLOSURES MADE BY THE SELLER AND ARE NOT THE REPRESENTATIONS OF ANY REAL ESTATE LICENSEE OR OTHER PARTY. THIS INFORMATION IS FOR DISCLOSURE ONLY AND IS NOT INTENDED TO BE A PART OF ANY WRITTEN AGREEMENT BETWEEN THE BUYER AND THE SELLER.

FOR A MORE COMPREHENSIVE EXAMINATION OF THE SPECIFIC CONDITION OF THIS PROPERTY YOU ARE ADVISED TO OBTAIN AND PAY FOR THE SERVICES OF A QUALIFIED SPECIALIST TO INSPECT THE PROPERTY ON YOUR BEHALF, FOR EXAMPLE, ARCHITECTS, ENGINEERS, LAND SURVEYORS, PLUMBERS, ELECTRICIANS, ROOFERS, BUILDING INSPECTORS, OR PEST AND DRY ROT INSPECTORS. THE PROSPECTIVE BUYER AND THE OWNER MAY WISH TO OBTAIN PROFESSIONAL ADVICE OR INSPECTIONS OF THE PROPERTY AND TO PROVIDE FOR APPROPRIATE PROVISIONS IN A CONTRACT BETWEEN THEM WITH RESPECT TO ANY ADVICE, INSPECTION, DEFECTS OR WARRANTIES.

Sellers, ___John Smith and Jane Smith___, are currently occupying the property.
Seller has owned the property for _5_ years.

I. SELLER'S DISCLOSURES. If explanation is needed, use attached sheet if necessary. Approximations should be labeled as such.

I. TITLE	YES	NO	UNKNOWN
A. Do you have legal authority to sell the property?	X		
B. Is title to the property subject to any of the following:			
(1) First right of refusal		X	
If yes, explain:			
(2) Option		X	
If yes, explain:			
(3) Lease or Rental Agreement		X	
If yes, explain:			
(4) Life Estate		X	
If yes, explain:			
C. Are there any encroachments, boundary disputes, or boundary agreements?		X	
If yes, explain:			
D. Are there any rights of way, easements, or access limitations that may affect the owner's use of the property?		X	
If yes, explain:			
E. Are there any written agreements for joint maintenance of an easement or right of way?		X	
If yes, explain:			
F. Is there any study, survey project, or notice that would adversely affect the property?		X	
If yes, explain:			
G. Are there any pending or existing assessments against the property?		X	
If yes, explain:			
H. Are there any zoning violations, nonconforming uses, or any unusual restrictions on the subject property that would affect future construction or remodeling?		X	
If yes, explain:			
I. Is there a boundary survey for the property? If yes, attach survey.		X	
J. Are the property's boundaries marked?	X		

Provided by USlegalforms.com. Copyright 2004 by U.S. Legal Forms, Inc.   page 1

1. TITLE	YES	NO	UNKNOWN
If yes, explain: Boundaries are fenced.			
K. Are there fences on the property?	X		
If yes, were the fences put up by the property owner?	X		
L. Are any trees or other flora on the property diseased, dead or damaged?			X
If yes, explain:			
M. Are there any covenants, conditions, or restrictions which affect the property?		X	
If yes, explain:			
N. Is the property accessed by public or private road?	(PUBLIC)	PRIVATE	UNKNOWN
If private, what yearly upkeep amount is paid by the property owner?			
If private, explain road upkeep in detail:			

2. WATER				
A. Household Water				
(1) The source of the water is:	(Public)	Community	Private	Shared
(2) Water source information:		YES	NO	UNKNOWN
a. Are there any written agreements for shared water source?			X	
If yes, explain:				
b. Is there an easement (recorded or unrecorded) for access to and/or maintenance of the water source?			X	
If yes, explain:				
c. Are any known problems or repairs needed?			X	
If yes, explain:				
d. Does the source provide an adequate year round supply of potable water?		X		
e. Are there any water treatment systems (softener, purifier, etc.) for the property?			X	
If yes, explain, and state if the system(s) is/are leased or owned.				
B. Irrigation				
(1) Are there any water rights for the property?			X	
If yes, explain:				
(2) If they exist, to your knowledge, have the water rights been used during the last five-year period?				
If yes, explain:				
(3) If so, is the certificate available?				
Explain:				
C. Outdoor Sprinkler System				
(1) Is there an outdoor sprinkler system for the property?			X	
(2) Are there any defects in the outdoor sprinkler system?			X	
If yes, explain:				

3. SEWER/SEPTIC SYSTEM			
A. The property is served by (circle one):	(Public Sewer Main)	Septic Tank System	Other Disposal System
If other, describe:			
B. If the property is served by a public or community sewer main, is the house connected to the main?	(Yes)	No	Unknown
If no, explain:			
C. Is the property currently subject to a sewer capacity charge?	Yes	(No)	Unknown
If yes, explain:			
D. If the property is connected to a septic system complete the following items (if no septic system, ignore these items):			
(1) Was a permit issued for its construction, and was it approved by the city or county following its construction?	Yes	No	Unknown
(2) On what date was it last pumped:			
(3) Are there any defects in the operation of the septic system?	Yes	No	Unknown
If yes, explain:			
(4) On what date was it last inspected:			
By whom:			
(5) How many bedrooms was the system approved for?			
(6) Are you aware of any changes or repairs to the septic system?	Yes	No	Unknown
If yes, explain:			

USLF
USlegalforms.com
The Forms Professionals Trust!

(7) Is the septic system, including drainage field, located entirely within the property's boundaries?	Yes	No	Unknown
If no, explain:			
E. Do all plumbing fixtures, including laundry drain, go to the septic/sewer system?	Yes	No	Unknown
If no, explain:			

4. STRUCTURAL

A. How old is the current roof? <u>10</u> years. (If unknown, mark Unknown.)		Unknown
Roof is constructed of: ☐ Asphalt Shingle, ☐ Wood Shingle, ☐ Slate, ☐ Metal, ☐ Tile, ☒ Asbestos, ☐ Unknown, ☐ Other:		

B. Has the roof leaked during your ownership?	(Yes)	No	Unknown
If yes, has it been repaired?	Yes	(No)	
Explain any roof repairs of which you are aware:			
C. Has the house undergone any conversions, additions, or remodeling?	Yes	(No)	Unknown
1. If yes, were all building permits obtained?	Yes	No	Unknown
2. If yes, were all final inspections obtained?	Yes	No	Unknown
Explain any conversions/additions/remodeling:			

D. Do you know the age of the house?	Yes	(No)
If yes, give year of original construction (if approximation, indicate such):		

E. Are you aware of:		
(1) Any movement, shifting, deterioration or other problems with walls, foundation, crawl space or slab?	Yes	(No)
(2) Any cracks or flaws in the walls, ceilings, foundations, concrete slab, crawl space, basement, floors or garage?	Yes	(No)
(3) Any water leakage or dampness in the crawl space or basement?	Yes	(No)
(4) Any dry rot on the property?	Yes	(No)
(5) Any repairs or other attempts to control the cause or effect of any problem described above?	Yes	(No)

Explain any 'Yes' answer(s) to 1-5 above. When describing repairs or control efforts, describe the location, extent, date, and name of person/company who did the work. Attach any reports and/or other documentation:

F. If you know of any defect(s) regarding the following items, mark the defective item with a check:

1. Foundation ☐	6. Fire Alarm ☐	11. Slab Floors ☐	16. Sidewalks ☐	21. Balconies ☐
2. Deck ☐	7. Doors ☐	12. Driveways ☐	17. Outbuildings ☐	22. Wood Stoves ☐
3. Exterior walls ☐	8. Door locks ☐	13. Attic Stairs ☐	18. Fireplaces ☐	
4. Chimneys ☐	9. Patio ☐	14. Windows ☐	19. Garage Floors ☐	
5. Interior walls ☐	10. Ceilings ☐	15. Window locks ☐	20. Walkways ☐	

If you checked any of the above items, explain the defect(s):

G. In the last 4 years, was a pest, dry rot, structural or "whole house" inspection done?	Yes	(No)	Unknown
If yes, which test(s), when, and by whom was the inspection done? (Attach documentation)			

H. Has the property had a problem with pest control, infestations, or vermin?	Yes	(No)	Unknown
If yes, explain:			

I. Are you aware of:		
(1) Any termites, wood destroying insects or pests on or affecting the property?	Yes	(No)
(2) Property damage by termites, wood destroying insects or pests?	Yes	(No)
If yes, describe:		
(3) Any termite/pest control treatments on the property in the last 4 years?	Yes	(No)
If yes, list company and where treated:		
(4) Current warranty or other coverage by a licensed pest control company on the property?	Yes	(No)

USlegalforms.com
The Forms Professionals Trust!

If yes, explain warranty and attach documentation:			
J. Have you made a homeowner's insurance claim(s) regarding the property in the last 4 years?	Yes	(No)	
If yes, explain when and why:			

5. SYSTEMS AND FIXTURES

If the following systems or fixtures are included with the transfer, do they have any existing defects:	YES	NO	UNKNOWN
A. Electrical system, including wiring, all switches, all outlets, and service		X	
If yes, explain:			

What type of wiring comprises the electrical system?	Copper	Aluminum	(Unknown)

	YES	NO	UNKNOWN
B. Plumbing system, including pipes, faucets, fixtures, and toilets		X	
If yes, explain:			
C. Hot water heater (mark one): (Electric) Natural Gas Other:_____ Age: _5_ years		X	
If yes, explain:			
D. Oven/stove: Electric (Natural Gas) Other:_____ Age: _3_ years		X	
If yes, explain:			
E. List ANY OTHER APPLIANCES TO REMAIN, attach separate sheet if necessary.			

	YES	NO	UNKNOWN
1. Refrigerator Age: _25_ years	(YES)	NO	UNKNOWN
If yes, explain: It leaks, smokes, and rattles.			
2. Age: _____ years			
If yes, explain:			
3. Age: _____ years			
If yes, explain:			

F. Cooling and Heating systems

Air Conditioning (mark one): (Central Electric)	Central Gas	Heat Pump	Window Unit(s) ____ # included in sale
Other (describe):			

Air Conditioning (continued):	Age of cooling system: _10_ years.	Zoned cooling? [Yes] (No)
Air Conditioning defects? (No)	Unknown Yes, explain:	

Heating system (mark one):	Electric (Natural Gas)	Fuel Oil	Heat Pump	Propane	Other:
	Age of heating system: _9_ years.		Zoned heating? [Yes] (No)		

Heating system defects? (No)	Unknown Yes, explain:	

Last date of servicing: Heating: 11/12/03	Cooling: 11/12/03	By whom: Anytown Alabama Servicers Co.

Are there rooms without heating/air conditioning vents?	Yes	(No)
If yes, which rooms:		

G. Security system (Circle One):	Owned	Leased	(None)	Any defects?:	Yes	No	Unknown
Describe security system:							
If defects are indicated, explain:							

H. Other:	Any defects?	Yes	No	Unknown
If defects are indicated, explain:				

6. COMMON INTEREST

A. Is there a Home Owners' Association?	Yes	(No)	Unknown
If yes, what is the name of the association?			
B. Are there regular periodic assessments:	Yes	(No)	Unknown
If yes, give amount per: Month: $	Year: $	Other: $	
If other, explain:			
C. Are there any pending special assessments?	Yes	(No)	Unknown
D. Are there any shared "common areas" or any joint maintenance agreements (facilities such as walls, fences, landscaping, pools, tennis courts, walkways, or other areas co-owned in undivided interest with others)?	Yes	(No)	Unknown

If any such areas exist, explain:

7. APPLIANCES, HEATING, PLUMBING, ELECTRICAL and OTHER MECHANICAL SYSTEMS

Instructions: Mark **INCL** if the item is included in the sale. If item is included in sale, mark **Yes** or **No** to indicate whether item is in working order. Indicate the item's approximate age (in years) in the 'age' space, if provided-- if age is unknown, mark '?' in space.

ITEM	INCL	Yes	No	ITEM	INCL	Yes	No
Attic Fan				Lawn Sprinkler Auto-timer			
Air Conditioner (central) age:10yrs	X	X		Lawn Sprinkler Backflow Valve			
Air Conditioner (wall/window) age:				Microwave Oven age:			
Air Cleaner/Purifier age:				Plumbing			
Ceiling Fan(s), # included				Pool age:			
Clothes Washer age:				Pool Equipment/ mechanisms age:			
Convection Oven age:				Range/Oven age: 3yrs	X	X	
Dishwasher age:				Range Timer			
Door Bells	X	X		Range Vent-hood			
Drain Tile System				Refrigerator age:25yrs	X		X
Dryer age:				Security System			
Exhaust Fans (bathroom)	X	X		Smoke Detectors (battery)	X	X	
Fireplace				Smoke Detectors (hardwired)			
Fireplace Mechanisms				Solar Collectors			
Furnace age:				Sump Pump			
Furnace Mechanisms				Toilet Mechanisms	X	X	
Freezer age:				TV Antenna/ receiver/ dish			
Garbage Compactor				TV Cable wiring			
Garbage Disposal				Water Heater age: 5yrs	X	X	
Garage Door Opener (GDO)				Window Treatments			
GDO Auto-reverse Safety Mechanism				Whirlpool/Hot-tub age:			
GDO Remote Opener(s), # included:				Wood Burning Stove			
Gas Grill				Yard Lights			
Gas Logs				Other:			
Heating System (central) age: 9yrs	X	X		Other:			
Heating System (supplemental) age:				Other:			
Humidifier age:				Other:			
Incinerator				Other:			
Intercom				Other:			
Lawn Sprinkler System				Other:			

Explanations: if any item above is NOT in working order, list the item and explain the defect in the space below.

8. GENERAL

8. GENERAL	YES	NO	UNKNOWN
A. Is there any settling, soil, standing water, or drainage problems on the property?		X	
If yes, explain:			
B. Does the property contain fill material?		X	
C. Is there any material damage to the property or any of the structure from fire, wind, floods, beach movements, earthquake, expansive soils, or landslides?		X	
If yes, explain:			
D. Is the property in a designated flood plain?	X		
E. Are there any substances, materials, or products that may be an environmental hazard such as, but not limited to, asbestos, formaldehyde, radon gas, lead-based paint, fuel or chemical storage tanks and contaminated soil or water on the subject property?	X		
If yes, explain: the roof is an asbestos roof			
F. Are there any tanks or underground storage tanks (e.g., chemical, fuel, etc.) on the property?		X	
If yes, explain, and give approx. position (attach map):			
G. Has the property ever been used as an illegal drug-manufacturing site?		X	

Provided by USlegalforms.com. Copyright 2004 by U.S. Legal Forms, Inc.   page 5

USLF
USlegalforms.com
The Forms Professionals Trust!

If yes, explain:		
H. If the property contains a wood-burning stove or fireplace, when was/were the chimney(ies) last cleaned?		
Detail date(s) and chimney(ies), or mark Unknown:		
I. Are you aware of any of the following regarding the property?		
Existing or threatened legal action ☐	Violation of any law or regulation ☐	General stains or pet stains to carpet or floor ☐
Transferable warranties ☐	Any locks without keys ☐	Unrecorded interests affecting the property ☐
Fire Damage at any time ☐	Appraiser or Mechanic's Lien ☐	Landfills or underground problems ☐
If any of the above are marked, explain:		
J. If any tests to detect **radon gas** have been done on the property, provide documentation. If radon gas has been detected on the property, explain when, where, by whom, and all other details:		

9. FULL DISCLOSURE BY SELLERS

A. Other conditions or defects:

	Yes	No
Does the Seller know of any other material defects affecting this property or its value that a prospective buyer should know about?		X

If yes, explain:

_____

_____

B. Verification:

The foregoing answers and attached explanations (if any) are complete and correct to the best of my/our knowledge and I/we have received a copy hereof. I/we authorize all of my/our real estate licensees, if any, to deliver a copy of this disclosure statement to other real estate licensees and all prospective buyers of the property.

11-13-05	*John Smith*	*Jane Smith*
Date	Seller	Seller

II. BUYER'S ACKNOWLEDGMENT

A. As buyer(s), I/we acknowledge the duty to pay diligent attention to any material defects which are known to me/us or can be known to me/us by utilizing diligent attention and observation.

B. Each buyer acknowledges and understands that the disclosures set forth in this statement and in any amendments to this statement are made only by the seller.

C. Buyer (which term includes all persons signing the buyer's acknowledgement portion of this disclosure statement below) hereby acknowledges receipt of a copy of this disclosure statement (including attachments, if any) bearing seller's signature.

DISCLOSURES CONTAINED IN THIS FORM ARE PROVIDED BY THE SELLER ON THE BASIS OF SELLER'S ACTUAL KNOWLEDGE OF THE PROPERTY AT THE TIME OF DISCLOSURE.

BUYER HEREBY ACKNOWLEDGES RECEIPT OF A COPY OF THIS REAL PROPERTY TRANSFER DISCLOSURE STATEMENT AND ACKNOWLEDGES THAT THE DISCLOSURES MADE HEREIN ARE THOSE OF THE SELLER ONLY, AND NOT OF ANY REAL ESTATE LICENSEE OR OTHER PARTY.

11-13-05	**Tom Brown**	
DATE	BUYER	BUYER

Lead-Based Paint Disclosure (Sales)

123 Any Street	Anytown	Alabama	38383
Street Address	City	State	Zip

WARNING! LEAD FROM PAINT, DUST, AND SOIL CAN BE DANGEROUS IF NOT MANAGED PROPERLY

Disclosure of Information on Lead-Based Paint and/or Lead-Based Paint Hazards
Lead Warning Statement

Every purchaser of any interest in residential real property on which a residential dwelling was built prior to 1978 is notified that such property may present exposure to lead from lead-based paint that may place young children at risk of developing lead poisoning. Lead poisoning in young children may produce permanent neurological damage, including learning disabilities, reduced intelligence quotient, behavioral problems, and impaired memory. Lead poisoning also poses a particular risk to pregnant women. The Seller of any interest in residential real property is required to provide the buyer with any information on lead-based paint hazards from risk assessments or inspections in the Seller's possession and notify the buyer of any known lead-based paint hazards. A risk assessment or inspection for possible lead-based paint hazards is recommended prior to purchase.

Seller's Disclosure

(a) Presence of lead-based paint and/or lead-based paint hazards (check (i) or (ii) below):
    (i) _____ Known lead-based paint and/or lead-based paint hazards are present in the housing (explain).

    _____

    (ii) __X__ Seller has no knowledge of lead-based paint and/or lead-based paint hazards in the housing.

(b) Records and reports available to the seller (check (i) or (ii) below):
    (i) _____ Seller has provided the purchaser with all available records and reports pertaining to lead-based paint and/or lead-based paint hazards in the housing (list documents below).

    _____

    (ii) __X__ Seller has no reports or records pertaining to lead-based paint and/or lead-based paint hazards in the housing.

Purchaser's Acknowledgment (initial)

(c) __TB__ Purchaser has received copies of all information listed above.

(d) __TB__ Purchaser has received the pamphlet *Protect Your Family from Lead in Your Home.*

(e) Purchaser has (check (i) or (ii) below):

    (i) __X__ received a 10-day opportunity (or mutually agreed upon period) to conduct a risk assessment or inspection for the presence of lead-based paint and/or lead-based paint hazards; or

    (ii) _____ waived the opportunity to conduct a risk assessment or inspection for the presence of lead-based paint and/or lead-based paint hazards.

Agent's Acknowledgment (initial)

(f) _____ Agent has informed the seller of the seller' obligations under 42 U.S.C. 4852(d) and is aware of his/her responsibility to ensure compliance.

Seller Initials: __JS__ __JS__   **Buyer Initials:** __TB__ _____   **Agent Initials:** _____ _____

Certification of Accuracy

The following parties have reviewed the information above and certify, to the best of their knowledge, that the information they have provided is true and accurate. **Penalties for failure to comply with Federal Lead-Based Paint Disclosure Laws include treble (3 times) damages, attorney fees, costs, and a penalty up to $10,000 for each violation.**

John Smith	11/13/05	Tom Brown	11/13/05
Seller	Date	Buyer	Date
Jane Smith	11/13/05		
Seller	Date	Buyer	Date
Agent	Date	Agent	Date

USLF
USlegalforms.com
The Forms Professionals Trust!

AGREEMENT TO AMEND/EXTEND CONTRACT

THIS FORM HAS IMPORTANT LEGAL CONSEQUENCES AND THE PARTIES SHOULD CONSULT LEGAL, TAX, AND OTHER COUNSEL BEFORE SIGNING.

December 21, 2005

RE: Contract dated November 13, 2005 between Tom Brown, (Buyer), whether one or more, and John Smith and Jane Smith, (Seller), whether one or more, relating to the sale and purchase of the following described real estate in Jasper County, State of Alabama known as 123 Any Street, Anytown, Alabama, 38383 (property address).

Buyer and Seller hereby agree to amend the aforesaid contract as follows:

1. The date for closing and delivery of deed is changed to January 21, 2006.

2. The date for furnishing commitment for title insurance policy or abstract of title is changed to January 4, 2006.

3. The date for delivering possession of Property is changed to January 21, 2006.

4. The date for approval of new loan is changed to January 10, 2006.

5. The date for lender's consent to loan assumption or transfer of Property is changed to January 10, 2006.

6. Other dates set forth in said contract shall be changed as follows:
   _____
   _____
   _____

7. Additional amendments:
   _____
   _____
   _____

All other terms and conditions of said contract shall remain unchanged.

DATED this the 15 day of December, 2005.

John Smith _____   **Tom Brown** _____
Seller   Buyer

Jane Smith _____   _____
Seller   Buyer

This report provided courtesy Greg Bell of Bell Inspection Service

Building Inspection Report

123 Main St Ormond Beach, Fl. 32176

Inspection Date:
06-20-2002

Prepared For:
John Doe

Prepared By:
Bell Inspection Service
P O Box 5175
Titusville, Fl. 32783

321-626-8840 Brevard
866-620-8840 Toll Free

Report Number:
02177

Inspector:
Greg Bell

123 Main St Ormond Beach, Fl. 32176 Page 2 of 13
This confidential report is prepared exclusively for John Doe
www.bellinspection.com
© 2004 Bell Inspection Service

Report Overview

THE HOUSE IN PERSPECTIVE

This is a single family home located beachside. All buildings on the beachside require a higher level of maintenance than mainland buildings. This home has been well maintained for a beachside house. The exterior has a few minor repairs that will help to extend the life of the exterior. The most serious condition is the electrical service mast. The drip loop is such that water runs into the mast which has caused it to start to rust. There is just a small area of rust visible below the soffit. The wall anchors have pulled out of the wall; this leads me to believe that the mast is under more stress than it should be. The meter can had no seal so I opened it to inspect. The rust has not made it down to this area yet which is a good sign.

The interior of the home is in good condition. The tile in the breakfast nook could have been installed in a more professional manner, but it is cosmetic only. During the inspection a new service door for the garage was installed. The French door off of master bedroom had a loose hinge on the left side; this item was repaired by the person installing the door. Most windows were missing screens. Where the back splash meets the counter in the kitchen it hasn't been caulked. You will see in the photo that the splash is starting to swell behind the sink but it is still solid.

CONVENTIONS USED IN THIS REPORT

For your convenience, the following conventions have been used in this report.

Major Concern: a system or component which is considered significantly deficient or is unsafe. Significant deficiencies need to be corrected and, except for some safety items, are likely to involve significant expense.

Safety Issue: denotes a condition that is unsafe and in need of prompt attention.

Repair: denotes a system or component which is missing or which needs corrective action to assure proper and reliable function.

Improve: denotes improvements which are recommended but not required.

Monitor: denotes a system or component needing further investigation and/or monitoring in order to determine if repairs are necessary.

Please note that those observations listed under "Discretionary Improvements" are not essential repairs, but represent logical long term improvements.

IMPROVEMENT RECOMMENDATION HIGHLIGHTS / SUMMARY

The following is a synopsis of the potentially significant improvements that should be budgeted for over the short term. Other significant improvements, outside the scope of this inspection, may also be necessary. Please refer to the body of thisreport for further details on these and other recommendations.

1. Improve the caulking in master bath shower and hall bath tub.
2. Caulk where backsplash meets counter in kitchen.
3. On each side of garage door where the vertical and horizontal bands meet there are holes that need to be sealed.
4. The electrical service mast is under more stress than it should be. Consult with a licensed and qualified electrician for repair.

This confidential report is prepared exclusively for John Doe
www.bellinspection.com

THE SCOPE OF THE INSPECTION

All components designated for inspection in the National Association of Certified Home Inspectors (NACHI) Standards of Practice are inspected, except as may be noted in the "Limitations of Inspection" sections within this report.

It is the goal of the inspection to put a home buyer in a better position to make a buying decision. Not all improvements will be identified during this inspection. Unexpected repairs should still be anticipated. The inspection should not be considered a guarantee or warranty of any kind.

Please refer to the pre-inspection contract for a full explanation of the scope of the inspection.

123 Main St Ormond Beach, Fl. 32176 Page 4 of 13
This confidential report is prepared exclusively for John Doe
www.bellinspection.com
© 2004 Bell Inspection Service

Structure

DESCRIPTION OF STRUCTURE

Foundation:	•Poured Concrete
Wall Structure:	•Masonry
Roof Structure:	•Trusses •Waferboard Sheathing

STRUCTURE OBSERVATIONS

Positive Attributes
Exterior wall construction is solid masonry. The inspection did not discover evidence of substantial structural movement.

General Comments
No major defects were observed in the accessible structural components of the house.

RECOMMENDATIONS / OBSERVATIONS

Exterior Walls
* **Monitor:** Exterior wall cracks above a lintel (a beam supporting masonry above an opening in a wall) suggests that the lintel may be marginal. This condition is not uncommon. If additional movement occurs, repairs will be needed.

LIMITATIONS OF STRUCTURE INSPECTION

As we have discussed and as described in your inspection contract, this is a visual inspection limited in scope by (but not
restricted to) the following conditions:
* Structural components concealed behind finished surfaces could not be inspected.
* Only a representative sampling of visible structural components were inspected.
* Furniture and/or storage restricted access to some structural components.
* Engineering or architectural services such as calculation of structural capacities, adequacy, or integrity are not part of a home inspection.

Please also refer to the pre-inspection contract for a detailed explanation of the scope of this inspection.

This confidential report is prepared exclusively for John Doe
www.bellinspection.com
© 2004 Bell Inspection Service

Roofing

DESCRIPTION OF ROOFING

Roof Covering:	•Asphalt Shingle
Roof Flashings:	•Metal
Chimneys:	•None
Roof Drainage System:	•Aluminum •Downspouts discharge above grade
Skylights:	•None
Method of Inspection:	•Walked on roof

ROOFING OBSERVATIONS

Positive Attributes
The roof coverings are in generally good condition. Better than average quality materials have been used as roof coverings.
The gutters are clean.

General Comments
In all, the roof coverings show evidence of normal wear and tear for a home of this age. The design of the roofing system is such that several vulnerable areas exist. There is a higher potential for unanticipated repairs. Annual inspections and ongoing maintenance will be critical to the performance of the roofing system.

RECOMMENDATIONS / OBSERVATIONS

Sloped Roofing
- **Monitor:** The roofing is in fair condition.
- **Monitor:** The design of the roofing system is such that a vulnerable area exists. There is a higher potential for leaks. Annual inspections and ongoing maintenance will be critical. This area is where the garage, breakfast nook meet into a flat area that directs the water to the front. Then into the arch around the breakfast nook window. Suggest to divert water away from that area around band of the window.

LIMITATIONS OF ROOFING INSPECTION
As we have discussed and as described in your inspection contract, this is a visual inspection limited in scope by (but not restricted to) the following conditions:

- Not all of the underside of the roof sheathing is inspected for evidence of leaks.
- Evidence of prior leaks may be disguised by interior finishes.
- Estimates of remaining roof life are approximations only and do not preclude the possibility of leakage. Leakage can develop at any time and may depend on rain intensity, wind direction, ice build up, and other factors.
- Antennae, chimney/flue interiors which are not readily accessible are not inspected and could require repair.
- Roof inspection may be limited by access, condition, weather, or other safety concerns.

Please also refer to the pre-inspection contract for a detailed explanation of the scope of this inspection.

123 Main St Ormond Beach, Fl. 32176 Page 6 of 13
This confidential report is prepared exclusively for John Doe
www.bellinspection.com
© 2004 Bell Inspection Service

Exterior

DESCRIPTION OF EXTERIOR

Wall Covering:	•Stucco
Eaves, Soffits, And Fascias:	•Aluminum
Exterior Doors:	•Metal •French Doors •Sliding Glass
Entry Driveways:	•Concrete
Entry Walkways And Patios:	•Concrete
Overhead Garage Door(s):	•Steel •Automatic Opener Installed
Surface Drainage:	•Graded Away From House
Fencing:	•Wood

EXTERIOR OBSERVATIONS

Positive Attributes

The aluminum soffits and fascia are a low-maintenance feature of the exterior of the home. There is no significant wood/soil contact around the perimeter of the house, thereby reducing the risk of insect infestation or rot. The auto reverse mechanism on the overhead garage door responded properly to testing. This safety feature should be tested regularly as a door that doesn't reverse can injure someone or fall from the ceiling. Refer to the owner's manual or contact the manufacturer for more information. The lot drainage was good, taking surface water away from the building. The driveway and walkways are in good condition.

General Comments

The exterior of the home is generally in good condition.

RECOMMENDATIONS / OBSERVATIONS

Exterior Walls

- **Repair:** Band around garage door has holes where the two bands meet (see photo) should be sealed to prevent further damage. There is an extra risk of hidden damage in such areas.

LIMITATIONS OF EXTERIOR INSPECTION

As we have discussed and as described in your inspection contract, this is a visual inspection limited in scope by (but not restricted to) the following conditions:

- A representative sample of exterior components was inspected rather than every occurrence of components.
- The inspection does not include an assessment of geological, geotechnical, or hydrological conditions, or environmental hazards.
- Screening, shutters, awnings, or similar seasonal accessories, fences, recreational facilities, outbuildings, seawalls, breakwalls, docks, erosion control and earth stabilization measures are not inspected unless specifically agreed-upon and documented in this report.

Please also refer to the pre-inspection contract for a detailed explanation of the scope of this inspection.

Electrical

DESCRIPTION OF ELECTRICAL

Size of Electrical Service:	•120/240 Volt Main Service - Service Size: 150 Amp
Service Drop:	•Overhead
Service Entrance Conductors:	•Aluminum
Service Grounding:	•Copper •Ground Rod Connection
Distribution Wiring:	•Copper
Wiring Method:	•Non-Metallic Cable "Romex"
Switches & Receptacles:	•Grounded
Ground Fault Circuit Interrupters:	•Bathroom(s) •Kitchen
Smoke Detectors:	•Present

ELECTRICAL OBSERVATIONS

RECOMMENDATIONS / OBSERVATIONS

Service / Entrance

- **Repair:** The service wires should form a "drip loop" where they meet the service mast on the exterior of the home. This ensures that water will drip off the wires, rather than run into the service mast.
- **Repair:** The service mast/conduit should be better secured to the exterior of the home.
- **Monitor:** The service mast shows evidence of rusting, suggesting the presence of moisture. This area should be monitored. If rusting continues, or if moisture is evident in the vicinity of the service box, a qualified, licensed electrician should be consulted. Rusted electrical components are unsafe.

LIMITATIONS OF ELECTRICAL INSPECTION

As we have discussed and as described in your inspection contract, this is a visual inspection limited in scope by (but not restricted to) the following conditions:

- Electrical components concealed behind finished surfaces are not inspected.
- Only a representative sampling of outlets and light fixtures were tested.
- Furniture and/or storage restricted access to some electrical components which may not be inspected.
- The inspection does not include remote control devices, alarm systems and components, low voltage wiring, systems, and components, ancillary wiring, systems, and other components which are not part of the primary electrical power distribution system.

Please also refer to the pre-inspection contract for a detailed explanation of the scope of this inspection.

123 Main St Ormond Beach, Fl. 32176 Page 8 of 13
This confidential report is prepared exclusively for John Doe
www.bellinspection.com
© 2004 Bell Inspection Service

Heating

DESCRIPTION OF HEATING

Energy Source:	•Electricity
Heating System Type:	•Forced Air Furnace •Manufacturer: Bryant
	•Serial Number: 1701A60559
Heat Distribution Methods:	•Ductwork

HEATING OBSERVATIONS

Positive Attributes
The heating system is in generally good condition. Adequate heating capacity is provided by the system.
General Comments
The heating system shows no visible evidence of major defects.

RECOMMENDATIONS / OBSERVATIONS

LIMITATIONS OF HEATING INSPECTION

As we have discussed and as described in your inspection contract, this is a visual inspection limited in scope by (but not restricted to) the following conditions:

- The adequacy of heat supply or distribution balance is not inspected.
- The interior of flues or chimneys which are not readily accessible are not inspected.
- The furnace heat exchanger, humidifier, or dehumidifier, and electronic air filters are not inspected.
- Solar space heating equipment/systems are not inspected.

Please also refer to the pre-inspection contract for a detailed explanation of the scope of this inspection.

This confidential report is prepared exclusively for John Doe
www.bellinspection.com
© 2004 Bell Inspection Service

Cooling / Heat Pumps

DESCRIPTION OF COOLING / HEAT PUMPS

Energy Source: •Electricity
Central System Type: •Air Cooled Central Air Conditioning
•Manufacturer: Payne •Serial Number: 1801E184702
Through-Wall Equipment: •Not Present

COOLING / HEAT PUMPS OBSERVATIONS

Positive Attributes
The capacity and configuration of the system should be sufficient for the home. Upon testing in the air conditioning mode, a normal temperature drop across the evaporator coil was observed. This suggests that the system is operating properly. The system responded properly to operating controls.

General Comments
The system shows no visible evidence of major defects.

RECOMMENDATIONS / OBSERVATIONS

LIMITATIONS OF COOLING / HEAT PUMPS INSPECTION

As we have discussed and as described in your inspection contract, this is a visual inspection limited in scope by (but not restricted to) the following conditions:

- Window mounted air conditioning units are not inspected.
- The cooling supply adequacy or distribution balance are not inspected.

Please also refer to the pre-inspection contract for a detailed explanation of the scope of this inspection.

This confidential report is prepared exclusively for John Doe
www.bellinspection.com
© 2004 Bell Inspection Service

Insulation / Ventilation

DESCRIPTION OF INSULATION / VENTILATION

Attic Insulation:	•Blown-in
Exterior Wall Insulation:	•Not Visible
Vapor Retarders:	•Unknown
Roof Ventilation:	•Ridge Vents •Soffit Vents
Exhaust Fan/vent Locations:	•Bathroom •Kitchen •Dryer

INSULATION / VENTILATION OBSERVATIONS

Positive Attributes
This is a well insulated home.

RECOMMENDATIONS / ENERGY SAVING SUGGESTIONS

LIMITATIONS OF INSULATION / VENTILATION INSPECTION

As we have discussed and as described in your inspection contract, this is a visual inspection limited in scope by (but not restricted to) the following conditions:

- Insulation/ventilation type and levels in concealed areas are not inspected. Insulation and vapor barriers are not disturbed and no destructive tests (such as cutting openings in walls to look for insulation) are performed.
- Potentially hazardous materials such as Asbestos and Urea Formaldehyde Foam Insulation (UFFI) cannot be positively identified without a detailed inspection and laboratory analysis. This is beyond the scope of the inspection.
- An analysis of indoor air quality is not part of our inspection unless explicitly contracted-for and discussed in this or a separate report.
- Any estimates of insulation R values or depths are rough average values.

Please also refer to the pre-inspection contract for a detailed explanation of the scope of this inspection.

Plumbing

DESCRIPTION OF PLUMBING

Water Supply Source: •Public Water Supply
Service Pipe to House: •Copper
Main Water Valve Location: •Inside garage
Interior Supply Piping: •Copper
Waste System: •Public Sewer System
Drain, Waste, & Vent Piping: •Plastic
Water Heater: •Electric •Approximate Capacity (in gallons): 40
•Manufacturer: Rheem •Serial Number: 0893808529
Other Components: •Sprinkler System

PLUMBING OBSERVATIONS

Positive Attributes

The plumbing system is in generally good condition. The water pressure supplied to the fixtures is reasonably good. A
typical drop in flow was experienced when two fixtures were operated simultaneously.

RECOMMENDATIONS / OBSERVATIONS

Fixtures

• **Improve:** Cracked, deteriorated and/or missing shower stall grout and caulk should be replaced.

• **Improve:** Cracked, deteriorated and/or missing bathtub enclosure grout and caulk should be replaced.

LIMITATIONS OF PLUMBING INSPECTION

As we have discussed and as described in your inspection contract, this is a visual inspection limited in scope by (but not restricted to) the following conditions:

• Portions of the plumbing system concealed by finishes and/or storage (below sinks, etc.), below the structure, or beneath the ground surface are not inspected.
• Water quantity and water quality are not tested unless explicitly contracted-for and discussed in this or a separate report.
• Clothes washing machine connections are not inspected.
• Interiors of flues or chimneys which are not readily accessible are not inspected.
• Water conditioning systems, solar water heaters, fire and lawn sprinkler systems, and private waste disposal systems are not inspected unless explicitly contracted-for and discussed in this or a separate report.

Please also refer to the pre-inspection contract for a detailed explanation of the scope of this inspection.

123 Main St Ormond Beach, Fl. 32176 Page 12 of 13
This confidential report is prepared exclusively for John Doe
www.bellinspection.com
© 2004 Bell Inspection Service

Interior

DESCRIPTION OF INTERIOR

Wall And Ceiling Materials:	•Drywall
Floor Surfaces:	•Carpet •Tile
Window Type(s) & Glazing:	•Double/Single Hung •Single Pane
Doors:	•Wood-Hollow Core

INTERIOR OBSERVATIONS

General Condition of Interior Finishes
On the whole, the interior finishes of the home are in above average condition. Typical minor flaws were observed in some areas.
General Condition of Windows and Doors
The majority of the doors and windows are good quality units.

RECOMMENDATIONS / OBSERVATIONS

Floors
 • **Monitor:** The installation of the tile floor is less than ideal in the breakfast nook. This can influence the long-term performance of the floor.
Discretionary Improvements
Install new exterior lock sets upon taking possession of the home.

LIMITATIONS OF INTERIOR INSPECTION

As we have discussed and as described in your inspection contract, this is a visual inspection limited in scope by (but not restricted to) the following conditions

 • Furniture, storage, appliances and/or wall hangings are not moved to permit inspection and may block defects.
 • Carpeting, window treatments, central vacuum systems, household appliances, recreational facilities, paint, wallpaper, and other finish treatments are not inspected.

Please also refer to the pre-inspection contract for a detailed explanation of the scope of this inspection.

123 Main St Ormond Beach, Fl. 32176 Page 13 of 13
This confidential report is prepared exclusively for John Doe
www.bellinspection.com
© 2004 Bell Inspection Service

Appliances

DESCRIPTION OF APPLIANCES

Appliances Tested: •Electric Range •Dishwasher •Waste Disposer •Refrigerator

Laundry Facility: •240 Volt Circuit for Dryer •Dryer Vented to Building Exterior •120 Volt Circuit for Washer •Hot and Cold Water Supply for Washer •Washer Discharges to Laundry Tub/Sink

Other Components Tested: •Kitchen Exhaust Hood

APPLIANCES OBSERVATIONS

Positive Attributes
The appliances are in generally good condition. All appliances tested responded satisfactorily.

RECOMMENDATIONS / OBSERVATIONS

LIMITATIONS OF APPLIANCES INSPECTION

As we have discussed and as described in your inspection contract, this is a visual inspection limited in scope by (but not restricted to) the following conditions

- Thermostats, timers and other specialized features and controls are not tested.
- The temperature calibration, functionality of timers, effectiveness, efficiency and overall performance of appliances is outside the scope of this inspection.

Please also refer to the pre-inspection contract for a detailed explanation of the scope of this inspection.

Chapter 14

Your Rights as a Seller

Anthony Duffy has nearly 30 years of experience in law. He's a seasoned real estate and business attorney for The Duffy Law Firm in Newport Beach, California. We asked him for legal advice regarding common scenarios For Sale By Owners face while selling.

"Like any important legal transaction, there are many challenges and potential pitfalls, associated with the FSBO process," says Duffy. "The following discussion addresses some of the common questions associated with the process, identifies some of the most common challenges and trouble spots facing the potential seller and provides a few tips on how to avoid the biggest legal traps associated with the process."

Piper: What should you consider when deciding to sell your own home?

Anthony: To FSBO or not to FSBO, that is the question. In today's volatile economy, every potential home seller would love to sell their property as easily and quickly as possible, while also receiving top dollar from the sale. Consequently, many of those potential sellers are choosing to sell their homes themselves, without the benefit of a real estate broker or agent. In fact, some estimates place the number of For Sale By Owners home sales at more than 25% of the total home sales in the country. To many potential sellers FSBO sales are attractive because they can (1) result in a dramatic cost savings to the seller by reducing or eliminating the sales commission typically paid to a real estate broker or agent, (2) reduce the amount of time that the seller's home remains on the market and (3) give the seller a great deal more autonomy in the home sale process.

Piper: What if a buyer shows up at your open house and wants to buy your home? Should you write the contract yourself, or should you assign that task to someone else? Also, what should you do if neither you nor the buyer have an agent?

Anthony: As in any transaction which has significant legal ramifications, taking on the responsibility of drafting and executing a real estate sales contract without the assistance of someone with demonstrated expertise in the area—such as licensed real estate professionals and, sometimes, legal counsel—can expose the innocent, but often uninformed, owner to various difficulties including liability exposure. Generally, real estate sale contracts must be in writing. Often buyers and sellers are not sufficiently informed regarding the legal requirements or of provisions commonly made in such contracts when prepared by professionals, and are therefore likely to omit important terms or make provisions that could have serious legal consequences. Accordingly, parties are rarely well-protected if they write the contract themselves.

Real property is considered unique, and contracts of sale can be enforced by a court ordering the parties to perform, through remedies such as specific performance, as well as awarding damages. Further, contracts for the sale of real property in California, for example, must exhibit a degree of specificity regarding various aspects of the transaction in order to be deemed valid. Some of the items which must be addressed with requisite specificity are (1) a description that is sufficiently clear to identify the property to be sold (including by street address and recorded legal description), (2) the purchase price, (3) the terms of sale, including how the purchase price is to be paid and, if applicable, financed and (4) when (and how) the offer to purchase will terminate.

The foregoing shows that the decision about whether to draft one's own real estate sales contract should be considered carefully. However, if the seller decides not to utilize a licensed real estate professional or an attorney to draft the contract, a variety of form real estate purchase and sale contracts are available that unrepresented parties can use. For instance, one form used often is a Residential Deposit Receipt and Real Estate Purchase Contract published by the California Association of Realtors. That contract form consists of three separate parts and serves three separate purposes: First, it acts as a receipt for the good faith deposit of the buyer. Second, it constitutes a contract of sale between the buyer and the seller. Third, it includes a separate agreement between the seller and any broker or brokers involved in the transaction for the payment of a commission.

For sellers and buyers who are committed to engaging in a real estate transaction without the participation of licensed professionals, utilizing recognized forms such as the previously mentioned, published by reputable real estate associations, title companies or even the Continuing Education of the Bar publications for attorneys, can provide a framework in which the parties can set forth the particular terms of their transaction. However, even where reputable forms are used by the parties, they are still generally well-advised to seek expert advice, even if just to review the contract. Issues can develop and unexpected circumstances may arise. These transactions are important enough to warrant seeking some professional help.

Piper: What if a buyer comes to your open house with an agent and expresses a desire to purchase your home; but you don't want to deal with a Realtor. What should you do?

Anthony: Some sellers do not want to deal with brokers, generally because they do not want to have their sale proceeds reduced by the brokers' commissions, which are generally a percentage of the purchase price. In a typical situation, if the buyer and seller each have separate brokers, a commission of 6% of the price may be charged, reducing the seller's proceeds. In other instances, the parties may agree to use a single broker, thereby reducing the commission.

Whether refusing to deal with buyers represented by brokers is advisable, however, depends on many circumstances. Brokers may provide valuable advice and solutions to problems that may arise, such as environmental, property condition, escrow or title issues. Paying the commission for such services may avoid future problems.

In a "hot" real estate market, where the potential buyers may exceed the available properties and the sale is without complexities or issues, a seller may be more inclined to deal only with buyers who do not have a broker. However, in flat or declining markets, sellers may not have the luxury of turning away ready, willing and able buyers simply because they have broker representation.

Another option available to the hypothetical seller is to agree to negotiate with the buyer through their broker/agent, but only upon the broker/agent's agreement to accept a reduced sales commission. If this option is chosen, the agreed-upon commission should be memorialized in the sale contract and escrow instructions, as well as any written broker engagement agreement.

The prudent seller should not attempt to convince the buyer to forego using a Realtor to assist him or her in their efforts to buy the home. Given the likelihood that the buyer and his or her Realtor have an existing contractual relationship, the buyer cannot terminate the relationship without being exposed to potential liability to the broker/agent. Further, the seller could be exposing himself or herself to legal liability to the Realtor for interference with an existing contractual relationship with the buyer. Also, if problems do develop in the sale or afterwards, the buyer may claim that the seller prevented the buyer from having adequate representation, which may create other exposure to the seller.

Piper: What rights do you have in selling your home?

Anthony: The question of what rights are available to a contracting party is inextricably linked to the question of what remedies are available if the party's rights are violated. In the area of real estate sales, California law provides a variety of remedies to a party that has been harmed, either intentionally or negligently, by the actions of another party to the transaction. For instance, if the harm suffered by the seller results from the lack of the parties' mutual assent (that is, the contract was never properly formed), the aggrieved party may rescind the contract. Common grounds for rescission are mistake, fraud, duress, menace or undue influence, or when there is a material failure of consideration. Additionally, he or she may elect to exercise their ancillary remedies, including canceling the contract, seeking to have a constructive trust or resulting trust imposed on the proceeds derived from the sale, and/or move for an order seeking to have title to the property cleared, such as by a quiet title action. Other remedies under California law provide equitable relief to the wronged party against an anticipated injury to his or her rights or interests.

In addition to the above, in the event that a buyer breaches the terms of the real estate contract, the seller can elect to affirm the contract and obtain specific performance (that is, force the buyer to perform according to the specific terms of the contract) or, as stated previously, treat the contract as terminated by the breach, and seek to recover monetary damages. .

Piper: What should you know about contracts? What should typically be identified in a contract?

Duffy: The foregoing represents a brief summary of some of the issues which any real estate seller who is contemplating participating in the process as a FSBO should consider. As in all legal transactions, it is highly recommended that the potential FSBO seller obtain qualified legal and/or licensed real estate broker/agent representation prior to embarking on the sale-related process. However, if the seller, despite the many reasons not to do so, decides to create his or her own contract, he or she should take special care to make sure that the requisite terms are set forth with specificity and clarity in the contract, including but not exclusively, the following:

+ The property to be sold is specifically identified.
+ The parties to the agreement are clearly identified.
+ The purchase price for the property, and terms of payment of that purchase price (for example, deposits, monthly installment payments over a specified term) are clearly identified.
+ Clear identification of the terms and manner of financing to be utilized.
+ Whether there are conditions, such as obtaining financing, that need to be satisfied before the transaction will be completed.
+ Whether the buyer is granted an option associated with the purchase.
+ The term of the agreement is clearly stated, as well as what events will effectively terminate the agreement.
+ Whether and/or how an escrow will be utilzed, who the escrow holder will be, the term of the escrow, the closing date, and the instructions to the escrow holder.
+ Obtaining preliminary reports and title insurance policies for both buyer and seller.
+ How the offer can be accepted should be clearly identified.
+ Whether and the amounts of any broker/agent commissions to be paid, to whom such commissions will be paid and who is responsible for paying it.
+ What material facts regarding the property must be disclosed.
+ What the seller's remedies are if the buyer breaches the agreement.

This is not an exhaustive listing, but should illustrate that, at a minimum, even if the parties understanding the consequences of not being properly and professionally represented decide to proceed alone, they should use one of the reputable forms published and available as described earlier.

Chapter 15

Safety While Selling: Protect Your Property and Your Family

*Just as important as preparing your home for sale
is protecting your safety for your family and belongings.*

Hot Tip

"There are several things that I always tell sellers. Never leave money lying around, be it on top of dressers or what they consider safely stashed in a drawer. Secure your valuable jewelry, preferably under lock and key. Any small, valuable items of décor in their homes, simply start packing now. And finally, but very importantly, remove all prescription medications from the bathrooms and/or kitchen and keep them somewhere else, such as the refrigerator drawer. The medicines have been a serious problem lately."

—Sandi Mitchell, real estate broker,
Empire Realty Associates

Safety is one of the main concerns real estate agents have every day on the job. Sometimes safety is forgotten and other times ignored. But whenever an agent has a home for sale, they are responsible for making sure nothing is stolen or broken and that their safety is in check when dealing with potential clients. The same is true when you sell your home. You want to make sure the safety of you and your family is protected at all times.

We talked to real estate agents about their top advice when it comes to safety while selling your home. In this chapter, we tackle core safety techniques, how to verify that buyers are who they say they are, how to advertise safely, fair housing laws and always handy safety tips. During the time your home is in the public eye, these are common recommendations from real estate sources for keeping your home safe.

✦ **Store away valuables:** Jewelry, medication, valuables, personal photos and other items need to stored away. Some recommend taking these items off the property completely or putting them in a safety deposit box. You will be moving shortly, why not get a head start?

✦ **Safety with children:** When you have showings or open houses, let your children stay with family or friends as a safety precaution. Also, if your home is for sale, you are going to have people coming to your door at any hour. If children come home from school and are home alone, advise them not to open the door to strangers. Potential buyers will call the number on the sign or try to reach you later. (Caller ID comes in handy. Let you children know how to avoid phone calls that may compromise your safety or privacy.)

✦ **Well-lit outdoor paths and entrances:** Promotes safety.

✦ **Advertising safety:** Try to avoid announcing that your home is for sale and vacant. (A lot of ads mention a home is vacant and can be seen anytime.) If you post pictures online or in fliers, newspaper or magazine ads, make sure it doesn't show your children or valuables.

✦ **Open houses and showings:** First, let buyers sign in with their name and number when entering your home, so you have a record of who entered your home. (Some recommend getting the car license plate and type.) As you do the showing, never go into small, enclosed spaces with a buyer. Let them lead, and you follow behind, so your back is never to the buyer. "I do not advise open houses for the general public," says Diane Matthews of Premier Properties in Easton, Massachusetts. "In my 13 years of experience, I have only sold one home during an open house and the buyers advised me that they fully intended to call me if I did not have the open house."

✦ **Prescreen buyers:** When you are setting up the appointment with the buyer, ask for his or her name, address and employer. Then verify the identity; call the employer, check if the address and number is valid. Also ask what he or she looks like, so you know who to expect when they come to your door. (When they arrive at an open house or showing, jot down the model of the car and license plate number, in addition to a description of the person, in case something happens. It's a safety precaution experts recommend often.)

✦ **Try not to show your home alone:** Whether you are showing your home or holding an open house, try to have someone with you (buyers will usually come with more than one person). Ask a family member, friend or neighbor to be there when you show your home. If you have to go it solo, make sure others know you are meeting with a potential buyer and at what time. Another option for solo sellers is showing your home by appointment only, making folks arrange appointments with you in advance. Always make sure you have your cell phone on you at all times. (Many experts suggest having a code word or phrase to tell a friend when you feel you are in a bad situation, uncomfortable or need help.) Experts say that if you are in a position in which you need to call police for help, do so.

✦ **Avoid revealing any confidential information:** Some people will ask how the security system works. While it seems natural during a conversation in which a buyer is asking how everything works and if it will be coming with the house, avoid sharing how a security system or safe works until you have a signed contract, recommends HouseWeb (*www.houseweb.com*).

✦ **What if you don't have an alarm system?** You have an option of installing temporary alarm components, such as motion sensors, during the listing. You can use motion detectors, cameras or other safety devices to help keep your home safe.

✦ **Weapons and guns:** Put these items in storage off the property or locked up safely.

✦ **Answering machine safety:** Check your answering machine to make sure it doesn't identify when you will and won't be home.

✦ **Never say…** "I can't show my house to you then because I won't be home." Just ask potential buyers what times work best for them, then select which times work for *you*.

✦ **The right words:** If you are ever at an open house or showing alone, tell visitors you are expecting a visitor soon; it helps deter them, if they have bad intentions.

✦ **Take security precautions:** Don't leave spare keys hanging around and don't leave calendars, itineraries or schedules out where visitors can see when you will and won't be home.

✦ **Be careful outside of the home too:** If a potential buyer who has never seen your home asks you to meet them somewhere, do not go, advises HouseWeb. Also, be wary of offers from buyers that have never come by.

✦ **Lockbox safety:** A lockbox is a box that securely stores your house keys. Real estate agents with "security keys" or "computerized key cards" can open the lockbox, get the keys and show your home while you aren't there. According to Prudential, an agent's security key tracks the time the agent visited your home, as well as the name of the agent and broker. But make sure agents call you first to let you know they are coming by, so you know who they are and when someone is entering your home while you are not there. (As a courtesy, Realtors are suppose to call you after they show your home to give you feedback on what the buyer did or didn't like—it helps you tweak your home for future visitors.)

✦ **Virtual tours:** A trend is online tours where buyers can see pictures of the inside of your home before they arrive. (Make sure children's photos are stored away and valuables aren't visible in the pictures.)

✦ **Keep doors locked at all times**.

✦ **State and federal fair housing laws:** Always treat every buyer the same and fairly. "It is illegal to discriminate against any buyer on the basis of race, religion, family status, national origin, etc.," advises ForSaleByOwner.com. "These are national laws and apply to any and all marketing efforts and selling practices. If in doubt, always consult with your real estate attorney. Any and all violations of Fair Housing Law carry stiff legal consequences."

✦ **Trust your gut instincts and common sense.**

What If Someone Gets Injured on Your Property?

Liability: If anyone becomes injured on the seller's property, the seller's homeowner's policy becomes responsible. Therefore, make sure walkways are clear, there is good lighting and that loose carpets do not become a hazard, as well as wet ceramic flooring, advises Diane Matthews of Premier Properties, in Easton, Massachusetts.

Pro-prevention:

✦ Repair broken steps, railings and walkways.

✦ Check bookcases, shelves and closets to make sure nothing will fall.

✦ Remove chemicals and hazards, if applicable.

✦ Is it snowing? Make sure the walkway is clear so the buyer doesn't slip and fall.

✦ Keep a first-aid kit handy.

Safety on Your Side

Robert Siciliano specializes in real estate safety. He is a Boston-based personal security consultant and president of three security-related companies. He has 18 years of security training in martial arts and as a personal bodyguard. He shared safety advice for when you are selling your home.

Piper: When folks hold an open house or do a showing, what are some safety tips?

Robert: Take a friend and bring a cell phone. Spend a few minutes considering all the vulnerable points within the home and how you would escape if necessary. When a couple shows up, require them to stay together. Often they split up, and while one has your attention, the other raids jewelry boxes and medicine cabinets for narcotics. In high crime areas, consider hiring an off-duty police officer to watch the property during a showing.

Piper: What is a good rule of thumb when selling your home?

Robert: Consider the fact you will be talking to strangers on the phone and letting them into your house for a showing. Make it a point to get some form of identification and make photo copies. Always be aware that there is a possibility that prospective buyers aren't who they say they are and that their intentions might not necessarily be to purchase a home.

Piper: There was a lady I interviewed who had let someone into her home to do a showing. She was skeptical at first, but she let him in anyway and regretted doing so. If you find yourself in a similar situation, what should you do?

Robert: Leave your own home. Seek safety.

For more information, you can reach Robert Siciliano at *www.RealtySecurity.com* or call (800) 438-6223. He also has Safety Minute Seminars (on real estate security) and can be contacted at PO Box 15145, Boston, MA 02215.

Your Plan of Action

How are you going to protect your safety? Here you can jot down your plan of action for keeping you and your family safe during this time. While safety sometimes gets put on the back burner, it is always a good idea to keep safety in mind as we sell. A home is your safe haven, a place of peace and where you go for shelter. Whether it is for sale or not, it is still where you go to find comfort. While you may have scores of visitors, the idea is to maintain the wholesomeness of your castle and carefully evaluate your safety. What is your safety plan?

_____

_____

_____

_____

_____

_____

_____

_____

_____

_____

_____

_____

_____

Chapter 16

Moving and Packing Tips: Making the Load Lighter on You

How many times in a lifetime will you move? Moving is one of those life-changing experiences. Just within a year, one of my friends moved to Maryland for a career-move, another friend moved because she got married and another traveled to the west coast to be closer to family. In addition, there was my friend who was going through a divorce and moved and another who took on a photography job in North Carolina. The list goes on.

It seems like a lot, but did you know that one in five people move each year? You and I may move 11 times in a lifetime, according to U-Haul. And most of us will rely on ourselves to get the job done.

"Moving is a great time to edit yourself. It's a great opportunity to have a new decorating look. Have a garage sale before you move," says *House Beautiful* editor-in-chief Mark Mayfield. "If people look at moving as an opportunity, as opposed to drudgery, it's a good opportunity to change your life."

In this chapter, we cover how to move efficiently and cost-effectively, the benefits of keeping track of tax deductible expenses, before-during-after moving day checklists, work-associated moving tips and more!

Do-It-Yourself Mover

Some three-quarters of movers are do-it-yourselfers, and they save about one-half to one-third the cost of a van-line move. The goal is often to save as much money as possible, move easily, pack as much into a tight space as we can and make it as painless as possible. U-Haul has been around since 1945, so we asked them for the inside scoop.

✦ **Plan your move in advance.** Make your reservations at least two to four weeks before your moving date. (Nearly 45 percent of all moves happen between Memorial Day and Labor Day.)

✦ **Avoid the weekend rush, move on a weekday.** Most do-it-yourselfers move on a Friday or Saturday. Usually, Sunday through Thursday offers the most equipment availability and rates may be lower then too. Also, if you move on a weekday, banks, utilities and government offices are open. You can take care of everything in an efficient way.

✦ **Get packaging supplies.** Ask your moving or storage company about packaging and selecting boxes. Another option is asking grocery stores for extra boxes you can use.

✦ **Pack strategically.** Select a "packaging room." Pack a few items a day to take care of your packing in a gradual process, so you aren't slammed with packing all at once. Mark each box with its contents and destination room, then you and your helpers will know where each box belongs in your new home. Pack items you know you'll need on moving day (towels, sheets, toiletries, a change of clothes, etc.). Have all your items packed before you rent a truck. Have a list of all your belongings before your pack. (Later in this chapter are tips on how to efficiently pack each item in your house.)

✦ **Allow time for the rental process.** When you pick up the rental truck, inspect it as when you rent a car. Be familiar with its features and how it works. Ask questions and read the user guide for tips on driving and safety.

✦ **Watch after your rental vehicle as if it were your own.** Check the oil, tire pressure and lighting system in the vehicle.

✦ **Always ask for any special rates.** You never know if there may be a special rate or deal going on that may apply to you.

✦ **Know the fees.** Find out all the fees associated with the service, so you are not surprised at the end by the cost.

When Working With Moving Companies

When Heidi was pregnant with her second child, her husband, Mark, had already transferred to Delaware for a new job, so they were unable to do the moving. They hired a moving company to take care of the whole moving process for them, which made moving easier.

If you opt to go with a moving company, get a price estimate to see who offers the best price and services. Ask about a few important items. What is their on-time record?

Find out what services they offer. Find out if the Better Business Bureau receives a lot of consumer complaints about the company.

When dealing with movers:

✦ **Check the contract:** Make sure everything you agree to is written in the contract, including the agreed-upon cost, how many hours the job will take and all the charges.

✦ **Be on time to meet movers to avoid charges:** When you know the time the movers are expected to arrive at your new home—the "estimated delivery time"—make sure you are at the house to receive the boxes. (If you aren't there, you may have to pay for waiting charges.)

✦ **Payment upon arrival:** It is usual for drivers to ask you for a payment before unloading items. Unless you have paid via credit card, you will make a payment according to the bill of lading terms.

✦ **Don't let the crew unload until you have the inventory sheet:** Many recommend having two people on hand when the delivery comes. That way one can check off all boxes, furniture and items on the inventory sheet as they are unloaded.

✦ **What the movers should do:** Movers are expected to place items in rooms indicated, plus reassemble any furniture/equipment they took apart to move from your old home to your new home. On the boxes for the movers, write where they goes, suggests Mark Mayfield. For example, if you have a box of books you want to put in the library, write "library" on the box so that the movers put it in that room. It will be harder if you have to walk your books from the basement to the library alone, without help.

✦ **Helpful hints:** Let the moving company know how many stairs are at your new house. During loading and unloading, examine all your items before signing a receipt.

✦ **Protecting your belongings:** Movers are limited by law, with regard to what they can give you for damaged or lost goods. It's also a good idea to check into renter's or homeowner's policies to cover any potential damage that may occur. Ask about any insurance the mover may provide.

Before You Move

When you get ready to move, don't feel compelled to take everything you ever owned with you. "By all means, get rid of stuff," says Mayfield. "If you aren't going to use it in the home, get rid of it. What is the purpose of storing it in the attic?" Hold a yard sale or donate to charities anything you don't want to take to your new home. One way to cut down on the stress of moving day is by preparing as much as possible in advance.

Moving Preparation Checklist

- ❏ Make arrangements with a moving company or reserve a rental truck. The sooner you make arrangements, the better.
- ❏ Two weeks before moving, contact your telephone, electric, gas, cable/satellite, refuse, and water company and any other services.
- ❏ Contact utilities in your new town about service start dates.
- ❏ Notify healthcare professionals (doctors, dentists, vet) of your move. If you are moving out of the area, ask for referrals and record transfers.
- ❏ Register children for school and ask for school records to be transferred.
- ❏ Fill out a change of address form for the post office.
- ❏ Fill out an IRS change of address form.
- ❏ Start using up food items so there is less left to pack and possibly spoil.
- ❏ Make arrangements for transporting pets and plants.
- ❏ Take inventory of belongings before they are packed, in case an insurance claim needs to be made later.

Preparation for Moving out of State

- ❏ Make travel arrangements with airlines, busses, car rental agencies and hotels.
- ❏ Transfer membership in churches, clubs and other organizations.
- ❏ Set up a checking account in your new area.
- ❏ Look into relocation companies that can help you move and find a new home in your new area.
- ❏ Learn as much about the area as possible before your trip.

Hot Tip

Moving Estimates

To help get an idea how much it will cost you to move, get written estimates from several companies to compare their services and costs. Moving estimates are based on the weight of your items, shipping distance, amount of packing and other services you will need to move. Many movers offer two types of estimates: binding and non-binding.

Binding estimate: You pay the binding estimate price even if the shipment weighs more or less than the estimated amount. But estimates only cover services and items *listed* on the estimate. If you add services or items, you will be billed for it 30 days after your shipment arrives.

Non-binding estimate: Usually lower than a binding estimate, the final cost is determined after your shipment is actually weighed. (But there isn't a guarantee the final cost will not be *more* than the estimate.)

Utilities Checklist

Make sure to disconnect and reconnect these utilities and services wherever you move:

- ❑ Electric.
- ❑ Water/Sewer.
- ❑ Trash.
- ❑ Recycling.
- ❑ Local telephone.
- ❑ Cable.

- ❑ Schools.
- ❑ Voter registration.
- ❑ Newspaper.
- ❑ Magazine subscriptions.
- ❑ Bills.

Moving Day

Moving day can be exciting, stressful and busy. The more you plan in advance, the easier the actual moving day will be for you. According to experts, you should set aside a whole day for moving to take care of everything you need to do.

Last-Minute Reminders

- ❑ Make sure all boxes, furniture and items are packed securely— whether you are doing it solo or using a moving company.
- ❑ Double-check rooms, closets, drawers, shelves, attic and garage to be sure they are empty.
- ❑ Carry important documents, currency and jewelry yourself or use registered mail.
- ❑ Carry travelers checks for quick available funds.
- ❑ Pack essentials, including checkbook, cash, credit cards, ID, medicine, moving-related paperwork, snacks, water, first-aid kit, washcloths and toys/books for children.

Your New Home

When you move into your new home—staring at those boxes and wondering what it will be like when you are finally unpacked—make sure you take care of a few important tasks, as well:

- ❑ Renew your driver's license, vehicle registration and tags.
- ❑ If applicable, shop around for new insurance policies, especially auto coverage.
- ❑ Locate the schools, hospitals, police stations, veterinarians and fire stations near your home.
- ❑ Take time to really know the area.

Moving for Work

If you are moving because of a job, many times your employer will give you a relocation package. A typical package usually includes a house-hunting trip, temporary living assistance, a relocation bonus and moving your household items. In return, you may have to promise to work for the company for 1-2 years, by signing a reimbursement agreement. If you decide to leave earlier, you will have to reimburse the company. But it varies, depending on the company. When Mark and Heidi moved from Virginia to Delaware, the company paid for their moving expenses and hotel stay while they searched for a new home; when Christina moved across the country from Utah, her company gave her several thousand to cover moving expenses.

If it is a corporate move, here are some handy questions to ask your employer:

✦ Can you select the moving company? Will the company arrange for the moving company to do an estimate on what it will cost to move?

✦ Does the company work with a relocation company that can help you move and find a home?

✦ Will the company purchase your home (done through a relocation company) and will they cover temporary living costs? What if you need help maintaining two households?

✦ Will the company compensate you for having to break a house lease?

✦ What type of moving insurance can you get? (Most will cover full replacement value coverage, but if you need more coverage than allowed—such as for luxury items and one-of-a kind items—you may need to pay for it yourself.)

✦ Will the company allow for a do-it-yourself move? What can you do to be reimbursed?

✦ Will the move be counted as business hours or designated vacation leave?

✦ What charges will you need to cover (extra labor, deliveries, extra insurance, etc.)?

✦ Will you get a relocation bonus for fees to cover your driver's license, utility deposits and vehicle registration?

✦ What if you have more than one vehicle—will the company move it for you?

Efficient Packing Tips

The experts at Penske Truck Rental (*www.pensketruckrental.com*) gave us pointers for packing efficiently. For every item you could possibly think of packing, they have advice on how to package it securely to get it safely from point A to point B.

Appliances, small: Pack small appliances in original container or a box cushioned with wadded paper. (Do not use shredded paper—it can clog the appliance.)

Appliances, major: Check with the appliance dealer for any special moving instructions. For all large appliances, remove loose fittings and accessories and pack separately. Tie down, tape or wedge all movable parts and doors.

Dishwasher/Washing Machine: Stuff towels between machine sides and tub to keep tub from rotating. Pad exterior well. Disconnect hoses, put in plastic bag, place in tub.

Freezer/Refrigerator: Defrost and dry interiors well. Fill interior spaces with lightweight linens, clothing or stuffed toys. If you want to lay your refrigerator down for moving, check first with the local dealer to determine if your brand can be moved like this. If so, make sure refrigerator stands upright for at least 24 hours before plugging in.

Gas Dryer: Have gas company disconnect.

Bicycles, Tricycles, Baby Carriages: Loosen, lower and turn handlebars at right angles to save space. Clean and cover chains and pedals to protect other items from being snagged or soiled.

Clothes: Dresses, coats, suits—anything hanging in closets—travel best in special, reusable, wardrobe boxes, which can be used seasonally as "extra closets" for wardrobe storage. Other clothes can remain folded in their regular dresser drawers.

Beds: Disassemble the bed frame. Tie rails and crosspieces together with rope or tape. Be sure to mark on tape to show where pieces fit together for reassemble. Use mattress protection bags to keep mattress clean.

Books: They're heavy, so use small boxes. Pack books flat, alternating bindings, and fill empty spaces with wadded paper.

Bureaus, Dressers: Fill drawers with small breakable items and cushion well with loose clothes. Secure drawers with pad or blanket (tape can remove the finish) and tie with rope. Do not overload drawers with heavy items.

Chairs: Wrap arms and legs to prevent scratches. Bundle armless chairs in pairs, seat to seat, with a folded blanket or other padding between and tie seats together.

Curtain Rod Hardware: Put the hardware in a plastic bag and tape to rod or pack in dresser drawers.

Dishes: Individually wrap each piece. If you use newspaper, wrap first in plastic bags to save dishwashing later. Place saucers, plates and platters on edge—DO NOT STACK FLAT. Cups and bowls may be placed inside each other and wrapped three or four in a bundle.

Glasses: Wrap each glass separately in newspaper or bubble wrap (remember to wrap first in a plastic bag to save washing later). Pack in sturdy boxes (dish packs are perfect for glassware as well as dishes).

Kitchenware: Pots, pans, etc. can be stacked in a box with a sheet of paper between them.

Lamps: After disassembling lamps, pack small bases in dresser drawers surrounded by loose clothing, and large bases in boxes stuffed with wadded paper. Box shades individually in boxes with plenty of tissue paper for stuffing. Don't use newspaper because it smudges.

Lawn Mowers: Drain fuel and oil before loading. Remove handle from hand mowers and place blade end in sturdy box. Mark properly.

Mirrors: Small mirrors can be well wrapped in paper and packed in boxes. For a large mirror, make a cardboard case by cutting pieces of corrugated cardboard. Mark GLASS on the outside to prevent mishandling. Always pack and store on end.

Rugs and Pads: After vacuuming rugs and pads, sprinkle with moth flakes. Roll up and tie with twine.

Paint and Flammables: Don't move it. The same goes for other flammables such as alcohol, solvents, lighter fluid, ammunition and greasy mops or rags. These can be dangerous items and must be disposed of properly before moving.

Paintings, Prints: Place in mirror boxes, wrap individually in corrugated cardboard, or wrap in cardboard cushioned with thick blankets and tie bundles with cord. Stand on sides.

Radios, TVs: Box upright and make sure items are well padded on all sides. For console-size equipment, surround with furniture pads, and then move and load upright.

Tables: For large tables, remove legs and tie together. Put hardware in small sealed envelope taped to underside of tabletop. Pad tops. Pad and tie spare table leaves. For smaller tables, pad top and wrap legs to prevent scratching.

Stereos, Compact Discs and Cassettes: Separately pack components and pack in well-padded box marked FRAGILE. Pack CDs upright in their cases in a sturdy box with tape-reinforced bottom. Tie CDs in small bundles before packing, then fill air space with wadded paper. Mark FRAGILE. Cassettes can be packed in a similar manner, although you can group them in larger bundles.

Tools and Gardening Equipment: Drain hoses, coil and pack in boxes. Fill remaining space with lawn sprinklers, small garden hand tools, etc. Tie rakes, shovels, and other long-handled tools together with rope or tape.

Pets: Your pet should always ride up front in the truck cab with you and never in the back of the truck. Be sure your pet is on a leash, in a kennel or cage when outside your truck and that it is always wearing an ID tag with its name, your name, a destination address and phone number (or a friend's or relative's).

Plants: The general rule when moving plants is to store them in plastic bags with holes punched for air. If possible, they should be placed in boxes. Temperature is the most critical factor. Temperatures below 34°F or above 94°F for much over an hour can be fatal. Plants are susceptible to shock when moving. Plants should be moist.

Valuables: Set aside jewelry, important papers and safe deposit box contents to be packed in a small container you can keep with you throughout the move. Car registration certificate, car ownership records, children's school records, insurance policies, medical and dental records, irreplaceable photos and snapshots and tax return records.

Selecting a Mover

Movers have a variety of costs and services. Call a number of companies so you can compare their services. Many recommend selecting a moving company that is an AMSA (American Moving and Storage Association)-Certified mover and van line. When you select a mover, Century21 Real Estate Corporation suggests that you:

✦ Know the rates and charges that apply.

✦ Understand the mover's liability for your items.

✦ Verify that pick-up and delivery times will work.

✦ Find out what claims protection you have.

Selecting a Mover

When you call movers, take comparison notes on their costs, services, claims protection and charges. Select a mover that suits your needs.

Mover	Cost Estimates, Charges and Service

Normal Services Offered

Most moving companies will have a representative come out and look at everything you have to ship. They will estimate what it may weigh, what shipping materials will be involved, how many hours it will take to load/unload and the number of boxes you may use. From there, they come up with an estimated cost. Most moving companies will provide you with the cartons and packing materials. They will also help with packing loose items, transportation and connecting and disconnecting your appliances. Find out exactly from the mover what they will and will not ship. Following is a list of what mover usually will not ship.

Movers usually do not ship:	Movers may move (but charge for):
Valuables.	Boats.
Combustible materials, explosives.	Recreational vehicles.
Plants.	Building materials.
Perishables.	Firewood.

Tax-Deductible Expenses

Did you know there were tax-deductible expenses when you sell your house and move? There are several tax-deductible expenses if you meet IRS eligibility requirements (visit *www.irs.gov*). For example, you can deduct some expenses for shipping, travel, moving, job-search costs and home buying expenses. Use the following chart to keep track of moving costs.

Shipping Expenses

Shipping	*Cost*
❏ Storage charges.	$_____
❏ Shipping charges (transporting, crating and packing).	$_____
❏ Insurance fees for household items in transit process.	$_____
❏ Household goods.	$_____
❏ Vehicle.	$_____
❏ Pet travel.	$_____

Travel Expenses

Move and Travel	*Cost*
❏ Personal vehicle (actual costs or track mileage).	$_____
❏ Mileage.	$_____
❏ Oil and gasoline.	$_____
❏ Tolls and parking.	$_____
❏ Vehicle rental.	$_____
❏ Childcare.	$_____
❏ Lodging.	$_____
❏ Loss of any or your property.	$_____
❏ Cost of any property stolen.	$_____
❏ Disconnecting, connecting utilities.	$_____
❏ Insurance (some type).	$_____

Expenses for Job Search

Job Search	*Cost*
❏ Resume prep and mailing costs.	$_____
❏ Telephone calls.	$_____
❏ Travel to interviews.	$_____
❏ Employment agency/job counseling fees.	$_____

Additional Expenses

Additional	*Cost*
❑ _____	$_____
❑ _____	$_____
❑ _____	$_____
❑ _____	$_____
❑ _____	$_____
❑ _____	$_____
❑ _____	$_____

List It

There is always so much to do to make sure the moving process goes smoothly. You have to schedule your moving arrangements, make sure you pack your antiques safely, ensure your pet is taken care of, grab those last-minute items stored in the attic and the list seems to go on and on. Here we wanted to offer space just for you to list what you need to get done.

❑ _____

❑ _____

❑ _____

❑ _____

❑ _____

❑ _____

❑ _____

❑ _____

❑ _____

❑ _____

❑ _____

❑ _____

❑ _____

❑ _____

❑ _____

❑ _____

❑ _____

❑ _____

Chapter 17

A Home Is an Investment: Savvy Financial and Tax Advice

We all want to know: How do we make the most money from the sale of our homes? In this chapter, we talk to experts about how to view your home as an investment and tax perks to lower your tax bill. Plus, there are some sound financial tips for any extra funds you make from the sale. Have a moment? Let's chat.

Viewing Your Home as an Investment

Norm Bour cohosts the "Real Estate and Finance Hour" in California and believes strongly in making the most with the money you have. We talked to him about looking at your home as an investment and how you are affected by taxes. He says "A home is an investment, whether intended or not, price appreciation or not. As the amount of principal is reduced, the amount of equity increases. This is nothing more than a paper gain until that property is sold. Many fortunes were made on a real estate foundation and the simplest method is to convert your primary residence into a rental and buy another." By doing this, you can "write off" all upkeep expenses, interest and taxes, as well as claim depreciation—the "paper loss" for the declining value. Norm goes on to explain, "as rent increases and the principal decreases, ideally the net results would be a mortgage-free home."

But as he points out, "whatever type of investment property you strive to own— from a condo to a single-family home to multiple units to commercial property—they each have their own advantages and drawbacks."

When selling a property, you are affected by taxes depending on whether it is a primary residence or a rental property.

For a primary residence, Norm says that you are permitted up to $250,000 of tax-free gain, if single, and up to $500,000, if married and filing a joint tax return, as long as ownership and use tests are met. This replaces the old law, which permitted unlimited gain as long as the owner moved "up."

The Ownership Test and the Use Test

Tax expert Gloria Wajciechowski says that, for the ownership test, "taxpayers must own the home for at least two years." For the use test, "taxpayers must live in the home as their main residence for at least two years. (Exceptions to the use test are members of the Uniformed Services or Foreign Service and individuals with disability.)

For an investment property, Norm explains, it gets a little tricky, but remember the term "1031 tax-deferred exchange," also referred to as a "like-kind exchange." It allows you to sell an investment or business property and pay zero taxes as long as the seller buys another investment or business property of a like kind.

Exclusion Rules

"To apply the exclusion rules for the sale of your main home to a rental home acquired through a like-kind exchange and converted to your main home, you must have lived in the home as your main home for the required two-year period," tax expert Gloria Wajciechowski says. "For sales after October 22, 2004, you must have owned the home for the entire 5-year period beginning with the date you acquired the home. Special rules apply for computing the excludible gain on property used for business or to produce rental income."

Other Investment Strategies

Another idea to consider is the lease-to-buy option when selling a home to a buyer. Or talk to your mortgage officer about seller financing options that work a sale more as an investment.

Tax Perks for You

As a seller, you have a great tax break: Married couples filing jointly can avoid taxes on up to $500,000 of home sale profits ($250,000 for singles)—no federal income tax—as long as you have lived in and owned the home for at least two of the previous five years. "The required two years of ownership and use during the five-year period ending on the date of sale do not have to be continuous," Wajciechowski says. "You meet the tests if you can show that you owned and lived in the property as your main home for either 24 full months or 730 days (365 × 2) during the five-year period ending on the date of sale." This is a capital gains tax that works to your advantage.

Gain or Loss on the Sale of Your Home

Wajciechowski also provides some useful information about determining gain or loss on the sale of your home, as outlines in IRS publication *523: Selling Your Home.*

The "basis" in your home is determined by how you got the home. Your basis is its cost, plus any increases or decreases to the basis, if you bought it or built it. If you got it in some other way (inheritance, gift, etc.), its basis is either its fair market value when you got it or the adjusted basis of the person you got it from.

The "adjusted basis" of your home is used to figure the gain or loss on the sale. It can include such items as additions/improvements, with a useful life of more than one year; special assessments for local improvements; amounts spent after a casualty, to restore damaged property; and some settlement fees—all of which will generally increase your basis. Some items that may decrease your basis include deductible casualty losses; depreciation allowed or allowable, if you used your home for business or rental purposes; and payments received for granting an easement or right-of-way.

To compute the gain or loss on the sale of your main home for tax purposes, you must know the selling price, the amount realized and the adjusted basis. Subtract the adjusted basis from the amount realized to get your gain or loss.

Selling price - Selling expenses = **Amount realized**

Amount realized - Adjusted basis = **Gain or Loss**

If the ownership and use tests are met and the gain from the sale of your qualifying primary residence is less than $500,000, if married and filing jointly, or $250,000, if single, you don't have to pay capital gains tax.

Real estate taxes for the year you bought your home may affect your basis, as shown in the following chart.

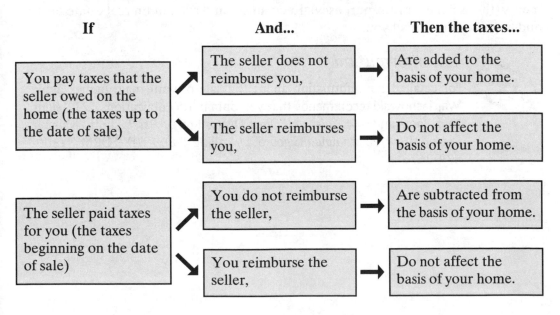

If	**And...**	**Then the taxes...**
You pay taxes that the seller owed on the home (the taxes up to the date of sale)	The seller does not reimburse you,	Are added to the basis of your home.
	The seller reimburses you,	Do not affect the basis of your home.
The seller paid taxes for you (the taxes beginning on the date of sale)	You do not reimburse the seller,	Are subtracted from the basis of your home.
	You reimburse the seller,	Do not affect the basis of your home.

Proportional Tax Break

If you don't make the two-year marker, you can get a proportional break based on how long you have lived in the home—as long as your move is due to a change in employment (at least 50 miles from your old job), health (doctor-recommended relocation for you or another "qualified person," such as a sick relative) or because of "unforeseen circumstances."

You can take a partial exemption for "unforeseen circumstances" such as:

✦ Divorce or legal separation.

✦ Qualifying for unemployment benefits.

✦ An employment change that leaves you unable to pay your living expenses.

✦ The birth of twins or other multiples.

✦ Death.

✦ Damage to the home from disaster.

✦ Condemnation or seizure of the property.

Property Taxes

As a seller, you don't have a great deal to do with property taxes, but if people complain about property tax, let them know that "higher property tax usually means better schools, better police and fire," because that's what those taxes cover, says Thomas Davidoff, assistant professor at the University of California, Berkeley, Haas School of Business.

Whenever you sell your home, just be sure to keep copies of your closing documents (this is handy for tax purposes). Keep an ear and eye out on real estate tax laws and how they may affect you.

Tax Information

For detailed tax information about the sale of your main home, Gloria Wajciechowski recommends that you obtain IRS Publications *523: Selling Your Home* and *544: Sales and Other Disposition of Assets*, both available free on the Web at *www.IRS.gov* or by calling 1-800-TAX-FORM (1-800-829-3676).

Chapter 18

How to Improve Your Credit and Score a Mortgage: Raising Your Score for When You Buy a Home

$12 gasoline = credit card
$355 car payment = car loan
$52 shopping = department store card
$125 = monthly student loan

Total: We all know about credit.

Credit is a part of life. When you go to buy a home, mortgage lenders look at key areas: your credit, job history, income, savings, reasons for past credit problems, equity in your home and the type of mortgage you want. Credit is one of the most important aspects, so we want to share how to improve your credit, what is considered a good score, how to get a credit report and how to score a mortgage. The better your credit history, the better your interest rate will be on your home loan—the less you have to pay.

"Examine your credit report and score; it will impact the price you will pay to buy a home," says Fannie Mae Foundation official Lynsey Wood Jeffries. "If your credit is poor, it may make sense to wait to buy a home until you have repaired your credit score, so that you will pay less."

Wood Jeffries gives us some starting pointers:

✦ **Credit score is affected by:** Timeliness of your payments to creditors, the level of your indebtedness and the length of your credit history. However, the algorithms that create the score are proprietary.

✦ **You can establish good credit by:** paying your bills on time for a significant length or time—credit cards, car loans, student loans, and so on.

✦ **Programs to help improve your credit:** Nonprofit organizations affiliated with the National Foundation for Credit Counseling are available to help consumers with their credit. You can find a list of organizations in your area at: *www.debtadvice.org/takethefirststep/locator.html*

✦ **Get your credit score for free:** Contact the three credit bureaus—Experian, TransUnion and Equifax—for reports, or visit *www.annualcreditreport.com* and *www.myfico.com*. (For more detailed contact information, consult the "Credit Information" section in the Appendix.)

How to Get Your Credit Report

Experts recommend checking your credit report at least yearly or semi-annually to ensure the information is correct. You can get your credit report from Experian, TransUnion and Equifax. When you request your report, you will be asked for your date of birth, social security number, current/previous address and, if it applies, your maiden name. You may have to pay a fee, or you may get it for free if your state has laws requiring that you get one or two free reports.

What Is on Your Credit Report?

Your credit report is a snapshot into your financial life. It shows your track record with your credit cards, student loans and other loans—when the accounts were started, on-time payments, late-payments, default and your overall debt. When you go through the mortgage process, always be up-front with your loan officer about your financial picture for two reasons: (1) it will all be revealed in the credit report and (2) you want them to have all the facts so they can help you effectively.

The Fannie Mae Foundation says a credit report reveals the following information about your credit:

✦ **Your identity:** Your name, social security number, date of birth, current/past employers, telephone number and current/previous address. Remember when you filled out that credit application? That's how this information is pulled.

✦ **Your credit:** It reports info about your credit cards and loans—credit limit, loan amount, balance, monthly payment, date opened, skipped payments, late payments, accounts sent to collections (such as medical or telephone bills) and repossessions. It shows your payment history over seven years, plus anyone else on your accounts (such as a cosigner or spouse).

✦ **Public record information:** Local, state and federal courts share additional financial information about you. For example, bankruptcy, tax liens (unpaid taxes), foreclosures, lawsuits, judgments and, depending on your area, unpaid child support.

✦ **Inquiries:** Some credit reports list inquiries made about your credit-worthiness, at times when you requested credit, and whether you were given credit based on the inquiry. (Some do this, but for example, Experian does not.) After seven years, most of the information on your credit history is deleted. If you've had a bankruptcy, it takes 10 years to be deleted (but that doesn't mean you can't get a mortgage). According to Fannie Mae Foundation, credit bureaus use a computer model to look at your credit report and then give it a credit score.

How to Improve Your Credit Score

So, how do you improve your credit score? We sat down with experts from the credit reporting company, Experian, and also sought insight from Thornburg Mortgage Home Loans president Ron Chicaferro. They share what we can do to repair our credit, manage credit habits easily and what is considered a good score.

Piper: Can you talk to us about credit and what we need to know?

Ron: A consumer's credit standing is one of the big items that all mortgage lenders look at when evaluating an application. Although it is against federal law to institute a minimum credit score, all lenders evaluate an applicant's credit by ordering a credit report, usually from three different credit-reporting companies. Each credit reporting company will show a numeric score. The lender will eliminate the highest and lowest score and use the middle score as the determining number. Every applicant is entitled to see and receive a copy of their credit report, because every applicant pays for the report. There are generally three levels of credit standing that lenders use: "A" credit, "A minus" credit and "Sub-prime" credit. The "A" credit borrower is the one to whom all lenders want to lend. Borrowers in the minus or sub-prime categories can obtain loans as well, but usually at higher rates.

Piper: How can you improve your credit so you can buy a home? Or how can you improve your credit to get a lower interest rate?

Ron: Most consumers are not surprised when a credit grantor (for a home, auto, furniture, etc.) tells them that they have "great credit" or that they have "some credit problems." If there is a credit problem on a credit report that the consumer feels is wrong, they can call the credit reporting company and see if a mistake was made. If the credit problems reported are true, there isn't much a consumer can do but try and have an extended period of good credit. That is, a consumer must make all of their payments in a timely fashion.

Eventually, the good credit will outweigh the bad and their rating will improve. That works for getting the best mortgage rate—the best rate is for the "A" credit borrower. The only way to get "A" credit is to make your payments on time and be prudent about how much credit you accept. The longer a consumer makes payments on time the higher their rating will become. Additionally, frequent users of credit cards—even if they make their payments on time—may see a lower rating if they're not careful. Consumers should only apply for credit when there is a need—not to have every credit card there is to have.

Piper: How long on average does it take to repair your credit?

Experian: The most reliable help for restoring credit will come from Father Time. There really is no way to "repair" a credit report when the negative information on it is accurate, except through the passage of time. Bringing your payments up-to-date and keeping them current is the best advice. Eventually the negative information on your credit report will be deleted and only the positive information will remain.

In the meantime, don't lose hope. You still may be able to obtain credit. As soon as you pay your debts, you begin to rebuild your credit history. Adding a string of on-time payments will help counter those old delinquencies.

After a year or two of keeping your account payments current, get a copy of your credit report and talk to your creditors about it. They may be willing to extend your credit based on the responsibility and reliability you have shown since overcoming your financial problems.

Delinquencies remain on your credit report for seven years. Most public record items remain on your credit report for seven years, although some bankruptcies may remain for 10 years. Inquiries remain on your report for two years.

Your credit score is a fluid number that changes as your credit report changes. Therefore, any change to your credit report could impact your score.

Piper: What are some tips to better manage your credit?

Experian: If they better manage their credit habits, their credit score will take care of itself because it only reflects what's in their report. When consumers review their Experian PLUS Score, they can see what their credit risk is, because the things that make them at risk in their credit report are the same things that impact all credit scores.

Here are some suggestions from Experian for keeping credit under control:

+ Pay bills on time. Delinquent payments and collections can have a major negative impact on a score.
+ Keep balances low on credit cards and other "revolving credit." High outstanding debt, compared to the overall available credit, can affect a score.
+ If consumers do open a new account to get a lower interest rate, they should make sure they don't do it right before a

major purchase, such as an auto or home. Also, they should be sure if they move their debt to a new card that they don't continue to charge on the old card as well as the new card, causing their overall debt to increase.

✦ Closing unused cards is not a short-term strategy to raise a consumer's score. Owing the same amount but having fewer accounts may even lower their score.

✦ For awareness, review credit reports regularly to know what is being reported. Realize, however, that this will not change or help to improve credit scores.

Piper: Numerically, what is considered a good credit score and what are the advantages?

Experian: A credit score is a number that reflects the information in a consumer's credit report and helps lenders decide how likely it is they will get paid back on time if they give a person a loan or credit card. Credit scores are also called "risk scores," because they help lenders predict the risk that a consumer will not be able to repay the debt as agreed.

The Experian PLUS Score range is 330-830. In general, a credit score in the low 700s is considered medium to low risk and once a consumer reaches the mid 700s and above, which is considered low risk, they will be eligible for the best interest rates and loan terms.

How to Avoid Late Payments

✦ **Automatic payments:** Get bills automatically pulled from your checking account. Keep track of it in your checkbook.

✦ **Online payments:** You can set up some accounts online for easy payments or to keep track of your accounts easily online.

✦ **Calendar:** Mark your bills on a calendar to pay them before they are due.

✦ **Travel:** If you travel a lot or head out of town, call your creditors and arrange payments in advance.

How to Score a Mortgage

We talked to a variety of mortgage experts for advice on how to score a mortgage and do so effectively. We got must-have information on how the mortgage process works, key questions to ask your lender, what we should all know about loans and so much more.

What Should Every Buyer Going Into the Mortgage Process Know?

According to Susan and Anthony Cutaia of Cutaia Mortgage Group:

"If you are purchasing a home, don't sign a contract until you have called your real estate attorney and checked to see whether or not he has time to review your contract in a timely manner so you can get out of it or modify it if he detects something that is not in your best interest.

Do not purchase furniture, car or any other large purchase until you have closed on the property (and unfortunately some people reading this will still fail to heed this excellent advice).

Don't close any credit accounts until you speak with a mortgage professional.

Inquire into your own credit history by contacting the three repositories…knowing your scores (although a mortgage company tri-pull may show slightly different credit scores, the credit history should be the same) will prevent any surprises at time of purchase or refinance."

What Should You Ask the Mortgage Lender?

To make sense of mortgage financing, homeowners need to know almost as much as their mortgage lender's employees. By asking a lot of questions, consumers can make sense of a highly technical process. Ron Chicaferro of Thornburg Mortgage Home Loans shares a quick list of what homeowners should be familiar with and ask questions about:

✦ **Does the lender charge "origination fees"?** Origination fees are usually one to two percent of the loan amount. Some lenders, such as Thornburg Mortgage, do not charge any "origination fees."

✦ **Does the lender sell their loans to some other company?** Most mortgage lenders sell their loans for a profit to other companies. The company selling the loan collects a "premium" when they sell the loan. Premiums are collected because they gave the consumer a higher rate than the market called for. Lenders like Thornburg Mortgage do not sell their mortgage loans.

✦ **Has this lender been in business for some time?** Stick with lenders that have had a good track record of handling mortgage loans in rising and falling interest rate environments.

✦ **Does the lender offer a loan modification option instead of a regular refinance?** Some lenders, such as Thornburg Mortgage, offer a borrower the option to modify their loan. That is, Thornburg Mortgage will allow a borrower to lower their rate or change loan programs without submitting any documentation. A modification can save the consumer literally thousands of dollars compared to a refinance.

✦ **Did my mortgage lender help me pick the right loan for me?** That's a question every consumer should ask before they sign any documents. Consumers are not all alike. Not everyone should pick the same loan. A one-year ARM (adjustable-rate mortgage) might be a better loan for one person and a five-year fixed-rate might be better for someone else. This is another area where your financial planner or advisor can help. Some mortgage brokers and lenders may do what's in their best interest that isn't always in the consumer's best interest.

How Does the Mortgage Process Work?

Ron Chicaferro of Thornburg Mortgage Home Loans explains:

"Once a consumer completes an application, the mortgage lender must send an estimated disclosure of costs to the borrower within three business days. This estimate should tell the consumer approximately how much their loan would cost. The application is given a "pre-screen"—that is, a quick review is performed of their income versus their expenditures. A credit report is also pulled at this time.

Most lenders should be able to tell an applicant that they are "conditionally" approved within 24 hours. All that's needed after that is a written verification of the applicant's income and assets. At the same time as this is being obtained, a title company is producing a "title report" that explains what liens are on the subject property.

An "escrow" is set up as well to handle the transfer of the property from the seller to the buyer. The escrow company (or in some states a title company) will coordinate with the borrower on where and when the documents will be signed, called the closing.

The timing on a mortgage loan depends a lot on how busy the mortgage lender is. Most reputable lenders will work to meet the closing date in your contract.

A reputable lender should not accept an application if they know they can't meet a time deadline. Loans for the purchase of a property are shown a preference by mortgage lenders over a refinance, because purchases need to close by a certain date. A good rule of thumb is that a purchase transaction will close in about 30 to 35 days and a refinance will close in about 40 to 45 days.

Most mortgage loans at most companies go smoothly, however, sometimes problems arise. Some consumers may say one thing on their application that is different from what the written verification says. That's when it's time for the borrower and the lender to sit down and talk. Most loans that are delayed are caused by information being obtained that was different or missing from the original application."

How Do You Select a Mortgage Lender?

According to Thom MacFarlane, "The best way to select a mortgage lender would be either by referral or by asking questions to determine how long your particular broker has been in business and the lender's principal resources of funding and by using one's intuition on the lender's competency and trustworthiness."

What Makes a Mortgage Company More Reputable?

Susan and Anthony Cutaia of Cutaia Mortgage Group tell us:

"A reputable mortgage company will stand behind their word. Too often borrowers will relate horror stories where they were promised one rate and got to the closing table only to find the entire deal had changed without their knowledge. There are valid instances when a mortgage program may have to change—instances that create new circumstances for the borrower, affecting debt-to-income ratios, and placing the borrower in another category, so he or she may no longer afford the same program, rate options, etc. However, if the program does change (and it doesn't matter how often), new disclosures are issued outlining the new program and any adjustments to pricing and/or rate. This is standard policy and the first sign as to whether or not a mortgage company is up to standards."

Going With a Lender	Going With a Mortgage Broker
"An important thing to remember is that a mortgage broker is not a lender. Lenders are companies that can use their own funds to close a loan with the consumer. The documents that the borrower signs has the lender's name on it—you will never see the name of a broker on those documents. Brokers are only middlemen and, for that reason, only add to the overall expense of the loan. Some consumers will use the bank where they have a checking account. Some will look on the Internet to find a lender. Once a lender is found, the consumer needs to ask each potential lender some questions. Consumers should call a minimum of three lenders." —Ron Chicaferro	*"While a lender and/or bank may have some good programs, they will be limited. Working with a professional mortgage broker allows the borrower the luxury of choosing from among many programs to find that right fit! There are other advantages as well: only one application fee, one credit inquiry, and only once that you sit down and explain your unique needs. Selecting a mortgage instrument is perhaps one of the most important decisions you can make. The right mortgage broker will understand this and take the time to incorporate your goals and objectives in a purchase and/or refinance of any property into careful analysis. Don't shop price—shop quality, integrity, information and knowledge; these are the attributes one should look for when selecting a company to serve their financing needs."* —Cutaia Mortgage Group

What Are Some Tips for Selecting a Mortgage?

Lynsey Wood Jeffries of Fannie Mae Foundation suggests:

- ✦ Shop around. Look for a low interest rate, minimal fees, and a type of mortgage that meets your needs (adjustable vs. fixed rate, 15 years versus 30 years).
- ✦ Generally, be cautious of lenders that come to you with offers, instead of you seeking their services. If it sounds too good to be true, it probably is.

What Should Everyone Know About Home Loans?

Lynsey Wood Jeffries also advises:

- ✦ Shop around, seeking the lowest interest rate—half a percentage point can turn into thousands of dollars saved or paid over the life of the loan.
- ✦ Consider the differences between fixed-rate mortgages and adjustable-rate mortgages (ARMs).
- ✦ Consider how long you want your mortgage to last—the longer the mortgage, the less you pay each month, but the more you pay over the life of the loan. Common terms are 15 years and 30 years.

✦ Learn about discount points, which you pay at closing and which can reduce your interest rate.

How Do You Lock in the Best Interest Rates?

According to Norm Bour of "Real Estate and Finance Hour," locking in an interest rate is a matter of skill, luck and timing. Mortgage rates move on a daily basis and follow the trend of the 10-year Treasury bond. It's best to follow the general direction of that index, whether it be up, down, or as we've seen for quite some time, fairly flat. Most lenders will not lock in a rate on an initial conversation, but will, at a minimum, pull credit, get an appraisal done, and request borrower documentation to be sure that the information they've been given is accurate and able to be proven. Most loan locks are for 30 days, but many can be longer.

Which Is Better: A Fixed-Rate Mortgage or an Adjustable-Rate Mortgage?

How can you judge the market to decide to go with an ARM? Are there better mortgage companies based on fixed or ARM? (Is there a cap on an ARM?) Norm Bour shares some additional information. He explains that the type of loan a borrower gets is very personal and is based on a number of factors, including the estimated time they plan on living in (or owning) the home and the borrower's ability to handle risk and uncertainty. A fixed rate loan is certainly advisable for retired persons or those on a fixed income, but for young professionals with good potential income, an ARM may be smarter.

Adjustable-rate loans are as varied as the days are long. Some are hybrids, meaning they are fixed for a certain number of years—2, 3, 5 or more—then they convert to an adjustable rate. These offer a great combination of security for a set time, but lower payments than a fixed loan.

Then we have the true ARMs—those that start below "regular'" interest rates. These are fairly easy to identify; they have a variety of names, one of the more popular being "option ARMS." If you see a mortgage offered at anything less than 4 percent or so, it's an option ARM, so named because the borrower has choices of which monthly payment to make:

✦ Minimum payment, which would incur negative amortization (neg am) and the principal balance could grow.

✦ Interest only, where the interest is paid, but no principal.

✦ Fully amortized, where the interest is fully paid and some principal.

All ARMs have caps—both annual caps, which control how much it can increase one year to the next, and lifetime caps, which determine how much it can go up over the course of the loan term. NOTE: The annual cap is more significant, generally.

Some companies specialize in ARMS and shy away from anything other than adjustable-rate mortgages.

Which Is Better: A Government Loan or a Private Lender/Conventional Loan?

Norm Bour says that government loans have their place, especially for first-time borrowers, in the form of FHA (Federal Housing Administration) loans, or for Veterans of the military, in the form of VA (Veterans Administration) loans. Both allow very low or no down payment options, but will have a form of mortgage insurance as protection for the lender, and are generally much more lenient with credit scoring.

How Secure Is It When a Mortgage Company Sells Your Mortgage to Another Company?

Norm Bour explains that loans are sold on the "open market" on a regular basis. The loan term remains the same and there is no downside to the borrower other than the chance of having the loan servicing "fall between the cracks." If your loan is originated by Lender A, and they sell to Lender B, the borrower will be notified in advance. If the payment due on the first of the month is paid to Lender A and that loan is sold later that month to Lender B, it's prudent to be sure it gets credited correctly. The likelihood of having your credit report show a mortgage delinquency is much higher when a loan is sold than at any other time.

When You Buy Your Second Home and Go to a Mortgage Lender, How Is the Process Different Than When You Bought Your First Home?

According to Norm Bour, in the world of residential lending, the purchase is either:

✦ Primary residence, where you get the best possible rate and term.

✦ A second home, which *should* give you a likewise term, but may be more difficult to qualify for. The income must support the original house—with no rental income—plus the second home.

✦ Investment property, which is the most difficult to get a loan for and requires more income and higher credit scores.

What are some borrowing basics everyone should know?

According to Lynsey Wood Jeffries of Fannie Mae Foundation:

✦ The most important advice is to seek education and counseling. An informed consumer will be able to find the lowest-priced mortgage for which they qualify and avoid predatory lenders.

✦ Shop for the best loan product with at least three lenders. Attending a homebuyer education class will also help with local referrals to reputable lenders.

Are There More Programs Available to Help People Own Homes?

Lynsey Wood Jeffries recommends participating in homebuyer education workshops. Shs says HUD approves counseling agencies (*www.hud.gov*), and other national networks of counseling providers include: NeighborWorks (*www.nw.org*), Housing Partnership Network (*www.housingpartnership.net*), National Council of La Raza (*www.nclr.org*), and the National Urban League (*www.nul.org*). There are also special, more affordable loan products available through government programs, such as FHA (for low-middle income people) or VA (for veterans), and nonprofit organizations.

Chapter 19

Now That You Have Sold Your House: Tips for Buying Your New Home

Buying a home is like starting a new year—a fresh start, new memories and new adventures to come. Some say buying a home is like falling in love. You can't quite define that feeling you get that makes it special, it's just a feeling that overcomes you. You utter the words, "This is the home." All of a sudden, you can envision your favorite painting above the fireplace in the living room. You can imagine throwing summer parties and picture gatherings with your friends at the kitchen table. Then, you realize you are standing in someone else's home. But, you want it.

We're going to help you get it!

The Grand Overview

We are going to take you through the home buying process with ease, including meeting with a mortgage officer, searching for a home, open houses, negotiating tactics and steps to closing. But, first, we want to share an overview of the process to help guide you as you go through the experience of buying a home.

Here is a checklist to help keep your progress on track:

❑ **Before house hunting:** Meet with a mortgage lender to get preapproved or prequalified.

❑ **When you find your dream home:** After you have a fully executed contract, select a mortgage and lender that works best for you. Let the lender know your whole financial situation so they can help you meet your needs.

❑ **The loan process:** You will fill out a loan application, then interview with a lender. A few days later, you'll receive a "Good Faith Estimate." (Make sure you receive a "Truth in Lending Disclosure" that discloses credit costs and terms, so you can compare loan programs or lenders.) Finally, your loan is submitted.

❑ **Before closing:** Keep in touch with your closing agent to make sure everything with your loan is going smoothly (as well as any other closing issues). Inspection(s) will be done, and the final walk-through will take place 48 hours before closing. Your closing agent will arrange the closing meeting. (See Chapter 10.)

❑ **Closing day:** Sign the paperwork and documents are recorded.

First Step: Meet With a Mortgage Officer

When you are buying a home, meet with a mortgage officer. Find out how much you can afford and get preapproved or prequalified, if possible. Then, when you go to make an offer on a home and give the seller your preapproval or prequalification letter, you show the seller that you're a serious buyer and that you can afford the home they are selling.

✦ **Prequalification:** You can do this over the phone in 10 minutes. You have a casual conversation with the loan officer about your income, debts and credit standing. Within minutes, you will find an estimate for how much you can afford. Many get prequalification letters. It's free.

✦ **Preapproval (better):** If you are a really serious buyer, go with a preapproval. It gives you an edge, because it is further along in the loan process and you find out exactly how much you can buy. You give the loan officer bank statements for the past two months, W2 forms for two years and recent pay stubs for the past month. You fill out a standard application for the preapproval. The loan officer pulls your credit report and lets you know your loan options.

Brightidea

Start Gathering This Paperwork

Your mortgage loan application usually requires the following documents:

✦ **Employment information:** Your current employer's name and address. If you have been employed less than two years, you usually have to provide your previous employer's name/ address. Previous two years of W2s and recent pay stubs. Students: If you weren't employed full time and you were in school the last two years, you will have to provide a copy of your diploma or transcripts. Self-employment: Federal tax returns for the past two years and a current profit and loss statement. Commissions, rental income, bonuses, interest dividends—if income is needed for you to qualify. (Also, if you want to disclose income from your alimony or child support, you will need to provide a copy of the divorce decree or separation agreement, plus proof of payment.)

- ✦ **Assets:** Two months of recent statements including checking, savings, money market and CD accounts; account statements for stocks, bonds, mutual funds; and any real estate you own, current leases, lender information and, if you own it, a copy of the deed.
- ✦ **Liabilities:** Your home address for the past two years, mortgage loan information, charges and credit cards, rental information, and child support and alimony payments.

Loan officers can help you find a mortgage that suits your financial needs. If you find you need a little help in improving your credit, your mortgage officer can be a great asset in helping you. Find a mortgage officer from a quality lending institution. Most recommend going with recommendations from friends and family who had a good experience.

Countrywide Home Loans senior vice president Doug Perry says if you don't meet with a lender and you spend time house-hunting, you end up either underbuying or overbuying.

Avoid Expensive Purchases While Buying a Home

When you go to buy a home, avoid a getting new car or credit cards—the additional debt will lower what you can borrow to purchase a home.

The Importance of a Good Loan Officer

It's not just about getting preapproved or prequalified; it's about getting a great loan officer with a wealth of knowledge in the field. Here's why:

I came across a family with five kids, three living at home. One son was in special education classes, the mom was suffering from a stigmatism, another son was juggling college and work to help support the family and the father was always working. They didn't have any credit, and they couldn't afford a down payment. But, their dream was to buy a home.

When my mom was little she use to tell me: "If there is a will, there is a way." So I always believe that, no matter your situation or circumstance, your dream or goal can be achieved.

"Will you help us get a house?" the family asked me, so earnestly as we sat on the sofa.

I nodded my head, promising we would get them in a house. I did my research. I found out that there are grants available for down payments, to help folks with financial need. Different localities help establish such programs.

I also took them to one of the best mortgage officers in Richmond. She helped handle a tremendous number of home loans.

Trust in people's abilities. I knew she was great at what she did and would be able to help them. She was able to look at their financial situation and help them establish their credit (using utility bills, rent payments, letters of recommendations), and we were able to help move them into a home.

A great loan officer will be able to look at your financial situation, help you bring it up to par to qualify for a loan and educate you about the different loan options available to you. A great loan officer is also, beyond the numbers, a compassionate individual who is understanding of every situation and educated and experienced in the field. A loan officer is on your team, he wants you to get into a house as much as you do.

There are numerous ways to find loan officers. You can ask for recommendations, research different options online or make phone calls to do your research. Once you are prequalified or preapproved for a loan, you will get a ballpark figure for how much you can afford. It's always much better to be preapproved for a loan, because a seller will consider you a better candidate for their home than another buyer that is only prequalified.

After you get a preapproval or prequalification letter in your hands, your search can begin.

The Search

Anne Riley loves selling homes in California. After her divorce, she threw herself into a new real estate career to support her family, as a single mom. She emerged as one of the best selling agents, handling high-priced homes. I think the secret to her success is the kind way she treats people and her keen observation of the industry.

She gave me great advice, that I passed on to my best friend who was looking for a home (you know it's great advice when you tell your friends). When you search for a home, you should select it based on these three factors and in this order:

1. Location: The location is the most important value of what you are buying.
2. The land.
3. The house.

She says to think about 20 years ago. Whatever neighborhood you bought a house in, you paid for the location at that time. The first thing that appreciates is location, the next important thing is the land, that also appreciates. After 20 years, the home is what *depreciates*.

You can search for a home using a real estate agent (usually called a "buyer's agent") or you can search solo. A buyer's agent's commission comes out of the sale price of the home. It is always advisable to have a real estate attorney look over your contract to make sure your rights are protected.

What Does a Real Estate Agent Do for You?

If you go with a real estate agent, Riley says that one of the best ways to select one is to start by going to open houses in the areas you are interested in. Here's why: You will see an agent who is taking their time on Sunday to meet with the public, their level of dedication to their career, and—because they are representing homes in the area you are interested in buying in—they have first-hand knowledge of that area.

Another great way to find an agent is to ask friends and family for referrals. Real estate agents rely on referrals. They try to have great rapport with their clients, so if their clients know someone who needs a home, they will be recommended.

When you are a buyer, the agent is your eyes and ears on the market. They go to the office every morning, pour their steaming cup of hot coffee and go to their computer to see what new homes are on the Multiple Listing Service—this exact listing of homes is available for you to see as a consumer at *www.realtor.com*.

But they should e-mail, call or drop a list of available homes to you that fit your requirements. Say you want three bedrooms, two bathrooms and a garage, and it needs to be in the range of $155,000 or below. Not a problem. The search takes a couple of seconds, and usually, the MLS program will automatically shoot them new homes that fit your needs. Realtors, such as Riley, use a "listing alert"—a "computer-driven alert program" that sends an e-mail directly to the buyer the moment any property within their search parameters comes into the MLS. Riley puts every client on it as soon as they start looking for a home.

They will arrange showings so you can see the homes you are interested in visiting and help carry you through the home search and from contract negotiations to closing.

Buyer's Agent, Anyone?

A real estate agent who represents a buyer is usually called a *buyer's agent*. Christine Fox of Ziprealty.com—a full-service real estate brokerage—gives some tips when it comes to agents helping you purchase a home:

✦ **Hire a real estate agent to assist with your search and find the right lender for your needs.** Agents have two things: the most current data from recent sales of comparable homes via the MLS and local knowledge about whether a neighborhood is cooling down. Because it's the seller who is paying the commission, there's no financial incentive to go it alone on your search.

✦ **Find an agent who you feel comfortable with and trust.** Buying a first home is a huge step for many individuals, and finding an agent you can trust will make the process that much easier for you. A good loan for you is not just about getting a low interest rate. There are closing costs and points, among the many other things to take into consideration.

If You Go Solo...

If you decide that you want to buy your home on your own, you can search for homes in multiple ways (and this is also advisable, even if you get a Realtor). Search *www.realtor.com* for the largest listing of homes available on the internet. Every home that is listed with a real estate company is listed on the MLS. This also includes homes listed through flat-fee listing programs, and discount brokerages also have their homes for sale on the MLS.

Also turn to your tried and true newspaper classifieds (online listings are also usually available), home magazines outside your grocery store, open houses and showings. In addition, drive through the areas you want to buy in and search for "for sale" signs.

If you would prefer to buy a For Sale By Owner home, in hopes that the cost would be lower, there are a number of free FSBO home magazines outside your grocery store and real estate sites to help you with this option, including *www.freelistingservice.com*, *www.forsalebyowner.com*, *www.owners.com*—and the list goes on. You can just search "for sale by owner" on the Internet to find such listings of FSBO homes.

If you opt to go solo, you should definitely consider having a real estate attorney to look over the sales purchase contract for you to make sure your rights and interests are protected in the transaction.

Finding the Right Home

What is important to you when you are searching for a home? I'll share an example. I had a friend who was searching, searching, searching. She spent months looking for a home—she criss-crossed the city and searched across numerous counties trying to find the perfect home. Then one day she narrowed her search and wrote down "Destination: West End." She liked the schools and the area, and she felt it would be a great place for her children to grow up and live. A couple of days after deciding where she really wanted to be, she found the house.

Sometimes in the fast pace of life and needing to move, we forget to sit down and decide what it is we are searching for—really.

It would be one thing if moving was just one task that stood alone. But, it is usually tied to another important part of our life that is changing too. So amid the rush, we need just a brief moment to settle in and know what we want.

Do you want certain schools for your children? Do you like a particular area? Do you want to be close to family and friends? Do you need to be close to work so you don't have to drive far? How many rooms do you want? What about a garage, two-door even?

Brainstorm What You Want in a Home

Take a moment and brainstorm what it is you are searching for in your new home:

_____

_____

_____

_____

_____

_____

_____

Price range: _____

Favorite location: _____

Number of rooms: _____

Number of bathrooms: _____

Needed Amenities: _____

Garage: Yes / No / Doesn't matter

Preferred schools: _____

Open Houses and Showings

You can look at scores of pictures online or in newspaper ads and magazines—but nothing beats actually stepping foot inside a home and knowing if it is "the one" or not. You will see scores of homes, whether by appointment or on your open house adventures on Sunday. Here you can keep track of homes you want to see and have seen, as well as your thoughts about the homes you come across.

House Search

Address: _____

_____

Contact info: _____

Description: _____

_____

_____

Appointment: _____

Did you see it: Yes / No

Address: _____

_____

Contact info: _____

Description: _____

_____

_____

Appointment: _____

Did you see it: Yes / No

Address: _____

_____

Contact info: _____

Description: _____

_____

_____

Appointment: _____

Did you see it: Yes / No

Address: _____

_____

Contact info: _____

Description: _____

_____

_____

Appointment: _____

Did you see it: Yes / No

Address: _____

_____

Contact info: _____

Description: _____

_____

_____

Appointment: _____

Did you see it: Yes / No

Negotiating the Offer, Getting a Loan and Closing

When you find the home, you will make an offer through your real estate agent. You may negotiate back and forth until your offer is accepted. When all the parties agree to everything in the contract, sign and date it, you have a fully ratified contract. Your purchase is now "pending."

Negotiating Techniques

American Home Luxury Marketing real estate agents Ed Smith and Mary Zentz share insight to successful negotiating tips as a buyer.

Piper: What is the best negotiating tip during contract negotiations?

Ed: As they say, "In life, you don't get what you deserve, you get what you negotiate." From the sale price and closing costs to who fixes what, your negotiating skills will have a profound impact on the overall transaction. You will likely live with the terms and conditions of your sales contract for years to come.

✦ **If the price is important, keep contingencies to a minimum.** Expect to pay more if you need to sell another property first, but an all-cash offer will typically result in a lower sale price. If not paying cash, buyers should have their financing in order before looking at properties. Many lenders will be happy to provide the buyer with a "letter of commitment." A seller may feel a higher level of comfort knowing that the buyer is prequalified, so include a copy of the commitment letter with the offer.

✦ **Know the market.** If you are buying in a hot market, don't expect much in terms of concessions on the part of the seller. A "lowball" offer in such a market typically spells disaster. An insulted seller will not take your offer seriously and may even counter back at *more* than full price!

✦ **In a buyer's market, you can be more selective.** There are probably many similar properties to choose from and the sellers are more receptive to offers below full price. While asking prices in such a market are irrelevant, knowing what other similar properties have sold for is crucial.

Piper: What is a successful negotiating technique?

Mary: Frequently buyers and sellers never meet. If they do, I precounsel my buyers that their entire goal is to charm the seller. If they don't meet, I share with the listing agent some information about my buyers that will hopefully pull on the heartstrings of their seller.

For example, the sellers lived in their home for 50 years, raised their family and is reluctant to leave, but health dictates. I tell them if the buyers are a young married couple hoping to have children in next year or two and who want to raise their children in that same environment. When a seller is out of state, I have the buyer write a letter to the seller and include it with the copy of the contract. This has helped my buyers win, more times than not, in multiple-offer situations in hot markets where my buyers' offers were never the highest.

Piper: What do you do in a multiple-offer situation?

Mary: In multiple-offer situations, I have made my buyers offer price $X over the next best offer. Sometimes this is $1,000 over other offers, as high as $5,000 over—your market will dictate.) Then, require proof of other offers. This has helped my clients win in multiple-offer situations where they really wanted the house, but didn't want to offer too much more than other offers. In those cases, I also put a cap on that amount, not to exceed a total purchase price of $X, in case the price goes too high.

After Your Contract Is Accepted

After your contract is accepted, send your lender a copy of the sales contract, the property amount, address and closing date. Now you start the final loan process.

You will complete the loan application and do a loan interview, and within about three days, you will receive a Good Faith Estimate.

You will also receive a Truth in Lending Disclosure, your loan will be submitted for a final review and your closing agent (real estate attorney, title company or escrow agent) will see if the conditions of the loan are met. It is also important to keep in touch with them to make sure the terms and conditions of the loan are what you are expecting. A lot of times at closing buyers walk away from the deal when the loan's terms are not what they expected. In advance of closing, find out everything about the loan, paperwork and costs.

A few days after your signed contract, you will get your whole-house inspection (plus any additional inspections you feel are needed) and select a title company, attorney (preferably real estate attorney) or escrow company to handle your closing. Also take care of getting your homeowner's insurance and switching over your utilities.

For more on inspections, review Chapter 11; to keep track of what happens between now and closing, see Chapter 10 (designed for sellers and buyers).

At least 48 hours before the closing, you will have a final walk-through to make sure the home is in the same condition (or better) than the day you signed the contract. Contact your closing agent in advance to go over the HUD-1 Statement that shows the costs you and the seller will pay and receive. (For a list of common paperwork you have to sign, review Chapter 12.)

Your closing will take place in your closing official's office and your loan kicks in officially. Then the sale is recorded at the local recorder's office, making the sale official.

✧ ✧ ✧

I hope you have a wonderful experience and find the perfect home. As you go through the home selling and buying process, feel free to e-mail me with any of your questions at info@pipernichole.com or visit our Website at *www.theforsalebyownerhandbook.com*. I look forward to hearing from you!

Thank you so much,

Piper

Appendix: Resources

Following is a handy list of resources to help you as you go through the home-selling process. Tips, contacts and sources are just a click or call away.

Credit Information

When you plan to sell your home, first meet with a mortgage officer to check your credit standing and your ability to buy a new home when your home sells. To check your credit or learn more about credit, consult these valuable sources:

Annual Credit Report: For a free credit report. PO BOX 105281, Atlanta, GA 30348-5281. Phone (877) 322-8228. Website: *www.annualcreditreport.com*. (Currently available for Western US, starts in the east coast September 2005.).

Equifax: PO Box 740241, Atlanta, GA 30374. Phone: (800) 685-1111. Website: *www.equifax.com*.

Experian: National Consumer Assistance Center, PO Box 2104, Allen, TX 75013. Phone: (888) 397-3742. Website: *www.Experian.com*.

Fannie Mae: Consumer Resource Center provides a listing of Fannie Mae approved lenders and answers consumer inquiries. Phone: (800) 732-6643. Website: *www.fanniemae.com*.

Federal Citizen Information Center: Check out "Your Credit Scores Publication." This site also has information on housing, family, education, and computers, just to name a few. Website: *www.pueblo.gsa.gov*.

Federal Trade Commission, Consumer Response Center: Free brochures about credit. 6th and Pennsylvania Avenue, NW, Washington, DC, 20580. Phone: (877) FTC-HELP. Website: *www.ftc.gov/credit*.

First Gov for Consumers: Banking, buying, credit, identity theft, consumer protection and more. Website: *www.consumer.gov/yourmoney.htm*.

Myfico.com: Here you can get a composite score. Phone: (800) 319-4433. Website: *www.myfico.com*.

National Foundation Credit Counseling: Nonprofit organization offering a program to help improve your credit. 801 Roeder Road, Suite 900, Silver Spring, Maryland 20910 Phone: (800) 388-2227. Website: *www.debtadvice.org*.

TransUnion LLC: Consumer Disclosure Center, PO Box 1000, Chester, PA 19022. Phone: (800) 888-4213. Website: *www.transunion.com*.

Where to Get Contracts

Lead disclosure form: Required if your home is built before 1978. You can get this form online (as well as a pamphlet) at the Environmental Protection Agency Website, *www.epa.gov*. You can get the required lead paint pamphlet and materials about lead paint hazards from the Department of Housing and Urban Development. Phone: (800) 424-LEAD (HUD's Lead Information Center). Website: *www.hud.com*.

Legal tips: Visit Attorneys' Title Insurance Fund at *www.thefund.com*.

Local association of Realtors or a law bar association: A way to get contracts that are tailored to where you live, up to standards, is to drop into your local association of Realtors or area law bar association—you can pick up a contract directly from these locations.

Office supply store: Many office supply stores offer contracts, but make sure you know what the contract says and include everything in the contract.

Online: You can find many contracts online. For example, *www.USLegalForms.com* provides contracts, according to your state, and scores of forms, depending on your needs.

Professional: If you have a lawyer handling your closing, you can discuss handling contract options with them. Another tip: Title companies or programs such as Assist-2-Sell's "Paperwork Only," will handle the paperwork for you. Some Flat Fee listing programs will handle from contract to closing for you, and some local discount real estate programs will help you with this. Check what suits your needs best and always ask questions, especially when it comes to costs.

To find a real estate lawyer in your area: *www.findlaw.com*.

What will the buyer pay, what will you earn? To see a sample HUD-1 Statement showing what costs buyers/sellers usually have at closing, visit *www.hud.gov*.

Home Inspections

American Society of Home Inspectors, Inc. (ASHI): 932 Lee Street, Suite 101, Des Plaines, Illinois 60016. Phone: (800) 743-ASHI or (847) 759-2820. Website: *www.ashi.org*.

National Association of Certified Home Inspectors (NACHI): PO Box 987, Valley Forge, PA 19482-0987. Fax: (650) 429-2057. E-mail: FastReply@nachi.org. Website: *www.nachi.org*.

National Association of Home Inspectors, Inc. (NAHI): 4248 Park Glen Road, Minneapolis, MN 55416. Phone: (800) 448-3942 or (952) 928-4641. E-mail: info@nahi.org Website: *www.nahi.org*.

USInspect: This is a great site for information on practically every type of inspection (mold, radon, roof, whole-house inspections, etc.) and sample inspection reports. Website: *www.usinspect.com*.

Tax Perks

Internal Revenue Service: For information about tax perks when you sell your home (as well as when you move.) Website: *www.irs.gov*.

Free Guides

Fannie Mae Foundation: The Fannie Mae Foundation provides three free guides available to the public. You can get the guides by calling (800) 688-HOME or request them online at *www.fanniemaefoundation.com*:

✦ *Opening the door to a home of your own.*

✦ *Choosing the Mortgage that's right for you.*

✦ *Knowing and understanding your credit.*

Mymoney.gov: Federal government's site for investing, saving and managing money. You can order online (*www.mymoney.gov*) the free guide *My Money Tool Kit*.

Safety While Selling

Robert Siciliano, real estate safety expert: Boston-based personal security consultant, president of three safety companies and leader of Safety Minute Seminars. PO Box 15145, Boston, MA 02215. Phone: (800) 438-6223.

Index

About the Author

PIPER NICHOLE is an award-winning writer, an editor for the NBC television affiliate's Website in Richmond, Virginia, and the author of hundreds of articles for the *Richmond Times-Dispatch* and a variety of other newspapers and magazines. She has also taken professional real estate training and passed both the state and national licensing exams.

If you have any questions while selling or buying your home, you can direct your questions to *www.forsalebyownerhandbook.com* or *www.pipernichole.com* or e-mail info@pipernichole.com.